THE EXTRA 2%

THE EXTRA 2%

How Wall Street Strategies
Took a Major League Baseball Team
from Worst to First

JONAH KERI

Foreword by Mark Cuban

BALLANTINE BOOKS   NEW YORK

ESPN
BOOKS

Copyright © 2011 by Jonah Keri
Foreword copyright © 2011 by Mark Cuban

All rights reserved.

Published in the United States by ESPN Books,
an imprint of ESPN, Inc., New York, and Ballantine Books,
an imprint of The Random House Publishing Group,
a division of Random House, Inc., New York.

BALLANTINE and colophon are registered trademarks of Random House, Inc.
The ESPN Books name and logo are registered trademarks of ESPN, Inc.

LIBRARY OF CONGRESS CATALOGING-IN-PUBLICATION DATA

Keri, Jonah.
The extra 2%: how Wall Street strategies took a major league baseball team
from worst to first / Jonah Keri.
p. cm.
ISBN 978-0-345-51765-4
eBook ISBN 978-0-345-51773-9
1. Baseball—Economic aspects. 2. Sports franchises—Economic aspects—
Florida—Tampa bay. 3. Tampa Bay Rays (Baseball team) I. Title.
GV880.K48 2011
331.88'11796357—dc22   2010054155

Printed in the United States of America on acid-free paper

www.ballantinebooks.com
www.espnbooks.com

2 4 6 8 9 7 5 3 1

First Edition

Designed by R. Bull

For Ellis, Thalia, and the esteemed Dr. F

FOREWORD

When I bought the Dallas Mavericks in 2000, they were coming off one of the worst stretches in NBA history. In the twenty years leading up to that point, the Mavs had won just 40 percent of their games. We had work to do.

One of the first steps we took was to invest in the product. Sure, that meant paying more for player talent than most other teams. But we made our investments count in many other ways too. We spared no expense on player facilities, even in the visiting locker room. Players notice these things. Every time another team rolls into town, every player can see what we've built, talk to our guys, and file that knowledge away for the future. To refine players' skills, we also hired the biggest coaching staff in the league. That way, when a big man needs extra work in the post or a point guard needs to work on his ballhandling, we've got specialized instructors who can take them aside and help develop their skills.

Having spent my whole career building technology companies, I was eager to bring that experience to bear with the Mavs. We've hired some of the brightest minds in basketball analysis and built a database that tracks everything from player personnel to game strategies. Wayne Winston, a professor at my alma mater, Indiana University, developed a proprietary measure that allows us to gauge the impact each player has on the court, beyond the usual box-score stats. More than just developing our own metrics, we've also learned a lot about how best to use them. While many teams use stats primarily as a player acquisition tool, we bring our analysts and coaches together. One of our top analysts, Roland Beech, travels to every game, working closely with our coaching staff on everything from lineups to set plays. Critically, everyone in the organization—from our best number crunchers to our most experienced coaches—buys into the system.

In the ten years since I bought the Mavs, we've won 69 percent of our regular-season games and made the playoffs every season. Players like Dirk Nowitzki deserve the lion's share of the credit for that progression—Dirk has evolved into a true NBA superstar, with other homegrown players developing alongside him or serving as valuable trade chips. But pure talent is never enough. Everything that we do revolves around the idea of finding that little edge, something that can transform our team from good to very good, and from very good to great.

One Major League Baseball team follows that same philosophy better than any other: the Tampa Bay Rays. When Stuart Sternberg turned over day-to-day control of the team to Matt Silverman and Andrew Friedman, he knew he was trusting his investment to two guys with limited baseball experience. But Sternberg felt that smarter thinking could trump their lack of experience. Silverman and Friedman had shown their potential while working on Wall Street. They could think about baseball in a different way, churning out ideas that their competitors had never seen or tried before. Like the Mavs, the Rays reached out to some of the sharpest analytical minds in the baseball world, bringing them into the fold. In Joe Maddon, they found a manager who wasn't merely accepting of new ideas—he thrived on them.

I see a lot of myself in Sternberg, Silverman, and Friedman. They have accomplished so much in such a short amount of time, turning a perennial loser into one of the top teams in baseball and growing the Rays into one of the model franchises in all of professional sports. Yet no matter what they do in the future, whether it's land a more lucrative TV deal, build a new ballpark, even win a

World Series, they'll always trail well behind the Yankees and Red Sox in terms of revenue streams, market size, and national cachet. Despite that reality, they embrace that challenge every day and continue to prove themselves on and off the field. Like me, they're always looking for new, subtle ways to beat the competition.

The Tampa Bay Rays are a shining example to anyone, whether you're running a professional sports franchise or a Fortune 500 company or a neighborhood gas station. Every day they look up and see the two biggest names in their industry, standing right on their turf. So they dream up new ideas, whether it's to find a new relief pitcher, improve their brand, or build their profit margin. No one idea is likely to make a huge difference. But collectively, those ideas make the difference between winning and losing, or between winning a little and winning a lot. Those ideas, working together, result in that little edge the Rays are constantly looking for—that *all* the best operators are constantly looking for.

No matter what kind of business you're trying to run, you should read this book. Then you too can understand what the extra 2% is all about.

—Mark Cuban
Dallas, Texas
September 2010

CONTENTS

THE EXTRA 2%

PROLOGUE

*I used to tell people I played for the Devil Rays
and they'd ask, "Who are the Devil Rays?"
Now, I think they know who we are.*
—B. J. UPTON

On the first day of spring training in February 2008, Scott Kazmir scanned his team's clubhouse, then swiveled his head back toward a pack of waiting reporters. The assembled media members wanted to know what the young pitching ace thought was possible for the coming season. Really, they wanted their first sound bite of the year. Kazmir was happy to oblige.

"What's possible? Play in October, that's possible," Kazmir proclaimed. "We have what it takes to win here."

There is no more optimistic moment in all of sports than the first day of spring training. Refreshed after a long off-season, young men descend on sprawling complexes in Florida and Arizona to catch up with old friends and make new ones. The sun beams down on freshly mown grass. Players slip into freshly laundered uniforms, feel the familiar pinch of their trusty spikes. The gate swings open, and seventy-five pairs of fresh legs saunter onto the field. At that moment, anything is possible. In spring training, every team is undefeated.

In that vein, Kazmir's prediction was typical. The flame-throwing left-hander had been hugely successful from the time he first stepped onto a Little League diamond. At twenty-four years old, he was a first-round draft pick who'd already matured into an elite major league talent, an All-Star, the ace of a major league pitching staff, the booty in what was considered one of the most one-sided baseball trades of the decade. Young, talented, handsome, and marketable, he was a few months from signing a contract big enough to leave him set for life. If any baseball player was going to be full of preseason bravado, Kazmir seemed a reasonable choice.

That is, until you remembered his employers.

For ten years, the team known as the Tampa Bay Devil Rays had plumbed the depths of Major League Baseball, averaging 97 losses a season. They finished last 9 out of 10 times. When they finished fourth in 2004 with a 70-91 record—the only time they'd reached 70 wins—it was viewed as a moral victory.

The D-Rays traded one of their best players to acquire a manager who left after three losing seasons. They attracted attention only after throwing tens of millions of dollars at washed-up former stars. Their owner alienated fans, local media, and local businesses. The Devil Rays were so reviled by players that when Torii Hunter, universally regarded as one of the nicest guys in baseball, was asked about the lucrative contract he'd signed with the Los Angeles Angels of Anaheim, he threw in a surprise non sequitur.

"I don't care how much money you give me, I'm not going to sign someplace that I don't like," said Hunter. "I wouldn't sign with the Tampa Bay Devil Rays."

Hey, at least that was better than Hunter's proclamation a few years earlier. Appearing on *The Best Damn Sports Show,* Hunter was asked if he'd rather take a Randy Johnson fastball to the head or play for Tampa Bay. He picked the beanball: "If he hits me, it's over with," Hunter quipped. "But if you play for the Devil Rays, you're stuck."

In a 2003 episode of the *Late Show with David Letterman,* Roger

Clemens read from the list of the "Top 10 Things Baseball Has Taught Me." Checking in at number four: "The best practical joke? Tell a teammate they're traded to the Devil Rays."

That long history of losing formed the backdrop for Kazmir's playoff prediction. The response to his forecast, then, was predictable.

"Nobody with the Devil Rays had ever said that," said Marc Lancaster, then a beat writer with the *Tampa Tribune,* "because it was ridiculous."

If a baseball team merely lost more games than it won every year, it wouldn't become cannon fodder for everyone from Gold Glove center fielders to talk show hosts. But the Devil Rays had much bigger problems than perennial losers like the Kansas City Royals or the Pittsburgh Pirates. They were more heavily mocked in their own community than even the biggest sad sacks in other sports, like the NBA's Los Angeles Clippers.

At the heart of the Devil Rays' failures was the team's owner, Vincent J. Naimoli. The New Jersey native had made his money as a turnaround specialist. When a company started hemorrhaging money, Naimoli would swoop in, slash expenses to the bone, ride out the worst of the business cycle, then reap the benefits of a lean, mean operation when the economy recovered. Unfortunately for Naimoli and fans in the Tampa Bay area, this was a terrible way to run a Major League Baseball team.

Dumping pricey, unproductive veterans and building with younger, cheaper, homegrown talent was a frugal, sometimes effective way for teams to turn their fortunes around. But Naimoli didn't stop there. A micromanager of the highest degree, Naimoli looked for any and every opportunity to save a few bucks, or find a few. The boss never considered—or cared to consider—the consequences of his extreme austerity. When Naimoli harangued the local Dillard's department store for using the Devil Rays logo without his permission, Dillard's responded by yanking all Devil Rays gear out of their stores. The St. Petersburg High School marching band was slated to play the national anthem before a game—until Naimoli told the school it would have to buy tickets to get into the park. The band canceled the gig, and the resulting firestorm over Naimoli's cheapskate tactic rankled locals. The boss's volatile temper and distrust of the media also hurt his reputation, and the team's. No reporter seemed to go more than a few months without Naimoli tearing him to shreds, usually over a trivial matter or a story that was factually correct.

The fans, already weary of a losing team, lost interest in forking over ticket money to the penny-pinching, cantankerous owner who ran the Devil Rays. More than that, some stayed away out of principle. A lousy team breeds apathy. A lousy team with a jerk for an owner makes people stay away in protest.

On the field, the Devil Rays found some success in the amateur draft, which should happen when you're picking in the top five nearly every year. Still, one can't help but wonder how the team might have fared had it ponied up for top talent.

In 2001, Tampa Bay owned the third pick in the amateur draft. The consensus best talent left on the board was switch-hitting Georgia Tech slugger Mark Teixeira. Everyone in baseball knew Teixeira wouldn't come cheap, and indeed, the four-year, $9.5 million major league contract that superagent Scott Boras landed for him was unorthodox and expensive. But the D-Rays had already spent tens of millions on aging sluggers like Vinny Castilla, Greg Vaughn, Fred McGriff, and Jose Canseco. Why they would suddenly refuse to spend an extra couple million for a potential cornerstone player made no sense; future washout pitcher Dewon Brazelton was the team's reward for its cheap approach. Would the Devil Rays' fortunes have changed if they'd spent more money on the amateur draft, scouting international talent, opening baseball academies abroad, and signing premium prospects from around the world? Almost certainly.

Naimoli compounded the team's problems with some perplexing hires. For the team's first general manager, Naimoli tapped

Chuck LaMar. At the time of his hire, LaMar owned a solid track record in scouting, minor league operations, and player development. He had presided over a Pittsburgh Pirates minor league system that fueled three straight division winners at the start of the 1990s. Next, working under John Schuerholz in Atlanta, LaMar played a key role in launching a Braves dynasty that would yield fourteen division titles in fifteen years. Despite his early-career success, though, LaMar was ill suited to run a big league team. What the Devil Rays needed, other than a new owner, was a general manager with a strong personality who could curb Naimoli's mood swings and push his own plan for the team, no matter how much the boss protested. LaMar wasn't that man. When the D-Rays predictably suffered through two losing seasons to start their history, Naimoli grew impatient and demanded that the club spend tens of millions of dollars to try to win immediately. LaMar could do nothing to curtail his boss, and Naimoli's plan failed spectacularly.

The Devil Rays' biggest problem under Naimoli, though, wasn't the owner's cheapness, his hiring and then keeping LaMar far too long, or even his legendary temper. It was the organization's complete lack of a coherent plan. Looking back on the Naimoli era years later, no one would ever believe this was the same franchise. In fact, Naimoli's biggest weakness was also the biggest strength of the people who would eventually take over the team. Every decision the new regime would make, right down to the smallest acquisition of a utility infielder or touch-up on the stadium's paint job, was part of a master plan to turn the D-Rays into winners.

That would take years, though. With Naimoli and LaMar in charge, the team flip-flopped between patient youth movement and the win-now mentality, frugal roster-building and reactionary free-agent binges. Off the field, Naimoli urged his charges to run the Devil Rays the way he'd run Anchor Glass, Doehler-Jarvis, Harvard Industries, or any of the other companies he'd resuscitated: on a shoestring budget, cutting as much inventory and overhead as possible. Naimoli failed to realize that a baseball team is very different from, say, a glass company. The Devil Rays fielded awful clubs.

Tropicana Field became a dreary, dirty, neglected building. Fans stayed away. National media mocked the franchise.

By 2005, Naimoli's final year as managing partner, the only question still hanging over the Devil Rays was why Major League Baseball hadn't followed through on its plan to fold the team three years earlier and put the good people of St. Petersburg out of their misery.

The Extra 2% is the story of how the laughingstock of professional sports rose to the top of the baseball world. The Tampa Bay Devil Rays went from worst to first in one season, transforming themselves from perennial losers to American League pennant winners. They won a second AL East division title just two years later, establishing their bona fides as long-term contenders. This wasn't just any old Cinderella story. No team in any major North American sport faces a tougher task than the Rays and their division mates in Baltimore and Toronto. In toppling the New York Yankees and Boston Red Sox, Tampa Bay took down the two marquee franchises in the game, two teams with mind-boggling fan bases, never-ending revenue streams, stratospheric payrolls, and front offices willing and able to make intelligent, aggressive decisions. In the process, the Rays established the makings of a national brand and laid the groundwork for a young, talented team that figured to win for years to come.

After the 2005 season, a new owner took over and made radical changes to the front office. By the time that new brain trust grabbed the reins, baseball had already gone through big changes. A statistical revolution had been bubbling beneath the surface for many years before Michael Lewis's *Moneyball* began its assault on bestseller lists. Teams began building predictive models and huge databases to store, manage, and manipulate data. The Oakland A's, led by general manager (and *Moneyball* protagonist) Billy Beane, embraced a new era of analytical thinking, becoming merely the most obvious example of a baseball team that could overcome limited revenue streams to achieve on-field success. While Beane's rapid adoption of statistical analysis made him a bit of an outlier in baseball circles, his was very much an insider's pedigree. Beane was a superstar athlete in high school, coveted by multiple teams in multiple sports. Though his big league career didn't last long, he still reached the Show. That made it easier for him to approach Sandy Alderson, the A's GM, in 1990 and ask for a job as a scout. Beane's scouting experience led to a front-office job as assistant general manager. Four years later, Alderson was gone and Beane was running the Athletics.

Unlike Beane and the heads of other major league front offices, the architects of the Rays' success weren't steeped in baseball. In fact, the franchise's top management team consists of the biggest group of baseball outsiders the game has ever known.

Andrew Friedman, the team's executive vice president of baseball operations, played college ball at Tulane, patrolling the outfield until injuries ended his playing career. That was the extent of Friedman's baseball experience before the Rays hired him as director of player development in 2004, with an eye toward eventually giving him control over the baseball side. Team president Matt Silverman never played, scouted, coached, managed, or performed any significant baseball functions in a high-level league. His baseball experience consisted of helping his former boss buy a share of the Rays, then assuming controlling interest in 2005. The Rays' owner, Stuart Sternberg, grew up a big baseball fan in Brooklyn. But his ability as a player never caught up to his passion for the game. Sternberg's closest brush with competitive baseball, other than his purchase of the Rays, has been coaching his sons' Little League teams.

In fact, the trio landed in baseball straight from jobs on Wall Street. Sternberg started as a part-time equity options trader in college, moved on to one of the largest specialist firms on the New York Stock Exchange, joined Goldman Sachs's merchant banking division, then struck out on his own and continued in private banking. Silverman worked with Sternberg at Goldman, coming up as an investment banker before teaming with Sternberg to arrange the purchase of a minority share, and later majority control, of the Rays. Friedman started as an analyst with Bear Stearns before moving on to the private equity firm MidMark Capital, where he worked as an associate. Though their backgrounds were somewhat different, all three men shared an ability to recognize value in a company and to pull off successful deals.

When Sternberg bought his initial stake in the team, he brought Silverman and then Friedman along with him. Since Naimoli remained the controlling partner, the three men couldn't make the sweeping changes they wanted—not all at once anyway. But the organizational culture started changing incrementally. For years, Naimoli looked for cost-cutting measures, for the sake of pocketing a buck. The Wall Street guys embarked on their own, constant quest for value. In their case, though, decisions boiled down to improving the *team*. If that meant spending significant money on a player or a new computer system or even new furniture, that was fine—as long as the organization came out ahead in the cost-benefit analysis.

Sternberg finally took over as managing general partner in October 2005. Silverman was named team president, while Friedman became the man as close to the general manager's title as Sternberg's Goldman Sachs habits would allow. The changes quickly accelerated. Where Naimoli used to preside over even the tiniest decisions, Sternberg, Silverman, and Friedman aggressively pursued top talent on both the business side and the baseball operations side, then delegated tasks accordingly. Where everyone from division heads to assistants had walked on eggshells in the old regime, fearful of a random Naimoli tongue-lashing, Sternberg and company used calculated, pragmatic techniques to solve problems. The results of the administration's more cerebral approach were most apparent on the field, thanks to the new GM.

To Friedman, every trade, signing, and draft pick was part of a greater process. The Rays searched for ways to create situations of, as Friedman called it, "positive arbitrage." In financial markets, arbitrage refers to the concept of simultaneously buying one asset and selling another, where the asset you're buying is cheaper than the one you're selling; an example would be buying Class A shares of a stock and selling Class B shares of that same stock, for a profit. Technically that kind of transaction wasn't really possible in baseball. But the basic idea remained the same: the Rays would look for value everywhere.

The Rays, and the rest of baseball, would quickly learn the extent of Friedman's deal-making chops. In his first off-season as the team's de facto GM, Friedman pulled off several trades, including the acquisition of young starting pitcher Edwin Jackson. A few months later, in the summer of 2006, he made five trades within the span of a month that netted the franchise five more players who were lightly regarded at the time: relief pitchers J. P. Howell, Grant Balfour, and Dan Wheeler; catcher Dioner Navarro; and utilityman Ben Zobrist.

Observers didn't think much of these deals at first. Here were six players, all with significant flaws. Jackson and Howell were one-time hot prospects who'd turned into pitching piñatas. Balfour's once-live arm seemed finished after a series of shoulder injuries. Wheeler was a generic relief pitcher who seemed out of place on a perennial last-place team. Navarro was still young enough to retain some prospect sheen, though this made two teams that had now given up on him. As for Zobrist, no one thought much about him at all.

All six pickups proved to be golden for the Rays. Howell, Balfour, and Wheeler became standout relievers who would engineer one of the biggest year-to-year bullpen turnarounds in baseball history. Jackson went from castaway status to solid midrotation starter and would later net a promising young outfielder in trade. Navarro matured into one of the most valuable catchers in the American League in 2008. Meanwhile, Zobrist added needed pop to the team's bench; when handed an everyday job, he became something more, shocking the league by becoming "Zorilla," a seven-position beast and dangerous hitter who ranked among the best players in the game in 2009.

There would be other, bigger moves on the Rays' journey to the top of the American League, including one blockbuster trade that knocked baseball on its ear. But it was Friedman's first batch of seemingly minor deals that typified the organization's new approach. The old regime zigzagged from one approach to the next, seemingly every year. Under Friedman, every baseball decision was carefully considered. No deal was too small to warrant consideration. Fringe relief pitcher goes on the market? Sure, we'll grab him if the price is right. Ben Zobrist is a 50-50 bet to become a decent twenty-fifth man on a future contender? And a 10,000-to-1 shot to develop into an MVP candidate? Okay, we'll take him.

Management's efforts were just as evident in other areas. To find new sources of talent, the Rays greatly expanded their international operations. Led by baseball operations special assistant Andres Reiner, they became the first team to open a baseball academy in Brazil, seeking to tap into a talent pool drawing from nearly 200 million residents. They traveled to the Czech Republic to sign a sixteen-year-old pitcher.

Off the field, they looked for ways to revamp their image and draw a new generation of fans. Stadium ushers, once ordered to crack down on fans bringing food to the ballpark and to generally act as enforcers, were retrained to provide a friendlier atmosphere at Tropicana Field, letting fans bring in outside food and generally becoming far more hospitable. Jumping on a concept in which a few teams had dabbled, the Rays built the biggest postgame concert series of any team in the majors. To better monetize and market those concerts and find additional revenue sources, the team formed Sunburst Entertainment, a spin-off company that would manage concerts, experiment with other sports such as the United Football League, and pursue other potentially profitable ventures. To win back the fans and goodwill lost under Naimoli, the Rays even made stadium parking free for two years, and it's still free for cars loaded with four or more people. Asked why he made that decision, Sternberg said he got the idea from the FREE PARKING space on a Monopoly board. Unorthodox? Sure. But this was the guy who stood at the gate for the 2006 home opener at the Trop, shaking as many fans' hands as he could. This was a 180-degree reversal from the old Devil Rays.

The new Rays never missed a trick. No conversations would be wasted, no ideas ignored, no course of action embraced or dismissed without considering the costs and benefits, the reactions and consequences. Just like that, the team's culture changed. These weren't just the new Rays; this was a team that was run differently from any other team in baseball. For Sternberg, every decision—how to sell tickets, which players to sign, how to treat his customers—would require smarter, more creative thinking. It was about gaining that little advantage on the competition.

"We've worked hard to get that extra 2%, that 52–48 edge," explained Sternberg. "We don't want to do anything to screw that up."

Eight months after Scott Kazmir made his bold prediction, Akinori Iwamura gleefully stepped on second base, ending Game 7 of the American League Championship Series and sending Tampa Bay to the World Series. As the players jumped onto a frenzied dogpile, sold-out Tropicana Field exploded into the kind of cathartic celebration that wiped away a decade of losing and mockery.

No longer was it ridiculous for the Rays to expect success. Not after they'd unlocked the secrets of "the extra 2%."

CHAPTER 1 | STALKING HORSE

Victory is yes after a thousand nos.
—RICK DODGE, former St. Petersburg city administrator

Big Jim Thompson stalked the floor of the Illinois state legislature, sweat soaking through his shirt and streaming down his brow. The Illinois State Senate had narrowly passed a bill that would pay for a new stadium for the Chicago White Sox. It was now up to the House of Representatives to approve the bill. That meant Thompson, the six-foot-six, 230-pound Illinois governor, now had to crack some skulls.

The Senate's vote had been contentious. Dissenting lawmakers blasted the bill. They asked why Illinois should shell out nine figures to build a new ballpark for White Sox owners Jerry Reinsdorf and Eddie Einhorn, both of them millionaires many times over, while the state's schools went woefully underfunded. Now House members were expressing similar objections. Worse yet for Thompson, the clock was ticking. The General Assembly had until midnight Central Time to pass the stadium bill. If the House failed to get the necessary votes, July 1, 1988, would be forever remembered as the day one of baseball's oldest franchises was forced out of town.

Twelve hundred miles away in Florida, St. Petersburg couldn't sleep. Hundreds of thousands of dollars had been spent on committees and feasibility studies. Millions more were spent to remove toxic chemicals from a downtown plot of land that once housed a coal gasification plant. Another $138 million would be spent on a domed, multi-use stadium on that site, which the city had begun building—*on spec*—to attract a major league team.

Giddy with anticipation, St. Pete's community leaders and baseball advocates watched the clock approach 1:00 A.M. Eastern Time. For months, speculation had grown that the White Sox wouldn't get their deal and would bolt for Florida. Local newscasts had long ago embedded reporters at the Illinois Statehouse, and live reports were now streaming in from Springfield, Illinois. St. Petersburg's hulking new stadium was half-completed, still awaiting an anchor tenant. In just a few minutes, the city would learn if the stadium plan variously described as courageous, reckless, and just plain *ballsy* would finally reel in the Major League Baseball team that the stadium's builders craved.

As the deadline approached, Governor Thompson's lobbying efforts intensified. He towered over House members, grasping shoulders, shaking hands, whispering threats to some, promises to others. Thompson saw the White Sox as a vital part of Chicago's very self, a valuable institution with a history stretching beyond anyone's living memory. The governor gradually swayed votes to his side. But every time he looked up, he would see that damned clock. All the pleading and cajoling was about to go to waste. With midnight about to strike, Thompson was still six votes short. The governor had only one move left.

He stopped the clock.

"We were live on the air, and twelve o'clock came and went," recalled Mark Douglas, a former reporter for WTSP-TV St. Petersburg who was embedded at the Illinois Statehouse. "John Wilson, our news anchor at the time, says, 'Mark, help me out here. I thought the vote had to be made by midnight.' Sure enough, the clock in the chamber was stuck at a few minutes before midnight. Since they'd stopped the clock, they had not officially reached their deadline."

Even by the down-and-dirty standards of Illinois politics, this was a jarring move. The state had seen countless Chicago aldermen rung up on racketeering and extortion charges, judges brought down for accepting bribes, mayors and state senators indicted or convicted on various charges. Two decades later, sitting governor Rod Blagojevich would be impeached and removed from office for a range of alleged infractions—including an alleged pay-to-play scheme in which he plotted to sell Barack Obama's vacated Senate seat to the highest bidder—and later convicted on a charge of lying to the FBI. But never in Illinois history had lawmakers stopped time to get what they wanted.

Thompson took full advantage. The governor secured the votes he needed, then put the bill up for vote. The proposal was approved by a thin margin: 60–55.

"It's a political resurrection from the dead," Thompson beamed afterward.

Meanwhile, the mood turned to shock and anger in St. Pete. The city had collected nearly twenty thousand entries to name the new stadium. Thousands of Florida White Sox T-shirts were chucked into the trash. The local media eviscerated Thompson and the rest of the Illinois General Assembly.

In a court order the day after the vote, David Seth Walker, the longest-serving circuit judge in Florida history, summed up the un-likely chain of events that got the Chicago stadium bill passed. Only twice in the history of man had the passage of time stopped, Walker proclaimed. Citing the Bible, Walker noted that the first in-stance occurred when Joshua was surrounded by enemies and feared he'd be overpowered upon nightfall. He pleaded to the Lord, who responded with a miracle—making the sun stand still. The second time happened in the Illinois legislature.

Major League Baseball had just begun to take St. Petersburg for a roller-coaster ride. With a completed, mostly empty stadium, the city wouldn't—couldn't—jump off.

⚾

Long before Vince Naimoli made baseball miserable for an army of sad, black, gold, green, purple, and teal-clad fans, the people of St. Petersburg pined for any major league club at all. But once an MLB team finally came to St. Pete, it stunk. Imagine you're a Chicago Cubs fan, doomed to follow a team with no hope of winning the big one . . . no matter what the theoretical odds say. Only instead of playing in picturesque Wrigley Field under bright blue skies, you watch your Cubbies lope after fly balls in a windowless warehouse somewhere in Indiana—a warehouse you waited half your life to get built. Use the Tampa Bay Devil Rays conversion system, where ten years of losing (most of those under the worst owner in sports) feel like a hundred, and you have a sense of the despair that rained down on St. Pete. It would take a complete management overhaul, a new generation of young star players, and a full-blown exorcism to finally turn the tide.

The city's baseball history wasn't always so glum. St. Pete had plenty of happy baseball memories dating back a lifetime before Major League Baseball ever arrived.

In 1902, the St. Petersburg Saints started play as a semipro team. The Saints eventually evolved into a minor league team, before folding in 1928. Another minor league club called the Saints emerged nearly two decades later. That team would later become the St. Petersburg Cardinals, and eventually the St. Petersburg Devil Rays, going through five different major league affiliations. St. Pete gained greater recognition as the birthplace of spring training in Florida. Starting in 1914 and spanning ninety-four years, the city played host to eight spring training teams. Babe Ruth played there. Bob Gibson pitched there. Casey Stengel managed there. Still, the city's baseball track record was far from perfect; St. Pete had suffered through its share of minor league attendance problems. It would take a while for the city to pop up on Major League Baseball's radar as a viable candidate for relocation or expansion.

Jack Lake was one of the first civic leaders to push for a big league team in the Tampa Bay region. By the late 1960s, the longtime publisher of the *St. Petersburg Times* was using his influence to rally local businessmen, politicians, and other influence peddlers to the cause. Those lobbying efforts eventually gained momentum. In 1977, Florida's legislature formed the Pinellas Sports Authority—named after St. Petersburg–encompassing Pinellas County—which the state hoped would play a leading role in attracting Major League Baseball to the area. Three years later, the St. Petersburg Chamber of Commerce formed a dedicated baseball committee. In 1982, the city offered a stadium site to the sports authority for $1 a year in rent, the first of many major concessions that local government would grant along the way. The next year, St. Pete's city council approved the new stadium project.

The ensuing two-year period marked a tumultuous time for St. Petersburg's stadium efforts. First, the county withdrew its support in 1984. The city and Pinellas Sports Authority countered with a lawsuit the next year and eventually prevailed. A public hearing followed, exposing passions on both sides. Stadium backers didn't want to see two decades of lobbying and goodwill wasted, even if they hadn't yet locked down a baseball team to actually play there. Local residents didn't want their tax dollars funneled into a new ballpark, a stance other cities would have done well to follow, given the billions of dollars in taxpayer money thrown into baseball team owners' pockets during the stadium-building boom that would soon follow. But against opponents' protests, the city council voted to proceed with the stadium project anyway. On November 22, 1986, St. Pete staged what it called "the World's Largest Groundbreaking."

As the stadium took shape, a handful of MLB owners began offering their support. Philadelphia Phillies owner Bill Giles was one of the first to speak out on St. Petersburg's behalf. Giles was a member of the National League expansion committee, and he had plenty of local knowledge—the Phillies had played their spring training games in nearby Clearwater since 1947. When St. Pete applied for expansion, Giles aimed to learn more about the city's credentials.

Giles took a group of Phillies personnel and outfielder Von

Hayes to St. Pete's new dome to see how the roof would play in a live baseball game. A Phillies coach hit a towering pop-fly to left field. Hayes looked up at the white, Teflon-coated fiberglass roof, squinted, then covered his head and scampered away. St. Pete officials looked on in horror—one pop-up and the whole deal was about to be blown. A few seconds later, Hayes started laughing. The dome's roof was made of the same material as the roof in Minnesota's Metrodome, and Hayes could see the ball just fine. Score one for the Philadelphia pranksters.

Giles and Mets owner Fred Wilpon also led a contingent of MLB executives who flew in to survey the market. The owners toured the new dome, explored the surrounding downtown area—by then seeing redevelopment—and surveyed the local traffic patterns, including the oft-lamented Howard Frankland Bridge. The three-mile bridge over Tampa Bay heightened the rivalry between the twin cities; the *Tampa Tribune* ran an editorial showing an island in the middle of Tampa Bay, near the bridge, as the ideal place for an expansion baseball team to play.

Giles weighed those and other factors and still came away impressed, reporting his findings to the rest of the committee. Putting a team in downtown St. Pete would tap into a large metropolitan area that could also draw from the twin city of Tampa, communities like Bradenton to the south, and even the greater Orlando area less than two hours away.

Still, St. Pete residents remained skeptical of MLB's interest. They didn't want to become that guy who gets all the compliments from female friends, before being deemed too nice to date. Indeed, when the White Sox began exploring a move south, they laid the flattery on thick.

"Florida is the last virgin franchise area in the country," Mike McClure, White Sox VP for marketing, said at the time. "It is the greatest opportunity in baseball since Walter O'Malley took the Dodgers west to Los Angeles."

Were McClure, Jerry Reinsdorf, and other White Sox execs being sincere in their at times over-the-top praise for St. Pete? Or were they using the threat of a move as a weapon they could wield against reluctant politicians who balked at building them a new stadium on the public dime?

It was a little of both.

"Reinsdorf initially [didn't want] to come to Florida," said Rick Dodge, St. Petersburg's longtime city administrator and one of the leading forces behind the city's drive to build the stadium and attract a team. "He owned the Bulls, he was really a Chicago guy. But even after Illinois passed legislation to build the new stadium, everything got delayed and nothing happened. He went from someone who was casually interested to, the further we got into this, the more he saw a potential market.

"There was never a misunderstanding," Dodge mused. "We were always the alternative if they couldn't get the deal done. But it's just like romancing someone. At some point you fall in love and you don't even know it."

Despite the White Sox letdown, St. Pete pushed ahead with stadium construction, and the Florida Suncoast Dome opened in the spring of 1990. The plan called for the stadium to host various sporting events, concerts, and other shows until a baseball team could be drawn to the area. At that point, the city would retrofit the Dome to meet the baseball-specific needs and requests of the team's owners. The Dome lured various musicians, Davis Cup tennis, arena football, and NBA exhibition games. The stadium would later find more use when its first anchor tenant, the NHL's Tampa Bay Lightning, took up residence in 1993.

Still, attracting a baseball team remained St. Pete's top priority for the stadium. And as Major League Baseball's 1991 expansion process evolved, St. Petersburg looked like one of the top candidates.

You could forgive Dodge for feeling like Charlie Brown, looking out at Lucy holding the football and wondering if this would finally be the time he'd get to kick. Again and again, baseball owners and other insiders had assured Dodge and other city officials that their time would come. They'd done so every time a team approached St.

Pete, only to back out when the owners either got the huge local public subsidy they'd been seeking all along or simply got cold feet.

The Minnesota Twins, Texas Rangers, Seattle Mariners, and Oakland A's all made overtures to St. Pete. Even the venerable Detroit Tigers secretly sent a delegation to Florida. Texas and Seattle would secure lucrative new stadium deals after first flirting with St. Pete. Detroit got its own new park, though the Tigers used less public saber-rattling to make it happen. Talks with Twins ownership progressed further, before the team opted to stay in Minnesota; state lawmakers would eventually fold and build a shiny new park for the Twins, though long after the team had mulled moving to St. Pete. Only the A's stadium situation remains in limbo to this day, with the team vying to move to San Jose and the Bay-sharing San Francisco Giants exercising nebulous territorial rights to block the move—some two decades after exploring a move to St. Pete.

St. Petersburg had become a stalking horse. The A's and Twins had failed to parlay the threat of a St. Pete move into a new stadium deal, at least directly. But several other teams leveraged local panic over a possible Florida move to get the favorable stadium deals they wanted. Best of all, team owners didn't have to make many threats themselves. The Commissioner's Office could make the threats for the owners while they remained above the fray, the downtrodden businessmen who just wanted to make an honest buck. To Major League Baseball and its owners, the message was obvious: Tampa Bay offered much more value as an exploitable, untapped market than it ever could as the home of a major league team.

"Bud Selig has been especially adept at playing the move threat card," said Neil deMause, author of the book *Field of Schemes,* which examines the large subsidies handed to MLB owners for new stadiums and the elaborate economic benefit projections that teams trot out to hoodwink the public, local governments, and themselves. (DeMause is proprietor of a blog of the same name as his book.) "He did it for years for the Marlins, and for the A's, in particular. I think he must have a boilerplate speech somewhere in his desk drawers that says, 'There's certainly no keeping the [put name of team here] in this city without a new stadium.'"

Baseball's stadium extortion game touched every team at some point, in some way—not just the sport's lesser lights. Several of MLB's sacred cows threatened to move to Tampa Bay, and Tampa Bay aggressively courted them all. Other teams invoked Washington, D.C., or Portland, Oregon, or Charlotte, North Carolina, or San Antonio to scare local governments into cutting a giant check. For a while, George Steinbrenner even made noise about moving the Yankees to New Jersey, a location still technically in the same metro market but worlds apart for many longtime Bronx Bomber fans. For all the pageantry and history the game offers on the field, off the field the business of baseball includes shady backroom deals, ruthless money grabs, and harsh threats. No matter who you root for.

Having failed to poach an existing team, St. Pete looked to baseball's first round of expansion since the 1970s as its best bet. The city lined up three potential ownership groups for its bid, per MLB instructions. There was a clear favorite, though: the group headed by car dealer Frank Morsani. The Morsani delegation had represented the city in its early attempts to bring an existing team to St. Pete and in the process built a great deal of local goodwill. Final say on the matter would fall to the league, however, not the city.

As Dodge and company would discover yet again, sitting at the mercy of the Lords of the Realm was a bad place to be. To St. Pete's great surprise and disappointment, MLB chose the Porter group, fronted by Washington attorney Stephen Porter and financially backed by Wisconsin's Kohl family, founders of the Kohl's department store chain. There were several reasons for MLB's decision. The league liked the wealth and influence that came with the Porter group, including the backing of Wisconsin senator Herb Kohl. There were also whispers that Morsani was somehow linked to the Mob, a charge that lacked evidence but might have colored baseball's choice.

"So we go to New York with the [Porter] group and meet with MLB," said Rick Mussett, St. Pete's longtime senior development administrator who worked alongside Dodge in the city's efforts to land a team. "And they just balked at the expansion fee, which was $95 million. Our mayor at the time, Bob Ulrich, had a famous quote about it, or at least famous here locally. He said they had deep pockets and short arms."

Opinions vary as to why the Porter group opted not to bid. Some contend that the Kohl family wasn't enthusiastic about ponying up the cash. Meanwhile, another late bidder emerged, eager to bring baseball to Florida: Blockbuster Entertainment CEO Wayne Huizenga. Huizenga wanted a co-tenant to play in South Florida's Joe Robbie Stadium with his Miami Dolphins. He lacked the Morsani group's long track record with MLB, but the league was impressed nonetheless.

St. Pete conspiracy theorists contend that MLB may have wanted an easy excuse to grant Huizenga a team despite his eleventh-hour interest. Choosing the Porter group—which lacked the resolve the other two Tampa Bay would-be bidders had—to represent the Florida Gulf Coast effort made the league's decision easier. The Huizenga-owned Florida Marlins and the fledgling Colorado Rockies nabbed the league's two expansion teams. Major League Baseball had locked out St. Petersburg at the last minute yet again.

For Morsani, this was the last straw. Bitter about MLB's broken promises and having been pushed aside in the expansion process, he sued the league. Years earlier, when Morsani appeared close to reeling in the Twins, MLB had stepped forward with a vow: wait your turn, and we'll reward you with the first available expansion team. Now, not only had the league passed on St. Pete as an expansion team, but it hadn't even given Morsani's group a chance to bid, choosing the Porter group to represent the city's interests instead. Morsani's creditors, already breathing down his neck, pushed Morsani to take the matter to court to try to recoup his losses. Slowing sales at his auto dealerships had taken a big bite from his personal fortune. Multiple futile attempts to bring a team to St. Pete had stripped away the rest of his cash, forcing him to file for bankruptcy. Morsani would eventually settle his case with MLB out of court.

For all the setbacks St. Pete suffered, when fresh opportunities came calling, local baseball boosters couldn't resist trying again. Pigheaded, slightly delusional, crazy . . . they were all of those things. In 1992, another of baseball's storied franchises came calling, this time the San Francisco Giants. Why the hell not, thought St. Petersburg's backers. In for a penny, in for another round of masochism. Besides, the city had already made contact with Giants owner Bob Lurie three years earlier. In a men's room. Dodge couldn't resist reaching out to Lurie—metaphorically at least.

"I said, 'I won't shake hands, but let me introduce myself,'" Dodge chuckled. "Lurie said he was having trouble getting a stadium deal. I said, 'Let's talk. Who knows, maybe one day we'll have a deal, and we'll look back at this first meeting and laugh.'"

Lurie made his fortune in real estate before buying the Giants from Horace Stoneham in 1976 for $8 million. The Giants had suffered through lean years for much of the 1970s and '80s, only to win the 1989 National League pennant and play in that season's Bay Bridge World Series. Despite that brief success, the Giants' home stadium remained a major albatross. Candlestick Park was a dump, a drab ballpark whose unique location on windy, bitingly cold Candlestick Point in south San Francisco made it a dreadful place for a baseball team to play.

The opportunity seemed too good not to explore. The Giants met the four criteria that St. Pete targeted in a team that might be receptive to relocation: a divided market, an unsatisfactory home park, a lack of support from local governments and citizens, and decreasing revenue.

By August 1992, negotiations had greatly intensified. All the major parties gathered at Bob Lurie's office in San Francisco. With Morsani out of the picture, Tampa businessman Vince Naimoli was now heading the new St. Pete ownership group. After so many failed attempts to secure a team, this looked like the moment St.

Pete had been craving for decades. Problem was, nobody was saying anything. The two delegations eyed each other like wallflowers at an eighth-grade dance, unsure who would, or should, make the first move.

Dodge broke the ice. "Let's do a deal," he blurted.

Lurie looked around the room, eyeing Dodge, then Naimoli. "Let's do it," he finally replied.

After ninety minutes, the two sides reached an agreement in principle. The Naimoli group would buy the Giants for $111 million and move the team to St. Petersburg for the 1993 season. It took just an hour for Lurie and his attorneys to draft a memo stipulating that a deal had been reached. The parties filtered out, Dodge making a quick pit stop on his way out. A few seconds later, Lurie sidled up to an adjacent urinal. The two men exchanged knowing smiles.

A couple hours later, Dodge, Naimoli, and company arrived at San Francisco International Airport, then breathed a sigh of relief when they found no members of the press waiting for them. Despite the extreme measures taken to preserve secrecy, Dodge's many attempts to recruit a team to St. Pete had put local media on high alert for the past half-decade. His suspicion turned out to be well founded. Word got out that a private plane transporting the St. Pete ownership group was on its way back from San Francisco and that there would be news. By the time the plane touched down at Tampa International, twenty media members were waiting—at 4:00 A.M. Dodge didn't comment as he strode through the throng. An hour later, though, he called a few key media contacts and told them there'd be a press conference that afternoon.

"I get a call at like five or six A.M.," recalled Marc Topkin, national baseball writer for the *St. Petersburg Times*. "We had just moved into a new house, my family was away, so I was sleeping on an air mattress. I hear the phone ringing, I don't know where the phone is because I plugged it in at the end of one of those eighteen-hour days when you don't know what's going on. So I hear the phone ringing, and it's Rick Dodge. I'm like, 'Hello?' And he says: 'We just bought the fucking Giants!'"

When word got out that a deal had been reached, MLB's reaction was a mix of anger and resignation. Commissioner Fay Vincent and most of the National League's other owners hated the pending move but seemed prepared to let the deal go through. People in San Francisco weren't nearly so accepting. San Francisco mayor Willie Brown lobbied Congress, demanding that MLB block the move; the league's antitrust exemption allowed baseball owners to make any decisions they wanted—including blocking franchise moves—without the threat of being sued on antitrust grounds.

As the 1992 season wound down, the pending move hit Bay Area Giants fans hard.

"My most searing memory was the final day of the season," recalled Mike Deeson, senior reporter for WTSP-TV in Tampa. "They had an a cappella group of women sing the anthem at Candlestick. There were so many die-hard Giants fans there, and they were just breaking down. Grown men had tears streaming down their faces."

Neither San Francisco's grief nor St. Pete's jubilation would last long. Lurie was eager to sell after a referendum for a new San Francisco baseball stadium failed, and the Naimoli group was eager to buy the team and move it to Florida. But Major League Baseball, for all its saber-rattling, preferred to exhaust all local possibilities before voting on a franchise move. National League president Bill White came out opposed to the Giants' relocation, prompting league owners to delay their vote until the Giants had exhausted all possible local ownership scenarios.

On November 10, 1992, National League owners voted 9–4 against the Giants' sale to Naimoli and his partners. In their stead, a new San Francisco ownership group stepped up, led by Safeway grocery store maven Peter Magowan. The price was $100 million—or $11 million less than the Naimoli group had offered.

Naimoli and the St. Petersburg city attorney filed lawsuits against the city and county of San Francisco (for tortious interference) and Major League Baseball. Florida's attorney general also filed suit against MLB, challenging baseball's precious antitrust exemption. As long as the league maintained that status it could thwart any attempt by a city to attract a team from another market. That MLB was now digging in its heels struck Dodge as the height of hypocrisy.

"What was so ironic was that you had the commissioner arguing that teams are not allowed to relocate," Dodge said. "And of course Bud Selig had stolen a team from Seattle and brought it to Milwaukee. It made them look pretty bad."

The case would eventually migrate to Capitol Hill, where a special committee was assembled to review MLB's antitrust status. There, Dodge would absorb another shot of cruel irony, the kind that only Major League Baseball could deliver. Sitting on the committee was none other than Wisconsin senator Herb Kohl—the same Senator Kohl who'd been part of the ownership group handpicked by Major League Baseball to bid for a Tampa Bay expansion team, only to have the group balk at the asking price. You couldn't make this up. To no one's surprise in Florida, the committee took MLB's side in the dispute.

Still, St. Pete pressed on with its legal challenges. The city convinced supporters to keep their spirits up, despite setback after setback. Slogans kept changing, but support lingered. "Rally 'Round the Stadium" had been the battle cry when the city broke ground on the Dome in 1986. "Join the Team" was the mantra behind St. Pete's first expansion effort. When the deal for the Giants fell apart, the city approached the 22,000 fans who had made season-ticket deposits in the event that a team finally arrived. Most of those 22,000 kept their reservations. About 7,000 took their support a step further, pledging a total of $350,000 to cover legal expenses as St. Pete pushed back against MLB and its antitrust exemption. "Join the Fight," the city implored.

In 1995, the fight appeared ready to pay off, as MLB made the surprise announcement that it would be expanding yet again. The St. Pete group knew that the pressure it exerted had forced the league's hand. Other cases had challenged the league's antitrust exemption in the past, and Major League Baseball managed to keep the exemption intact each time. The more immediate concern was the discovery process that would have ensued had litigation proceeded further.

Major league teams, especially lower-revenue teams, have long claimed that turning a profit can be a momentous struggle. Those claims have helped drive public opinion for new stadium deals: the league claims that teams are losing money and that without a new, publicly funded stadium, those teams will have no choice but to move. Independent studies by *Forbes* have concluded that such claims are overstated, its investigators having produced annual team finance estimates and franchise values that counter the league's claims. If an antitrust case were ever to go to court, the league would be forced to open its books, something it desperately strives to avoid. With multiple plaintiffs poised to bring those figures to light, granting an expansion team to St. Pete seemed the far easier solution, as it would prompt the plaintiffs to drop their cases.

Still, St. Pete was taking no chances. Launching a new campaign called "Bringing It Home," the city upped its season-ticket reservation total to 31,000, while also winning commitments for all forty-eight luxury suites in the Dome. Now everyone just had to sit back and wait.

The franchise award presentations would take place at the Breakers, a luxury resort in Palm Beach, Florida. Dodge, Naimoli, and everyone watching and waiting in St. Pete cautiously hoped for victory at last. Prospective team owners had spent months plotting out projected attendance and merchandise sales and accounting for likely expenses, all while budgeting for MLB's announced $110 million expansion fee. But the league had one more last-minute surprise in store: the expansion fee was now $130 million.

When Naimoli got the news, he was livid. On top of that $130 million, the two expansion teams would have to relinquish their rights to $5 million per year from baseball's central fund for the first five years of their on-field existence, making the effective franchise fee $155 million. The league also changed the terms of the already limited expansion draft, forcing the two expansion teams to choose from a particularly thin cast of fading veterans and nonprospects when stocking their rosters. For a brief moment, joining the ranks of Major League Baseball didn't seem like all that great a deal.

Naimoli huddled with St. Pete representatives, before both sides swallowed hard and accepted baseball's terms. Still, even after agreeing in principle to MLB's heightened demands, no one was quite sure what would happen next.

"I remember sitting there with all the owners and the mayor," said Dodge. "They have us come into the room, and still no one's said anything. I hear someone yelling at me from across the room."

It was Jerry Reinsdorf, the White Sox owner who would have taken his team to St. Pete seven years earlier if not for the clock-stopping tactics of Big Jim Thompson and the Illinois legislature.

Dodge looked up, still not sure what would happen. "He throws his arms around me, leans over, and says, 'Ricky, this one's for you.' That's when I knew."

More than two decades of negotiating, lobbying, lawsuits, and heartbreak had finally ended. St. Petersburg's team, the Tampa Bay Devil Rays, joined the Arizona Diamondbacks as MLB's two newest ball clubs. For the Devil Rays' home opener three years later, the ball used for the ceremonial first pitch was passed from person to person, starting at old Al Lang Field, where the city had hosted so many thousands of minor league and spring training games, and finishing in the new Dome, where Naimoli stood waiting. When the ball arrived in the stadium, the sold-out crowd roared.

That was the last moment when Devil Rays fans would have reason to cheer for a long, long time.

CHAPTER 2 THE WRONG CEO

Do you know who I am? I'm Vincent Joseph Naimoli,
owner of the Devil Rays!

—VINCENT JOSEPH NAIMOLI, (former) owner of the Devil Rays

The waiters and guests in linen togas were a nice touch. So were the dozens of staffers dressed as gladiators. Fig trees draped with lights dotted the property, a stunning, exclusive club on the Italian island of Sardinia. Scantily clad dancing girls entertained roving packs of wealthy middle-aged men, many of them able to sneak only occasional peeks with their wives cinched to their arms. The food? Unlimited caviar, mountains of shellfish, mouth-watering desserts. But for all of the night's excess, one figure became the toast of this historic party. Positioned in the middle of an enormous spread was a giant ice sculpture of Michelangelo's *David*. Thirsty? No problem. An endless supply of Stolichnaya vodka streamed from David's meticulously crafted penis.

It was June 2001, and Tyco International chief executive officer Dennis Kozlowski spared no expense for his second wife Karen's fortieth birthday party. The $2 million gala—disguised as a shareholder meeting to excuse his dipping into company funds—would become known as the Tyco Roman Orgy. Captured in all its gaudy glory on a camcorder, the orgy would epitomize the overheated lifestyle many CEOs enjoyed during the stock market's boom around the turn of the century. An exorbitant salary and unlimited perks weren't enough to slake Kozlowski's greed. To finance his $18 million New York apartment, $6,000 shower curtain, half the orgy tab, and a lot more, Kozlowski looted his own company with impunity. Four years after "the Vodka-Shooting Penis Seen Round the World," a jury convicted Kozlowski and fellow Tyco executive Mark Swartz of swindling $600 million from the company's coffers.

Vince Naimoli was the polar opposite of Dennis Kozlowski. Rather than blow company funds on luxuries, Naimoli defined austerity as owner of the Tampa Bay Devil Rays. Instead of taking a callous approach to public perception, Naimoli obsessed over it. Instead of delegating tasks to underlings while he lived the high life, Naimoli weighed in on even the smallest decisions. Yet despite avoiding the oh-so-public pitfalls that doomed Kozlowski's tenure as Tyco chief executive, Naimoli would also run his organization into the ground. Just as Kozlowski's downfall became fodder for a million MBA-level management classes, Naimoli's reign as managing partner of the Devil Rays offers a cautionary tale for businesses of all kinds and sizes, a perfect primer on how not to run a company. In very different ways, both men were classic examples of "the Wrong CEO."

Naimoli's failures are stunning to behold today, given what transpired after he left. A new management team, plucked straight from Wall Street, would later take over, effecting huge change in every facet of the Devil Rays' operations. Friendlier marketing and community outreach turned the D-Rays from pariahs into local darlings. Savvier business plans jump-started a once-flaccid revenue stream. Most obviously, the team itself went from league doormats to two-time AL East champions much faster than anyone expected. It's instructive to break down the Naimoli era piece by regrettable piece. Only then can you truly appreciate the sheer competence that followed as soon as he left.

Naimoli's career in business started far more auspiciously than the way it ended up with the D-Rays. Trained in mechanical engineering before acquiring an MBA and a degree from Harvard Business School's advanced management program, Naimoli made his fortune in manufacturing. His trademark skill was his ability to pull a company out of a hole. Executing an effective corporate turnaround typically requires a level of thriftiness that borders on cruelty. Inventories are slashed to the bone. Payrolls too.

In 1983, Naimoli sought a $75 million takeover of Anchor Hocking's faltering glass division. To make the deal work, he needed investors. Naimoli approached Wesray Capital, a private equity firm that became known as one of the first to specialize in leveraged buyouts. In a leveraged buyout, the buyer borrows heavily to acquire controlling interest in the targeted company. This deal, which took all of three weeks to consummate, seemed ill advised at first, with the rebranded Anchor Glass Container Corporation losing $1 million a year. After consolidating operations and firing a bunch of people, Naimoli moved the company and its remaining 120 employees from Lancaster, Ohio, to Tampa. He held the line on salaries after the move, hoping that Florida's lack of state income tax might forestall complaints. That initial thriftiness kept Anchor afloat as the economy emerged from recession, allowing the company to benefit when conditions turned for the better. Naimoli's cost savings would pay off in a big way. A hostile takeover plucked the company away in 1989, at a huge profit for Naimoli that included a $20 million golden parachute and $14 million more from a leaseback deal on Anchor's facilities.

Naimoli would build a streak of successful turnaround stories over the next few years. He took over auto parts maker Doehler-Jarvis when the company was teetering on the brink of bankruptcy. Naimoli again took a hatchet to any assets that struck him as nonessential. The company then convinced its biggest customer, Ford, to pay more for its transmission cases, boosting Doehler-Jarvis's margins and enabling a return to profitability. At another auto parts firm, Harvard Industries, Naimoli took over a month after bankruptcy, sliced and diced operations and personnel, and again reaped profits in short stead.

He went to extremes to cut costs. All expenses had to go through him, including office supplies. Are you done writing that memo? Good, now use the other side of the paper for the next one. If you were one of his executives traveling to a company branch, you could expect to bring a satchel full of mail with you—stamps weren't free, after all. Vince Naimoli was Ebenezer Scrooge, and he was damn proud of it.

"People ask how I turned these companies around," wrote Naimoli in his 2009 vanity press book *Business, Baseball, and Beyond*. "All had one thing in common: too much fat. If you skim the fat, much as you would do to a pot of chicken soup, you will have a healthier product."

A CEO who aggressively cuts costs can earn all kinds of glowing adjectives. Thrifty. Aggressive. Shrewd. But as Naimoli would find out, the baseball world had a different word for an owner obsessed with pinching pennies: cheap.

To his credit, Naimoli's merciless approach proved invaluable in bringing a team to St. Petersburg. City officials recruited him to head up the city's efforts to land a team after used-car dealer Frank Morsani dropped out. Why the city chose Naimoli remains a bit of a mystery. Some say he benefited from the recommendation of Tampa resident and New York Yankees owner George Steinbrenner, who was a friend. Whatever the case, Naimoli was enthused about the task of bringing baseball to Tampa Bay. He'd seen the overtures made by the Twins, White Sox, and other teams toward the area, as well as the region's failed attempt at an expansion team. But when he failed to lure the Giants out of San Francisco, Naimoli went into full ball-breaking mode.

Joining forces with the St. Petersburg city attorney, he filed lawsuits against the city and county of San Francisco and MLB. The risks for the league went well beyond simple financial damages. Two things terrified the Lords of Baseball: the opening of their books and the repeal of MLB's antitrust exemption. As long as the status quo endured, team owners could cry poverty and bully local municipalities into building palatial new stadiums on the public dime. With St. Pete and also Florida's attorney general filing suit, the Lords of the Realm knew the threats wouldn't go away quietly. In his own way, Naimoli posed an even bigger threat.

"He was the right guy to get the team here, unquestionably," said *St. Petersburg Times* columnist Marc Topkin. "The city had been used so much. It took threatening lawsuits, it took screaming, it took stomping around. It took all that to finally get the team."

After years of waiting, and eight years' sitting on a stadium with no anchor tenant, St. Pete residents were ready to embrace the Devil Rays and the owner who'd helped land their major league franchise. Fans lined up outside Tropicana Field on a Thursday night, clamoring to claim tickets for the inaugural season when they went on sale that Saturday morning. When the ticket windows opened, the line stretched more than four blocks. The home opener sold out within minutes, and Naimoli predicted twenty more games would do the same that day.

That first opening day would be the highlight of the Naimoli era.

The first hints of trouble appeared well before the first pitch was thrown at the Trop. The local media's first dose of Naimoli skepticism dated back to the city's attempt to land the Giants. Reporters knew Rick Dodge had led a mysterious group to San Francisco, met with Bob Lurie, and were now positioned to move the Giants to St. Pete. But no one in the sports world had heard of Naimoli, who'd kept a low profile. This wasn't a big problem per se. Plenty of sports team owners had run successful operations by staying out of the spotlight. But Naimoli took secrecy to a new level. The plane that shuttled the San Francisco delegation back to Florida that fateful night made a late-night stop in Dallas. Naimoli hopped off there, ahead of next-day business meetings for his other enterprises. When the plane touched down in Tampa at dawn, Dodge was left to answer all the obvious questions. Naimoli wouldn't have any contact with the media for more than a week.

"That was kind of the first sign that this isn't someone used to a high-profile position," said Topkin.

The next wave of questions popped up in the months and weeks leading up to the inaugural 1998 season. Naimoli had been through multiple situations in his career where he held the upper hand, and he had aggressively used that leverage to his advantage. That approach backfired with the Devil Rays. He solicited multiple bids from vendors for everything. If Tropicana Field needed carpets, he would demand fourteen bids from carpet providers. Merely to be in the running, each vendor had to buy Devil Rays season tickets. One vendor would prevail. The other thirteen would cancel their tickets at season's end and make hash of Naimoli's name and his organization in the community.

In the summer before the Rays' first season, the St. Petersburg/Clearwater Area Convention and Visitors Bureau printed a visitor's guide showing the Devil Rays logo and promoting the future team. It could only help the Devil Rays. Naimoli didn't care. He demanded $750,000 for the right to use the team's logo on the cover of the guide. Then there was the infamous Dillard's snafu of 1998: Naimoli demanded that the department store pay for the right to sell Devil Rays gear. Dillard's figured the D-Rays needed them more than they needed the D-Rays and yanked all team merchandise from their shelves.

At the heart of Naimoli's hardball approach was a sense that local government, businesses, and baseball fans owed him for bringing the Devil Rays to life. There was no questioning the hard work and enthusiasm he'd put into the job. Naimoli had used the same powers of persuasion that once helped him buy auto parts companies to round up a group of partners who'd help bankroll the Devil Rays' operations. He attended to every little detail leading up to that first opening day, showing the same micromanager's technique that had paid off in his previous endeavors. But observers wondered why he couldn't share the credit with others or be a little more self-aware. A few weeks before opening day, speculation began spreading over who would throw out the first pitch for the first game. The Devil Rays recruited a group of Hall of Famers for the honor. One reporter suggested that Naimoli also tap a civic leader like Jack Lake or Rick Dodge, men who'd spent many years stumping for baseball in St. Petersburg.

Naimoli scoffed. "There is no one but me who got the team."

Another major problem was the team's string of broken promises. Sponsors paid heavily for the right to display signage at the Trop or associate themselves with the Devil Rays in any way during the inaugural season. Naimoli spread the word throughout the organization and throughout the region: the Devil Rays were going to draw 4 million fans in their first season, so business partners would have to pay a premium to get a piece of the action. The strategy worked at first, as Tampa Bay ranked among the major league leaders in sponsorship revenue in 1998. But when the team drew 2.5 million fans—seventh in the American League but 1.5 million fans short of Naimoli's prediction—sponsors were irate.

"I spent the first ninety days playing rope-a-dope," said baseball marketing maven Mike Veeck, who worked for four major league teams and several minor league clubs. Veeck joined the Devil Rays at the end of their first season and constantly dealt with the anger fostered by broken promises. "I called every sponsor, heard every horror story. Every meeting started horribly. Never had I been subjected to such animosity. My plan was just to go in and lead with, 'Here I am, take a shot,' and literally let people punch themselves out until they got exhausted."

Though Mike Veeck inherited his dad's showman's touch, he was also far more patient and tolerant than Bill ever was. Bill Veeck, a longtime major league owner and author of the classic baseball autobiography *Veeck—As in Wreck,* would've had major problems with Naimoli. The Devil Rays' first owner was a humorless dictator, loath to experiment with new ideas or promote any fun in the workplace—the antithesis of the Veeck philosophy. By stark contrast, Bill Veeck would've loved what the new guard later did in Naimoli's stead: bringing in attractions ranging from a touch tank full of rays to an old-school video arcade, promoting theme nights like "Baseball Nightclub" and "Senior Prom for Senior Citizens," and stacking the schedule with postgame concerts.

Mike Veeck could at least close his eyes and try to put himself in Naimoli's shoes. But empathy was often a monumental task. The huge attendance shortfall, the pissed-off sponsors, and a 99-loss opening season made Naimoli madder than anyone around the team had seen to that point. In February 1999, he led a lawsuit against Danka Business Systems, alleging that Danka owed sponsorship fees and suite payments. A few weeks into the team's second season, Naimoli took a meeting with St. Pete's mayor and other city officials, with Veeck by his side. The goal was to figure out a way to pay for a $65 million renovation of the Trop; while the team was brand-new, the stadium had been around for a decade. The talks didn't go very far before Naimoli dropped a bombshell: if the Devil Rays didn't get better attendance soon, he would move the team out of town.

"He said to me, 'I guess I showed 'em!'" recalled Veeck. "I said, 'You just signed your death warrant.'"

St. Pete wasn't New York or Boston. The local media had given Naimoli a wide berth to that point, and the owner's reputation, while flagging among some in the business community, remained mostly positive among the broader public. But marching into the mayor's office and threatening to leave town before the Devil Rays played their hundredth home game? This would not stand. The following Sunday, the *St. Petersburg Times* ran a two-page spread of letters from readers—all of them inviting Naimoli to stick his threat somewhere uncomfortable.

The Naimolisms escalated. In December 1999, after a slightly improved Devil Rays team lost 93 games in its second season, Naimoli again showed off his litigious side, suing the Pinellas County property appraiser—over a $38,571 tax bill.

A few months later, the Devil Rays backed out of supporting a fund-raiser for the medically needy because the event was held at the St. Petersburg Coliseum instead of the Trop.

Speaking before the Chamber of Commerce in what his hosts

believed was a friendly meet-and-greet, Naimoli laced into local businessmen for not supporting the team. He then slammed the host hotel, the Hyatt Regency Westshore, for canceling its season tickets. The audience reacted with silence. (Shockingly, an uptick in ticket sales did not follow.)

One of the Devil Rays' biggest Naimolified public relations disasters involved the St. Petersburg High School band. The team invited the band to perform the national anthem—only to have the appearance canceled after band members were told at the last minute they would have to pay to get into the ballpark.

"Vince became his own worst enemy," said WTSP-TV reporter Mike Deeson. "He became a tragic figure, almost like a Shakespearean play. The hero who couldn't get out of his own way."

Most of Naimoli's PR disasters were driven by an obsession with money. These weren't your typical concerns over eight-figure player salaries either. Some of the stories about Naimoli's cheapness defy belief—until you hear the same tales told by former employee after former employee.

The most famous yarn involved his contempt for technology. Naimoli thought email was a fad. He insisted on reading and signing off on the smallest documents. Naimoli wouldn't buy Internet access and by extension wouldn't arrange for email for Devil Rays employees. Tom Whaley, director of corporate sales from February 1999 to December 2000, recalled the steps he had to take to convince clients he worked for the Devil Rays and could be trusted.

"I set up my own email account: WhaleRay@yahoo.com," Whaley chuckled. "I thought it would be three weeks and then I'd get rid of it and get a Devil Rays account. Never happened. I remember one conversation in particular with a national food company. The guy on the other end said he felt odd sending information to a private email account. 'Don't you have company email?' he kept asking me."

Naimoli's Internet boycott continued for several more years. As late as 2003, if a Devil Rays employee wanted to sell group tickets or negotiate sponsorships, he had to buy his own Internet access and send emails from DevilRaysDude99@aol.com. According to data compiled by Northwestern University's Media Management Center, 62.4% of U.S. households had Internet access in 2003. The vast majority of businesses with more than a few employees had access. Every team in baseball was wired. Every team but the Devil Rays.

Naimoli looked for all sorts of ways to squeeze an extra dollar. The Devil Rays' owner initially planned to name the upscale watching area behind home plate at the Trop the Clearwater Mattress Club. Aides talked him out of that name, convincing Naimoli that a local mattress chain was not an appropriate title sponsor for the team's elite seating area. The Devil Rays came up with a marginal upgrade, secured sponsorship from Kane's Furniture, and called the area the Kane's Club. Ticket-holders took an elevator down to their exclusive seats. When the doors opened, they revealed . . . couches. Yes, for the thousands of dollars you had to pay for the best seat in the house, your reward was a pitch from a furniture salesman in a cheap suit who thought you might be interested in a sofa.

Another factor working against Naimoli was his lack of experience with running a sports franchise. "He was used to doing business deals the way business guys do them behind closed doors," said Topkin. "They can be nut-cutters, they can be SOBs, and that can be a successful way to do business. But baseball was a public trust, in a community that was looking to embrace the person who brought the team here."

Naimoli's nut-cutting methods did occasionally work. When he needed financing for stadium improvements or other ventures, he would meet with multiple bankers and pit them against each other to get the best deal. When concessions operators approached him, he'd find a way to beat the price down as much as possible without chasing them away.

Naimoli's problem was that he never knew when to quit. His combination of ego, pride, combativeness, and obsession with getting the best deal led to requests that he believed should be honored but that others saw as ridiculous, if not insulting. He once sent a letter to the city of Tampa asking why he didn't have a free, reserved parking space at the airport. Meanwhile, Naimoli forced team employees to buy specially designed Rays license plates if they wanted to park in Tropicana Field's empty main parking lot on workdays . . . or else be forced to park much farther out and walk a quarter-mile to their offices. This was in stark contrast to his successor Stuart Sternberg, who offered two years of free parking to everyone at Tropicana Field as a token of goodwill . . . and a sop to everyone who suffered through the Naimoli years.

The coup de grâce was Naimoli's "personal and confidential" letter to Hillsborough County, in which he complained that a "pesky raccoon" was intimidating his wife and daughter at their sprawling estate.

"What I'd like to know is why," Naimoli wrote, "when I reportedly pay the highest or one of the highest property taxes in Hillsborough County and probably one of the largest supporters (mostly anonymous) of charities in our area—I can't get equal treatment on Raccoon Rabies Protection."

The night before the Rays' first home opener, local television news stations were planning to go live with reports. Mark Douglas, now a reporter for WFLA-TV Channel 8 in Tampa, recalled his colleagues setting up live location shots all over the stadium.

"We were all going live, it was a huge moment in sports history," Douglas recalled. "We'd been reporting that things weren't quite finished, and a few guardrails weren't up yet, that the roof had a small leak—in the grand scheme of things just a scramble to the finish, some small, last-minute construction stuff. Vince didn't like that. So he threw us all out."

A few years earlier, just before MLB was set to announce the winners of the second round of expansion, Mike Deeson, the WTSP reporter, got word that the Tampa Bay group would name its team the Devil Rays, a tidbit that hadn't been reported to that point. Deeson called John Higgins, the team's senior vice president and general counsel. How does the name "Devil Rays" sound, Deeson asked. Higgins went silent for ten seconds before telling the reporter not to run with that name or he'd embarrass himself. The long pause told Deeson he had the story right, and he ran with it. Naimoli was livid. When local and national media assembled at the Breakers resort in Palm Beach for the new franchise announcements, Naimoli tore into Deeson—in front of all his peers.

"He can stutter at times, but it was much worse back then," Deeson said. "He looked at me and yelled, 'Y-y-you had no right to do that. Y-y-you spoiled it for everybody!' All the old New York sportswriters were there. They just kept mocking him."

Those out-of-town writers would feel Naimoli's wrath too. In 2004, a visiting Baltimore reporter bought a small pizza at a Tropicana Field concession stand, then brought it back to his seat in the press box—standard practice. Naimoli tore the reporter a new one. "Bringing food into the press box is a health department violation," Naimoli shouted, again in front of a large group of other reporters. "And I'm not going to get fined for it!" The Devil Rays' owner threatened to revoke the reporter's credentials. Only a last-second intervention by Rick Vaughn, head of public relations throughout the team's existence, enabled the reporter to finish his assignment (and his pizza).

Naimoli's short fuse began to earn him comparisons to various hot-tempered public figures, even fictional ones. A *St. Petersburg Times* spoof depicted him as Tony Soprano. Naimoli flipped out. First, he pulled all *Times* papers and newspaper boxes from the Trop, severing ties—albeit briefly—with one of the region's biggest providers of Devil Rays coverage. He threatened to sue the *Times*. Then he contacted the American Italian Anti-Defamation League, seeking further recourse. Far smaller slights also set him off. When radio hosts criticized Naimoli, he'd often respond by calling the station immediately with a rebuttal. Eventually, reluctantly, he stopped that practice—only to have Vaughn continue to call on his behalf.

For all the abuse Naimoli heaped on local businesses, government, and the media, Devil Rays fans remained mostly unaffected—until the team implemented Draconian policies at the

Trop. As attendance dwindled, some enterprising fans began looking for ways to sneak down to better seats. Management installed
extra ushers all over the stadium, ordering them not only to prevent
such seat upgrades but also to loudly chastise any fan who gave the
slightest indication he was trying such a move. If the ushers opted
to let a sneak-down slide, even in the ninth inning of a blowout
game with 5,000 people in the stadium, they risked losing their
jobs. Meanwhile, threatening signs dotted the stadium. Do not
walk on the field, several signs warned, or you will face criminal
prosecution and incarceration.

The Devil Rays also banned outside food. Many other teams had
the same policy. But the way personnel enforced the rule, and who
did the enforcing, was unique. Not surprisingly, ushers were the
first line of defense against the scourge of peanut butter and jelly
sandwiches. If they failed to detect the contraband, though, the
Devil Rays had a backup plan: Detective Naimoli. The owner sat in
the stands for most games, bringing him closer to the action, and to
the fans. If he spotted a fan eating outside food, he'd walk over and
ask where he entered the stadium. He would then call, find out
who was manning that entrance, and have that person fired on the
spot.

Naimoli's threats turned the D-Rays' stadium crew into un-
flinching supercops of snack prevention. A group of seniors hopped
a bus to one game during that period. One couple within the group
approached the stadium entrance, the wife in a wheelchair. Security found a bag of cashews on her and yanked them away. The eld-
erly lady explained that she was diabetic and needed the nuts for
her diet. The gate agent yelled back that no exceptions were toler-
ated. The husband jumped into the fray. After more arguing,
the couple finally turned around, and the husband wheeled his wife
back to the bus. There they sat for three and a half hours, until the
game finally ended and the group returned. Local press got hold of
the story. Some reporters might've sat on it, or at least downplayed
it, under different circumstances. But this was Vince Naimoli. The
story came out. Naimoli refused to apologize. By the franchise's

fourth season, the fans had completely turned on the Devil Rays' owner. When the team held a send-off ceremony at the Trop for Cal Ripken in 2001, fans serenaded Naimoli with a chorus of boos.

"Someone with the Rays once said to me, 'I didn't think one person could keep five thousand fans out of the seats—until I met Vince,'" said Deeson.

He may not have been helping, but he didn't stop trying. Naimoli was also a micromanager of the highest degree. His own employees felt Naimoli's presence most of all. He sat in on sales and scouting meetings. He frequented the press box, presumably on pizza patrol. He'd sometimes fly on the team plane and even ride the team bus, especially when the D-Rays were in New York. That way he could hitch a postgame lift from the stadium to his NYC apartment—which was completely out of the way for everyone else—rather than spring for cab fare.

In his defense, Naimoli's attention to detail made it clear that he cared. He remained oblivious to numerous problems, though. The Trop aged quickly under his stewardship, for one. Bob Andelman, author of the book about Tampa Bay's quest to get a stadium, *Stadium for Rent,* once joked that the bathrooms were so poorly maintained that "there's a sink . . . that's been running since 1998." When Sternberg finally took over for Naimoli in 2005, the new regime spent eight figures just to perform basic maintenance and aesthetic upgrades such as painting and repairs.

Naimoli's unique brand of ownership made the Devil Rays' offices a miserable place to work. Even those who got along reasonably well with Naimoli, or had little contact with him, felt the effect of his presence. The boss's big temper and quick trigger finger put everyone under him on edge. Blaming others gave you a chance to survive the latest rampage; acting surly became a natural reflex.

"There was just this *toxicity* to the office environment," Whaley winced.

This wasn't Naimoli's problem, as far as he was concerned. "You know, Harry Truman said it right," he once told a reporter. "'The buck stops here.'"

If the buck stopped with Naimoli, the Devil Rays' credibility also ended with him. Every year several baseball teams will put up lousy records, play uninspiring baseball, and fail to attract fans. But the Devil Rays became something worse: hated by the community and the laughingstock of baseball. What could you say after Naimoli spotted a Mets scout coming out of his private bathroom, then threw him out of the stadium and banned him for life? Or when he punted a Japanese reporter from the Trop for the same reason? When, during a mop-up relief appearance by disappointing first-round draft pick Dewon Brazelton, he incited fans around him to boo his own player? When, after his assistant received a set of chairs as a gift for her office, Naimoli screamed and threatened to fire her if she kept the chairs, since they'd prevent her from doing work?

One fifteen-word remark perfectly captures the essence of Naimoli's reign. In July 2004, St. Petersburg police officer Scott Newell stopped Vince's wife Lenda for running a red light. Naimoli stormed out of the car and blew up at Newell, then tried to scare him off. Finally, Naimoli pulled out his ace in the hole.

"Do you know who I am?" he shouted. "I'm Vincent Joseph Naimoli, owner of the Devil Rays!"

What Naimoli needed more than anything was someone who could rein in all his worst tendencies so that his attributes—his commitment to the team, his shrewd negotiating skills, his ability to get more bang for his bucks—could shine. At first, he did have a few people around who could stand up to him. The Devil Rays' ownership group included several seasoned local business leaders. But the franchise's escalating money problems, the unique challenges of owning a ball club, and the change of going from men in charge to partners with vastly different opinions gradually caused the group to splinter.

A few other people looked like they might make worthy foils for Naimoli, in the process softening some of his harder edges. As head of marketing, Veeck would frequently overrule Naimoli's decisions, then let him know exactly why he disagreed. But friction between

Veeck and others within the organization, along with a family illness, drove him out after just seven months.

In April 2001, Naimoli appeared at a surprise press conference. The franchise was said to be hemorrhaging cash and also had intractable disputes between the partners. Wearing a Hawaiian shirt that caught everyone off guard, Naimoli forced a smile and announced that he would give up his title of managing general partner to spend time traveling and relaxing and that a new chief operating officer would be named. A few weeks later, longtime baseball architect John McHale Jr. took the COO job. But Naimoli returned at the same time, reinstalling himself as managing partner and CEO. McHale, one of the few people in the organization with both the gravitas and experience to speak his mind to Naimoli, left after nine months.

Naimoli's brother Raymond might've been the best hope of all to bring order to the franchise. Raymond Naimoli didn't have one specific job; he did a little of everything. Most important, he served as a middleman between Vince and team employees. If someone had a good idea and Vince hated it, Raymond might convince his brother that it was something worth pursuing. But in the winter of 1998, after the team's first season, Raymond passed away. His death did more than take away a much-needed buffer.

"It was sad—it really just took a lot out of Vince," said Veeck. "Ray was the one person to really say no to Vince. I said no too, but that didn't mean he'd listen. But Ray said no and he would listen. I liked Vince. But he was an intense guy who said the first thing that popped into his head. Ray softened it a little. Ray was the yin to Vince's yang."

Without Raymond, McHale, or anyone else to offer counsel, the Devil Rays were left with a group of people who were new to their jobs, who struggled to adapt, and who wouldn't stand up to the boss. Larry Rothschild's first and only major league managing job came with the Devil Rays. Chuck LaMar's first and only stint as a general manager started in 1998, the D-Rays' inaugural season. In the postmortems written about the Naimoli era, LaMar and others within the organization were frequently described as yes men. More than that, Rothschild, LaMar, and company were hired for jobs they couldn't make work. Rothschild was a respected pitching coach, but ill suited for the manager's chair. LaMar had a long track record as a scout and player personnel man, but lacked the key traits to be a successful general manager, including an ability to bend Naimoli's will when necessary.

More than anybody, though, it was Naimoli who didn't fit the role for which he was cast.

"Naimoli was General Patton," said Dodge. "No one was better in a time of war than Patton. And it took a big son of a bitch with a gigantic ego to win the war and get a team in St. Petersburg. But when the war was over, people needed a peacetime general. No matter what he did, Vince just couldn't transfer to peacetime."

CHAPTER 3 THE LAMAR PRINCIPLE

What a terrible trade for the Phillies.
What were they thinking?
—Kevin Stocker, the shortstop traded by the Phillies . . . for
Bobby Abreu

Some people are born deal-makers. Like that kid flipping baseball cards who knows Dwight Gooden is your favorite player. Sure, you can have the card in his right hand, the really cool one with Gooden firing his trademark fastball. Just give him that Rickey Henderson card, and maybe that card in your dad's closet—you know that really old one? With Nolan Ryan's signature on it? You remember them. Later in life they'll sweet-talk Dad into lending his 'Vette, cajole a college admissions board into early admission. They'll memorize Alec Baldwin's "Always Be Closing" speech from *Glengarry Glen Ross*. Make the most deals and you win a Cadillac. Finish second, steak knives. Third prize is you're fired.

Deal-makers pursue careers that reward their skills. Wall Street is built on them: bond traders and commodities traders, market makers and merger-and-acquisition specialists. A few of these deal-makers make it all the way back to their roots, going from swapping cardboard likenesses of major league players to trading the genuine article, the kinds of transactions that can win or lose pennants, make a baseball team millions of dollars or lose tens of millions.

Chuck LaMar was never cut out to be a deal-maker.

"I grew up as a baseball man, as a scout," LaMar said with a laugh. "In the areas of scouting and player development, I felt like I was as prepared as anyone. There were other areas, however, that . . ."

He paused, chuckled again. ". . . That I was not as prepared for, that I wish I would have been, looking back."

Like Vince Naimoli, the Devil Rays' owner who'd mastered the art of turning failing manufacturing companies around only to find his overbearing and thrifty ways counterproductive when running a baseball team; like Larry Rothschild, the highly respected pitching coach who could get the most out of a young arm but struggled to manage personalities and outwit opposing field managers; like Naimoli and Rothschild, LaMar gained a fine reputation, only to be thrust into a job he was ill equipped to handle. Together, the three men oversaw the first three-plus years of the Tampa Bay Devil Rays' existence, with disastrous results.

Raised in Houston, LaMar grew up in a baseball family, his father coaching Little League and his brother Danny becoming a high school star and first-round pick of the Cincinnati Reds. After coaching at the high school and college levels, LaMar was hired in 1985 by the Reds, first as a full-time scout, then as a scouting supervisor. That era saw the Reds lay the foundation for the young squad that won the 1990 World Series, though LaMar played only a minor role. The Pittsburgh Pirates hired him away in 1989, making LaMar their director of minor league operations. By then, Barry Bonds, Bobby Bonilla, and Doug Drabek had already matured into young stars for the Bucs. But LaMar still oversaw the development of a few complementary players who played on the Pirates' three straight division winners from 1990 to 1992. Tim Wakefield's transition from light-hitting corner infielder to ace knuckleball pitcher began in the minor leagues, with LaMar running the farm.

LaMar's reputation got the biggest boost from his time with the

Atlanta Braves. John Schuerholz hired him to be the team's scouting director in 1991, a job he would hold for three years before moving to director of player development for two years. The Braves were about to start their run of fourteen division titles, with the biggest contributions coming from homegrown players: Tom Glavine, Steve Avery, Ron Gant, David Justice, Mark Lemke, Jeff Blauser, Chipper Jones, Javy Lopez, Ryan Klesko, Mark Wohlers, and many others. Those players were already in the organization when LaMar jumped on board. Still, he deserves credit for the Braves' drafting, signing, and bringing along several prospects who flourished when he was long gone, among them Andruw Jones, Kevin Millwood, Jason Schmidt, Odalis Perez, and Jermaine Dye.

Some credit, and some blame. Millwood was an eleventh-round pick and Dye a seventeenth-round pick; such late-round picks are usually orchestrated by area scouts and cross-checkers, with the scouting director typically keeping close tabs on the first ten rounds at most. Schmidt was a steal as an eighth-round pick. But the Braves' top draft picks in LaMar's three years as scouting director were huge whiffs. In 1991, the Braves drafted Mike Kelly number two overall. The Arizona State outfielder never landed a full-time big league job, hitting a career .241 in 684 MLB at-bats. The next season the Braves focused on toolsier, higher-upside talent, selecting high school pitchers Jamie Arnold and Jamie Howard with their top two picks. Arnold threw 108.1 innings in the majors with a 5.73 ERA; Howard never made it. The Braves' top pick in 1993, high school outfielder Andre King, also never reached the majors, though at least the Braves could claim waiting until number 66 overall as a good excuse that time. Meanwhile, the Braves missed out on the following players in '91 and '92: Shawn Green, Cliff Floyd, Jason Kendall, Johnny Damon . . . and Manny Ramirez.

"If there's one thing you don't want to do in the draft, it's waste high picks," said *Baseball America*'s John Manuel. "That's exactly what the Braves did."

Despite his mixed track record, LaMar benefited from a Braves halo effect. Several other baseball executives also parlayed their affiliation with the 1991–2005 Braves into high-profile jobs else-where. The Washington Nationals raved about landing Stan Kasten as the team's president, pointing to his tenure as president of the Braves. They made no mention of Kasten's spotty track record with the Atlanta Hawks, which included some glory years in the 1980s with Dominique Wilkins but also curious decisions like making a zillionaire out of Jon Koncak, a player who could best be described as the opposite of Dominique Wilkins. The Kansas City Royals thought they were getting a scouting savant when they hired Day-ton Moore to be their new general manager after a long stint in At-lanta that included numerous roles; the Royals since then have been so abysmal that the baseball blogosphere snarkily mocks Moore's moves as part of "the Process."

LaMar offered a lesson that any business should heed: Look be-yond the résumé. Companies hunting for their next great executive don't hire someone solely for having previous experience with Apple or Google. They look for candidates who made Apple and Google tangibly better. LaMar had his share of accomplishments in the scouting and player development realm, no doubt. With Atlanta, he learned the importance of building from within from legendary scout Paul Snyder, general manager John Schuerholz, and manager Bobby Cox. Still, LaMar's claim to fame was being the Zelig of the National League.

From the beginning, Tampa Bay ownership's goals differed wildly from the timetable set forth by LaMar. Naimoli and his part-ners pushed for a five-year plan that would culminate with playoff contention. These were successful businessmen who were used to turning profits quickly; Naimoli built his whole career out of quickly hoisting companies from the brink of insolvency to prof-itability. But five years was an unrealistic projection for an expan-sion baseball club in the Devil Rays' position. When the D-Rays took the field for the first time, they faced the Yankees in the middle of their dynasty; the Orioles coming off two straight playoff berths; the tradition-rich, deep-pocketed Red Sox; and the big-market Blue Jays just a few years removed from back-to-back World Series. The

Rays would play an unbalanced schedule, with nearly half of their games against the Beasts from the East.

History is littered with examples of expansion teams that needed much more than five years to challenge for the postseason. The Toronto Blue Jays didn't make it until their ninth year. The Montreal Expos needed eleven years to finish above .500, thirteen to play into October. The San Diego Padres took sixteen years just to climb above fourth place. The Seattle Mariners waited nineteen years to crash the dance. Still, the Devil Rays' owners could point to more recent examples in making their case for rapid success. The Colorado Rockies didn't merely draw huge crowds; they also made the playoffs in just their third season. Closer to home, the Florida Marlins raised expectations even more: all they'd done was win a World Series in their fifth season, just a few months before the Devil Rays first took the field. The success of the Rockies and Marlins, and later Tampa Bay's expansion cousins in Arizona, would push the Devil Rays into a series of disastrous decisions that set the franchise back for years.

Still, LaMar was optimistic, if not quite as bright-eyed as his bosses. "I thought that within a seven-year period we could truly not only have a nucleus of players throughout our system, but that we would also be ready to win. The way we would do it, with our payroll, in our division, would be through scouting and player development."

In the 1997 expansion draft, Tampa Bay and Arizona each got to choose thirty-five players from the other twenty-eight major league teams' forty-man rosters and minor league systems. But each team could protect fifteen players, plus three more after each round of the draft, and the D-Rays and D-Backs were prohibited from picking anyone who'd been taken in the 1996 and 1997 amateur drafts or any player eighteen or younger when signed in 1995. That left few top commodities with which to build a team. Amateur draft restrictions were even uglier. Tampa Bay and Arizona made their first amateur draft picks in 1996; that meant that neither team was likely to start producing major league talent via the draft until at least a couple years of big league play had gone by. Tougher still, both teams would be limited to picking at the end of the first round in their first three years of drafting (draft order is usually based on reverse order of the previous season's standings), thereby missing out on some elite talent. The players picked from 1996 through 1998 ahead of the Devil Rays' and Diamondbacks' draft slots included Pat Burrell, Mark Mulder, J. D. Drew (twice), Brad Lidge, Troy Glaus, Michael Cuddyer, Lance Berkman, Jayson Werth, and CC Sabathia.

Even in the most optimistic scenario, those restrictions, combined with historical precedent, suggested it would take a while for the Devil Rays to catch up to the rest of the league. In the fragile early days, proper talent evaluation becomes vital for a team trying to make up ground. But before the Devil Rays ever took the field, LaMar made one of the biggest talent evaluation gaffes in a generation.

With their third pick in the '97 expansion draft (sixth overall), the Devil Rays selected a twenty-three-year-old Venezuelan outfielder named Bobby Abreu. In the minor leagues, Abreu had established himself as a player with diverse and precocious skills. Playing in Jackson of the Texas League at just twenty years old, Abreu hit an impressive .303/.368/.530 (batting average/on-base percentage/slugging percentage) with 50 extra-base hits in just 400 at-bats. As a twenty-one-year-old at Triple A Tucson the next year, Abreu banged out a .304/.395/.516 performance. Left in Triple A the next year despite his big numbers, Abreu posted a still solid .263/.389/.459 line, showing speed on the base paths and in the outfield—a strong enough effort to earn a cup of coffee with the Astros before the end of the '96 season. Abreu started at Triple A the next year, then hit .250/.329/.371 in 59 games with the Astros. Despite his impressive minor league track record at a young age, some early signs of holding his own in the big leagues, and a mix of skills that included extra-base power, speed, a patient batting approach, a strong throwing arm, and playable defense, Houston left Abreu unprotected in the expansion draft. Here was a chance for the Devil

Rays to fulfill their promise of building through the acquisition of young talent, with the goal of crafting a winner a few years down the road.

LaMar had other plans. He'd arranged to swap Abreu to the Philadelphia Phillies for shortstop Kevin Stocker. The Devil Rays wanted defensive help for their pitching staff, and D-Rays scouts liked Stocker's glove. On offense he'd shown he could take a walk, putting up respectable on-base percentages of .335 or better in four of his first five major league seasons. He had playoff experience. But the warning signs were flashing. Stocker struggled with injuries, hit just .252 in the four years after his debut—suggesting his .324 average as a rookie was a fluke—and hit just 14 homers in five seasons. He was also four years older and four years closer to free agency than Abreu; LaMar saw him as just a stopgap for a couple years, in stark contrast to the Devil Rays' youth-targeted mandate.

So why'd they make the deal?

"Obviously we did not evaluate Bobby Abreu like we should have," said LaMar. "I personally had never seen him, I had never seen him play a game, never an at-bat. But to tell you how inexact a science the scouting world is, there you have [then Astros GM, now Rays senior vice president of baseball operations] Gerry Hunsicker, one of the finest baseball men in the game. They didn't evaluate him right either!"

LaMar felt that the Devil Rays could build a bullpen through the expansion draft, but that starting pitching would be hard to find, so any help they could get on defense, they would immediately take. It was all part of a teamwide goal, he said, to avoid losing 100 games in the team's first season. LaMar admitted that goal was nearsighted. The Devil Rays never identified Abreu as a potential impact player, and plenty of teams have passed on plenty of good players over the years. But by placing particular importance on losing 99 games instead of 100 in their debut season, and picking veterans over younger players, the D-Rays sabotaged their (supposed) long-term plan.

When the Phillies and Rays met up years later in the 2008

World Series, Stocker fired off his tongue-in-cheek comment about Philly making a terrible trade. Not so terrible, as it turned out. Stocker was out of baseball three years later. Through the 2010 season, Abreu had played in more than 2,000 major league games and totaled well over 2,000 hits. Along the way, he would curse Tampa Bay yet again. After the 2008 season, with Abreu a free agent, the Rays made the highest offer for Abreu, an attractive two-year contract for a player who'd lost his defensive prowess but remained an effective hitter. Abreu spurned the Rays for a smaller one-year deal with the Angels. Forced to their backup plan, Tampa Bay instead signed Pat Burrell to a two-year, $16 million deal, the worst free-agent contract ever handed out by LaMar's successor . . . by a mile.

As badly as the Abreu/Stocker trade backfired, few predicted Abreu's rise to stardom at the time. The Devil Rays' signing of thirty-three-year-old relief pitcher Roberto Hernandez, on the other hand? Incomprehensible.

There is no commodity in baseball more pointless than a high-priced, veteran closer on a bad team. Fans don't feel any better if the closer saves two more games than a cheaper replacement might, lifting the team to 65 wins instead of 63; there's little to no marginal revenue gain from winning games at that rock-bottom level either. In the Devil Rays' case, signing Hernandez wasn't merely a pointless move. Cash-strapped, the club would eventually pay Hernandez nearly $17 million. Hernandez did a respectable job, piling up 101 saves in three years. The Devil Rays could have saved millions of dollars and added prospects much sooner had they quickly cashed in Hernandez's shiny closer status in trade. Instead, they waited three years, shipping out Hernandez and Cory Lidle—a starting pitcher who would have two strong years in Oakland—for young, slugging outfielder Ben Grieve. Though Grieve didn't pan out, the D-Rays at least made a move with the future in mind.

By signing Hernandez, though, the Devil Rays did more than blow a big wad of cash. They also sacrificed a first-round draft pick. Under baseball's arcane compensation rules, free agents are divided into different classes based on often counterintuitive criteria. In the off-season of 1997–1998, Hernandez was classified as a Type A free agent. That meant that any team that signed him to a free-agent contract would have to sacrifice a first-round draft pick in the amateur draft (or a second-rounder if the team had already lost its first-rounder), assuming it was in the latter half of the first round. By inking Hernandez, Tampa Bay gave up the 29th overall pick in the 1998 draft.

This wouldn't be the last time the Devil Rays jettisoned high draft picks for the right to sign veteran players to rich contracts. In the 2000 draft, Tampa Bay chucked its second-, third-, and fourth-round picks as compensation. For their trouble they got:

- Juan Guzman, a thirty-three-year-old starting pitcher who threw 1⅔ innings in Tampa Bay before his arm exploded.
- Steve Trachsel, a starting pitcher coming off a season in which he'd gone 8-18 with a 5.59 ERA. Trachsel offered the added bonus of being the slowest-working pitcher of his generation, thus driving Devil Rays fans mad with his lousy and slothful performance. He went 6-10 with a 4.58 ERA in 23 Tampa Bay starts before getting shipped out.
- Gerald "Ice" Williams, an outfielder perhaps best known for charging Pedro Martinez after being hit by a pitch and missing in his wild swing at the star pitcher. Williams lasted a year and a half in Tampa Bay. In 2001, he hit .207 with a .261 on-base percentage before the Devil Rays released him. In 2000, Williams hit 21 homers; he also made nearly 500 outs, ranking near the league leaders in that dubious category despite missing 15 games.

All told, the Devil Rays paid three draft picks and $20 million, getting light-hitting prospect Brent Abernathy (acquired when they traded Trachsel) and replacement-level performance from three forgettable veterans for their trouble. Other teams have similarly miscalculated the value of draft picks, and only recently have most teams gotten serious about spurning mediocre Type A free agents. But there's never a good excuse for a non-contending team to toss away a chance at an upper-tier prospect.

The Devil Rays made a slew of big-money signings in their first few seasons, most of them players whose past performance didn't remotely warrant such largesse—never mind their inevitably lousy future performance. Wilson Alvarez got five years and $35 million. Rolando Arrojo got more than $20 million. The Devil Rays would later sign an army of lumbering, past-their-prime sluggers in an off-season that set the franchise back for years. But less splashy deals for players like Hernandez, Alvarez, and Arrojo also hurt the team in multiple ways. Naimoli gave LaMar a budget each year, with the understanding that he would spend the money he was given. But rather than make good on his promise to focus resources on player development, LaMar snatched up the first veteran free agents who would agree to take Naimoli's money. He threw in preference for players with Florida connections, foolishly surmising that such connections would bring in lots more fans, even when the product on the field remained lousy. They did not.

Naimoli's goal was to avoid 100 losses in the team's first season, do better than 95 losses in its second season, and vie for a division title by year five. The Devil Rays did achieve those first two (modest) targets, going 63-99 in 1998 and 69-93 in 1999. But those goals, combined with Naimoli's meddling approach, sabotaged the team's building efforts.

"Vince micromanaged so much that there were deals Chuck wanted to make that Vince wouldn't let him make," said *St. Petersburg Times* baseball columnist Marc Topkin. "Quinton McCracken, who was a fringe player but became a fan favorite early on, was one of those guys. He had a good year, you knew his value was never going to be higher, and Chuck had some people maybe talking about trading for him. But McCracken was their fan favorite that first year. So Vince wouldn't let Chuck make the deal."

What Naimoli couldn't see and LaMar failed to understand was the *opportunity cost* of the big-ticket contracts they doled out—and the veterans-for-prospects trades they weren't making. For a few million dollars a pop, Tampa Bay could have opened baseball academies in multiple countries. Convert just one sixteen-year-old prospect signed for $20,000 into a viable big league player and you've made back your investment. History told the Devil Rays that fans would show up for the first few seasons regardless of the quality of the product on the field, owing to the honeymoon period that teams get when they enter the league (or build new stadiums). Signing Hernandez, Alvarez, Arrojo, and others wasn't going to stop the Devil Rays from losing no matter what. If they had diverted more money to drafting and developing players and less to sinkhole veterans, the Devil Rays could have hastened their rise to contender status by several years.

"Looking back, we should've just kept fighting and pouring more money into scouting and player development so that you have a chance to find a player to hit a home run—versus putting it into major league payroll when you're just going to win so many games anyway," LaMar lamented. "Looking back, we were trying to have our cake and eat it too, trying to build through scouting and player development and also trying to win a certain amount of major league games. And looking back, who cares about sixty-three or sixty-five or sixty-seven wins—let's take our lumps, but load up with that nucleus of players. It's something that I wish we had back."

Credit LaMar for being able and willing to identify his former organization's worst practices and his own mistakes. As a first-time GM with a get-along personality, he was ill equipped to take on an overbearing boss like Naimoli. So he followed the same script that many general managers, and by extension many corporate middle managers, swear by every year. Get an annual budget from the boss, then spend every penny while you can. Why look for creative ways to invest capital when there are easier, faster ways? Never challenge authority. Take the road most traveled so you won't be second-guessed.

The early success of the Diamondbacks blew the Devil Rays further off LaMar's preferred course. Arizona improbably won 100 games and the NL West title in its second year of existence. The D-Backs had deeper pockets than their Gulf Coast counterparts, and they dug into them. The difference for Arizona was who they acquired. Instead of nabbing midmarket talents at lofty prices, the D-Backs trolled for bigger fish. They signed Randy Johnson, who became one of the biggest bargains in the history of free agency. Though Matt Williams was getting a little long in the tooth, Arizona recognized that he could provide more value as an everyday third baseman than, say, a closer like Roberto Hernandez ever could. The Diamondbacks also started with a stronger nucleus, identifying several young players who would become solid major league contributors. More broadly, though, the Diamondbacks didn't offer a blueprint that the Devil Rays could easily copy. The D-Backs spent more money than Naimoli and company could ever hope to raise and larded their books with back-loaded contracts, creating a huge long-term debt load that would eventually weigh them down for years. They also got really lucky. Veteran Luis Gonzalez had a huge breakout in his thirties; older players like Jay Bell and Steve Finley similarly found fountains of youth, excelling in Arizona at ages when players historically have declined. Williams, for one, would later be linked to a Florida clinic that sold human growth hormone and various performance-enhancing drugs.

None of this stopped Naimoli and his overeager partners from drooling with envy. Emboldened by the Diamondbacks' success, the Devil Rays' owners approved a $60 million budget for the 2000 season, up nearly $25 million from the year before. The GM had his marching orders: sign brand-name players who will not only win games but also put butts in the seats. Now. The problem with that plan was the horrendous timing. The free-agent market was paper-thin that off-season. "You had John Olerud, you had Greg Vaughn, and you had Gerald Williams, okay?" LaMar said.

Bad talent market or not, the Devil Rays pressed on. LaMar acquired Williams, Vaughn, and power-hitting third baseman Vinny Castilla, the three pickups joining a lineup that already included Tampa native and original Devil Ray Fred McGriff and injury-prone powder keg Jose Canseco. The D-Rays dubbed their new lineup "the Hit Show." For the first time, the team got significant national media attention for their on-field product. Few pundits thought the ploy would work. In baseball as in business, quick fixes rarely do. But the Devil Rays' owners were happy to see the team finally getting attention. Happier still were the new additions.

"They want to win," Vaughn said upon signing with the Rays. "They want to win now. They don't want to wait. You couldn't ask for a better situation." Indeed, the thirty-four-year-old Vaughn couldn't have asked for better than a contract that would pay him $34 million over four years, given the sky-high attrition rates of plodding, mid-thirties sluggers with no discernible baseball skills other than power.

The Hit Show needed an extra "S" to properly illustrate its catastrophic effects on the Devil Rays. Vaughn had a decent first season in Tampa Bay, hitting 28 homers with an .864 OPS, but that was down from a combined 95 homers in the previous two seasons. His production plunged off a cliff from there, leading to his eventual release in 2003. Pumped to the hilt with the latest chemical enhancements, Canseco bashed 31 homers by the 1999 All-Star break, before a back injury started a precipitous decline. Castilla completely tanked in Tampa Bay, hitting just .221/.254/.308 with 6 homers in 2000; released the next season, he quickly regained his power stroke in Houston, even added a 35-homer, 131-RBI season at age thirty-six in Colorado. McGriff remained a quiet, steady performer for several more years; the Devil Rays tried to cash him in for useful prospects the next season, only to land the feckless combination of Jason Smith and Manny Aybar.

Like the Diamondbacks, the Devil Rays deferred big chunks of the contracts they doled out. Unlike the Diamondbacks, they wound up with crippling debt but very few wins. The D-Rays won just 69 games in 2000, the same as a year earlier with a payroll about 40% smaller. Even more jarring, attendance actually got worse, dropping from roughly 1.6 million in 1999 (10th in the AL) to around 1.4 million in 2000 (13th in the AL). Meanwhile, the

Moneyball A's won the AL West with a payroll half as big as Tampa Bay's in 2000, while the White Sox won the AL Central with a $35.7 million payroll, in line with the Devil Rays' expenditures the year *before* they shot the moon. Five other teams with smaller payrolls enjoyed winning records that year.

The Hit Show's spectacular failure sent the Devil Rays into a tailspin. Manager Larry Rothschild lost his job fourteen games into the following season, starting a bizarre managerial chain reaction that would eventually lead the Devil Rays to trade established outfielder Randy Winn to Seattle for the rights to manager Lou Piniella—a straight-up player-for-manager deal that had never been done before and hasn't been done since. With Naimoli's finances now stretched tight, ownership ordered a huge fire sale over the next couple of years, knocking the team's payroll from twelfth in the majors in 2000 to dead last two years later. The Devil Rays not only chopped major league talent; they also phased out their Latin American operations almost entirely, cutting off an essential pipeline of young talent. When Commissioner Bud Selig proposed contracting two teams, the Devil Rays were one of the candidates considered, their financial woes having already drowned out the optimism that flowed through Tropicana Field for that first pitch in 1998.

And then there was the losing. In 2001, the Devil Rays lost 100 games for the first time, then tacked on 106 more losses in 2002. Only once in the eight-year Naimoli-LaMar era did the team manage even 70 wins or avoid last place in the AL East. The losing didn't just beat up fans and management. It also wore on the players.

"You just hated to be going through what we were going through," said Carl Crawford, a second-round Devil Rays draft pick in 1999 who played through much of the old regime's reign, then stayed when new ownership took over. "Losing so much started to take a toll on you, and you started to think bad things about yourself. You just wished that things would change."

"You would just kind of get the vibe when a lot of veteran guys would sign [with the Devil Rays], that it would just be them on their last legs," recalled Scott Kazmir, who played in Tampa Bay from 2005 to 2009. "We were just a team that would get beat up by everyone in the American League East. We didn't really have any goals. We were just out there not having the confidence, not thinking that we could beat anyone."

Crawford and Kazmir shook their heads in disbelief as they recounted the bad old days. Both would become stars for the new Rays, young veterans and team leaders who lived through the darkest times and then the brightest. The new regime would transform the team's fortunes so quickly that Kazmir and company went from that defeatist attitude to making preseason playoff predictions nearly overnight.

Meanwhile, LaMar stuck around to the bitter end of Naimoli's reign. The GM got his first contract extension at the end of the Devil Rays' first season, then improbably nabbed another two-year deal in 2004, after his five-year contract expired. When LaMar was finally fired by new ownership after the 2005 season, he left his job as the fifth-longest-tenured general manager in baseball—despite a ghastly 518-777 record, a .400 winning percentage, and an average of 97 losses per season. Naimoli first hired LaMar based on his track record. He gave him his first contract extension because he thought LaMar was the right man to lead the Devil Rays to winning baseball. He then appreciated LaMar's efforts to keep costs down: "I'm not saying I like this quotient, but if he had a quotient of the cost per win, I think he would come out far ahead," Naimoli told the *St. Pete Times*. By the end, it seemed, neither man was going to leave until a third party forced them out, and that's exactly what happened after the 2005 season. LaMar and Devil Rays fans were left to wonder what might have been.

"Looking back, it wasn't the players we signed that I regret," LaMar said. "It was not being able to look at Vince and the ownership group and say, 'Gentlemen, trust me. We cannot do this.'"

CHAPTER 4 NEW BLOOD

The only thing that keeps this organization from being recognized as one of the finest in baseball is wins and losses at the major league level.
—CHUCK LaMar

There are few jobs in baseball less glamorous and more taxing than that of the area scout. These road warriors cover wide swaths of territory in pursuit of baseball talent. Their cars become their homes on their long, lonely drives down drab highways, burger wrappers and soda cups strewn all over the passenger seat. The area scout dreams of uncovering that hidden gem, the player other teams miss who goes on to stardom. The area scout isn't the person who makes the final decision on whether or not to draft a player. He doesn't even have a direct line to the scouting director, much less a team's general manager. For every player an area scout touts, a cross-checker—itself a pretty thankless, often lonely job—must travel to see that player perform, then report back to his bosses. Area scouts do gain credit if the team drafts and signs the player. But until that moment, the scout can only hope that someone will listen to him.

Fernando Arango understood the drawbacks of his job. Arango covered five states in his role as area scout for the Devil Rays:

Arkansas, Kansas, Missouri, Oklahoma, and Nebraska. His region was nowhere near the baseball hotbeds of California, Florida, and Texas. But the relative lack of talent in his area could also mean fewer eyes on some intriguing players, thus causing a few to slip under the radar. One spring Arango drove to the tiny town of Republic, Missouri, to catch a high school tournament. One player stood out. This one kid, a burly third baseman, just a junior, was smacking line drives all over the park. Arango introduced himself, and the two hit it off. Both scout and player were students of the game, happy to talk about the finer points long after others would tune out. Arango saw a rare mix of natural ability and baseball intelligence in the third baseman. He got the player's contact information and promised to keep in touch.

The following year, Arango's prospect accelerated his education. A strong student with an affinity for math, he earned all his high school credits by January 1999, then transferred to Maple Woods Community College in Kansas City. Arango went back to see the young man play. This time there would be no covert operation. Several major league scouts and representatives, including former Kansas City Royals manager John Wathan, also showed up to see various players. The high school third baseman, now playing as an oversized shortstop, launched two long home runs over the fence in left-center, into a thicket of trees.

"The ball sounded like a cannon went off," Arango recalled. "It wasn't even fair for him to use an aluminum bat."

No way we'll get this guy, Arango thought to himself. Still, when he met with his cross-checker, Stan Meek, as well as scouting director Dan Jennings, Arango filed a glowing report on the player. Meek had gone to see the young man in action, but wasn't nearly as impressed as Arango.

"He was this paunchy, thick-bodied kid," Jennings recalled. "Stan said to me, 'I saw this kid strike out two or three times, I don't know what position he'd play, I can't do anything with him. I can't write him up.'"

Undaunted, Arango told his bosses, "All I want to say about this guy is that someday he'll hit 40 home runs in the big leagues."

Jennings wasn't ready to dismiss Arango's report or his ranking of the top prospect in Arango's five-state area. So he sent in R. J. Harrison, a national cross-checker (who would take over, years later, as scouting director). Harrison's verdict: "I can't do anything with this guy."

Even after two emphatically negative reports, Jennings wanted to give Arango's find one last shot. The Devil Rays invited him to a pre-draft workout. No other team extended an invite. Not even the Royals, who played twenty minutes away.

Arango met his young protégé over Grand Slam breakfasts at a Denny's. The more they talked, the more Arango loved the smarts and grounded approach that went with the kid's talent. A huge contingent was waiting when Arango arrived at Tropicana Field. Jennings and Meek were there, along with fifteen other talent evaluators, Chuck LaMar, even Vince Naimoli. They watched a big group of draft hopefuls take their turns. Finally, the Missouri kid got his chance.

What happened next depends on who's telling the story. Arango claims his prospect looked like Lou Gehrig. Jennings saw no such thing.

Arango observed a 60-yard dash in 7.1 seconds, a good time for a player that size. The Devil Rays tried him at his college position of shortstop, where Arango says he handled an array of sharply hit grounders and showed good instincts for a big man. Jennings looked at the player's body, then suggested maybe he should catch. He'd never caught before and was worried he'd make a bad impression. Arango told him to relax, put on the equipment, and humor everyone for a few minutes. His first throw to second base came in a flash: 1.89 seconds. That time was phenomenal for a high school catcher and solid for a college catcher; several big league catchers show similar times. Only this player had never caught at any level.

Then he got in the batter's box and started roping line drives all over the park. Growing up, his dad had taught him to hit the ball with authority to right-center. Do that consistently, his father told him, and he could one day hit .300 in the big leagues. Jennings wasn't impressed. "Where's the power?" he muttered. Arango got the message. "They'd like you to hit it a little farther," he told his pupil. On the very next pitch, the kid crushed the ball off the top of the left-field foul pole. Arango smiled. He was going to get his man.

Jennings said he and the other scouts in attendance—all except Arango—remained concerned about the kid's thick build. They also focused on the negatives rather than the positives as Arango and Jennings both fell into a bit of confirmation bias. Jennings didn't like the player going down on one knee more than once to field grounders at short. He was also concerned about the player's performance at catcher: messy footwork and iffy throwing mechanics, despite a few good throws. At bat, he worried about the player's approach more than the results. "He's sitting very deep on his back leg, uppercut swing, back shoulder dipping pretty good," Jennings said.

"We go back upstairs, and I pose the question to the room," Jennings recounted. "'This kid Fernando's got on his list, you see anything different today than what we've seen before?' Nope, no one saw anything. We left the workout with the same identical issues that caused us not to have him high on our board."

When draft day arrived, Arango waited. And waited. The Devil Rays weren't going to take his guy in the first round, he knew. But after the third, fourth, and fifth rounds passed, with the kid still undrafted, he started to wonder if his prediction of forty-home-run seasons had simply been forgotten. The D-Rays weren't the only team passing. On and on the draft went, and still no news. There were a bunch of reasons for the snub. The Devil Rays went after Florida players aggressively, giving them preference over other prospects—and Florida-raised veteran free agents priority over non-Floridians—in a constant quest for local identity and support. It was a shortsighted practice that never paid tangible dividends and often hurt the team. They still worried about the player's build, as

Jennings had earlier, and wondered what position he would play. This was especially odd, since the player didn't get much chance to try out at third base, his natural position, or first, where Arango thought he could also fare well. Many skeptics also wondered about his age: he was born in the Dominican Republic, didn't move to the United States until high school, and always looked old for the age he was supposed to be. Meanwhile, the player's agent was new to the gig, and that uncertainty raised fears that just signing the guy could become dicey, even in the later rounds. Besides, the Devil Rays had their targeted names up on the draft board, and the draft was flying by. Jennings wasn't ignoring Arango's projection per se. There was just so much other stuff going on that they didn't give it much thought. By the time you get past the tenth round, most players have no shot of ever sniffing the big leagues, let alone becoming productive regulars, let alone becoming the kind of superstar Arango envisioned. No big deal.

With the first pick of the thirteenth round, the Devil Rays selected Jason Pruett, a left-handed pitcher out of a Texas community college. Seventeen picks later, the Cardinals threw their own dart. With the 402nd overall pick in the 1999 draft, St. Louis grabbed the player Arango had wanted all along. A pudgy kid from Missouri named Albert Pujols.

Arango was crushed. He quit his job and went to work at a sports agency. It didn't take long for the Devil Rays to realize their mistake. The player who once carried the weight of his *abuela*'s rice and beans carved his body into granite. Pujols crushed the ball the minute he got to the minor leagues. He continued to mash in spring training of 2001, impressing St. Louis brass so profoundly that the Cardinals tossed him into their opening day lineup, despite Pujols having played only three games above A-ball to that point. He hit .329 that year with 37 homers, a .403 on-base percentage, and a .610 slugging percentage, one of the greatest performances by any rookie in major league history.

Arango never forgot his initial scouting report, and neither did Pujols. Late in Pujols's third season, he reached 39 home runs.

Arango called Pujols with a message: he and his wife had a bottle of champagne chilling that they would open as soon as Pujols cracked number 40. The next day Pujols called back. Arango already knew what he was going to say.

"I got forty," Albert Pujols told one of the few scouts who had believed in him, "and forty-one too. You can go ahead and call the Devil Rays now."

To be fair, twenty-eight other teams missed on Pujols too. But the D-Rays' whiff on the greatest player of the past decade epitomized the team's early struggles in building a productive farm system. Tampa Bay would eventually become known as a scouting and player development powerhouse, one built partly on high draft picks, but also on a smarter approach than the competition. That reputation would take a while to bloom, though. Before that, the D-Rays were a team that struggled to build the talent pipeline it needed to win at the major league level. Those failures were the results of poor choices, cheapskate spending habits, and in the case of the thirteenth-round pick turned future Hall of Famer, plain old bad luck. That and failing to listen to baseball's equivalent of a foot soldier—the overworked, underpaid, underappreciated area scout.

For almost as long as there's been commerce in this country, there have been debates on how to regulate commerce. Grant too much unfettered power to the largest companies and you risk widespread malfeasance and potential monopolies. Throw up too many restrictions and those companies suffer, the economy suffers, and people lose their jobs. These debates cover every industry imaginable and show no signs of going away: Should the government overhaul the financial sector to prevent the kind of market manipulation that built a housing bubble and a near economic collapse and made the biggest banks too big to fail? Should regulators blow up coal mining companies given the heavy environmental damage and lapses in worker safety the industry has caused, or lay the hammer to oil companies like BP that callously drill deep into the ocean floor without any feasible plan if disaster strikes? Or does the threat of an energy crisis make it necessary to allow energy providers to run their businesses any way they choose? Evaluating the boundaries and definition of free markets will always rank among our society's biggest challenges.

Major League Baseball has no such dilemmas. It's not a free market and doesn't pretend to be one. To keep fans' interest, both teams must have a reasonable chance to win on any given day. To address this issue, rich teams—typically those in the largest and most profitable markets—share hundreds of millions of dollars in revenue every year with poorer teams. Still, by comparison, the amateur draft looks like full-blown kibbutz living. The team that finishes with the worst record in the major leagues gets rewarded with the top pick in the draft the following year. Meanwhile, success is penalized: win the World Series and you'll wait until the end of the first round to make your first pick. Picture the top producer at an investment bank getting a $5 bonus and the worst producer getting promoted to vice president and you've nailed the MLB draft.

Few teams have reaped baseball's equivalent of government cheese for longer than the Devil Rays. For ten straight years, the D-Rays lost enough games to draft in the top ten (though they would willingly surrender the first of those ten). Their futility earned them four number-one overall picks, with no selection lower than eighth. That collection of top draft picks helped form the core of a team that would wash away a decade of embarrassment in Tampa Bay. But despite several successful picks, the team's many draft misses during Chuck LaMar's decade as general manager remain damaging to this day.

By the time a baseball man rises to the position of GM, his scouting days are usually all but over. General managers seldom travel to small-town ballparks to follow A-ball prospects in other organizations who could someday make for interesting trade targets. They don't venture to the Dominican Republic to find sixteen-year-old diamonds in the rough. And with apologies to Billy Beane and his legendary chair-tossing skills, they rarely pull the strings on draft day, at least not after the first round; LaMar had little say in who the Devil Rays drafted beyond the early rounds. But he did assemble the team of scouts, coaches, and instructors who helped identify and mold some of that talent—including a few late-round picks—into winning major league players.

One of them was scouting director Dan Jennings. "He's fun to talk to, a great storyteller from Alabama," said *Baseball America's* John Manuel. "The classic scout that you drum up in your head." Jennings's scouting proclivities mirrored LaMar's: he loved strapping pitchers who threw blazing fastballs. For position players, he targeted speed and athleticism first—he'd find the athletes, the team could turn them into ballplayers.

Thanks to Major League Baseball's restrictions on expansion teams, Tampa Bay and Arizona were forced to pick at the end of each round in each of their first three drafts. Both franchises cried foul, complaining that the decision was unfair to a pair of expansion teams starting from nothing. Making matters worse was the challenge both teams faced in building complete scouting and player development departments from scratch. Simply forming and implementing an organizational plan and getting to know the preferences and quirks of everyone from the scouting and farm directors on down can take several years. Without the benefit of high picks, and with everyone simply getting to know each other's philosophies, the Devil Rays' first three drafts went horribly.

Dipping into the high school ranks—as they would many times in the ensuing years—the D-Rays grabbed an outfielder from North Carolina with the twenty-ninth overall pick in 1996. But Paul Wilder was a six-foot-five, 240-pound bruiser, far from the speed demons Jennings preferred. Wilder didn't play a single game in the big leagues, nor did the team's second- or third-round picks. The Devil Rays didn't draft a significant major league contributor that year until fifth-rounder Alex Sanchez, a slap-hitting speedster who hit a career .296 with little power and 122 stolen bases—while playing all but 43 of his career games with other teams. The D-Rays didn't find another good major leaguer until thirty-fourth rounder Dan Wheeler.

In 1997, Tampa Bay led off with a prototypical pick. With the thirty-first selection, the Devil Rays took Jason Standridge, a six-foot-four, 215-pound right-hander out of an Alabama high school, the kind of power pitcher who sets scouts' hearts fluttering. But again the pick bore little fruit: Standridge appeared in just eighty major league games (started just nine) and compiled a 5.80 ERA. The next seven picks? Kenny Kelly, Barrett Wright, Todd Belitz, Marquis Roberts, Doug Mansfield, Eddy Reyes, and Jack Joffrion, who combined to appear in thirty-nine major league games. Toby Hall, drafted out of UNLV in the ninth round, became a useful big league catcher for a few years. The draft yielded no one else of note for the next *sixty* rounds, until Heath Bell became a throw-a-dart success in round sixty-nine—with a different team, years after the Devil Rays failed to sign him.

The Devil Rays' first two drafts underscored the risks that come with drafting raw high school athletes, especially when the top pick comes well after the top ten. But the D-Rays weren't going to deviate from their plan, even after some of the earliest high school picks flamed out.

"We were facing tough competition in the American League East," said LaMar. "We also had the mentality that it was going to be rough going for a while, but that we wanted to eventually build a championship organization. We also knew that our payroll, for the most part, was not going to be what some of the other clubs would have. So we took the chance on high school players, knowing that if you hit on them, you had a chance to hit big."

LaMar shot himself in the foot after the 1997 season, blowing the Devil Rays' first-, second-, and third-round picks in '98 by signing veteran free agents Roberto Hernandez, Wilson Alvarez, and Dave Martinez; the Hernandez and Alvarez deals cost the team a combined $63 million in salary. Vince Naimoli and his let's-win-now-at-all-costs partners weren't as involved with these signings as they were in the creation of the ill-fated Hit Show. But LaMar did feel some ownership pressure to bring in proven veterans for the Devil Rays' debut season—though he should have known better than to blow the team's top three draft picks in the process. Two years later, the D-Rays would sacrifice their second-, third-, and fourth-round picks by signing another passel of veterans. As short-sighted, ill advised, and counterproductive as it was to blow tens of millions of dollars on aging veterans in those early Devil Rays years, punting high draft picks to sign them was even more indefensible.

"We'd be sitting there waiting to pick, and in the meantime our draft boards were getting decimated—it was difficult to keep morale," said Jennings. "You look at some of the drafts we had after that, and we ended up doing okay. But overall, they still didn't have the impact we were looking for."

Despite losing valuable picks, Jennings and his staff of scouts and cross-checkers finally found some draft success in '98. The Devil Rays grabbed Aubrey Huff in the fifth round, Joe Kennedy in the eighth, and Brandon Backe in the eighteenth, landing one very good major league hitter and two serviceable big league pitchers. Still, Huff, like Toby Hall before him, was a college draftee. After three years of drafts, the Devil Rays had scooped up a handful of players who would go on to become useful major leaguers. But the master plan to stock the farm system with high-upside high school-ers had yet to get started—owing to MLB's draft restrictions for the first three Tampa Bay drafts, the free-agent largesse of LaMar and the Devil Rays' owners, and a bunch of plain old whiffs.

It was the 1999 draft, however, where a few real signs of promise finally emerged. Despite losing out on Albert Pujols, four of the team's top five picks would make it to the big leagues. In the third round, the team pulled a Devil Rays exacta, not only targeting a big high school right-handed starter but also grabbing a local kid in Doug Waechter, a product of St. Pete's Northeast High School. Another imposing high school righty, Seth McClung of West Virginia, came in the fifth round.

The best Devil Ray of the bunch—in fact, the best Devil Ray

ever for quite some time—would prove to be the team's second-round pick, high school phenom Carl Crawford. Skeptics wondered if Crawford merely looked good in high school owing to poor competition in the Houston circuit in which he played. He didn't play in the big showcases that other top prospects attended. His split focus on football and baseball led critics to wonder if he could refine his raw baseball tools into playable skills. Crawford proved the doubters wrong, honing his baseball skills and becoming a major league All-Star. For Jennings and the Devil Rays, Crawford's rise helped vindicate their approach.

"If someone is going to surprise you, it will usually be someone with athletic ability," Jennings opined. "In my seven years [with the Devil Rays], the greatest compliment I ever had came from [Tampa Bay's future head of scouting] R. J. Harrison. He said, 'You try to hit a home run every round, don't you?' That kind of defined us."

However, it was the Rays' first pick in the 1999 draft that would prove to be the biggest risk—though for reasons they didn't anticipate. In their debut season, the Devil Rays had finished with the worst record in the American League and the second-worst record in the majors. Thanks to baseball's quirky alternating league system (which has since been changed) for determining number-one picks, plus the end of MLB's three-year restriction on high draft picks, Tampa Bay gained the right to call out the first name of the 1999 draft. The consensus top two picks that year were Josh Beckett, a big Texas high school right-hander who'd already been compared to Nolan Ryan and Roger Clemens, and Josh Hamilton, an obscenely talented high school player from North Carolina with more tools than Home Depot. Both players fit the high-upside mold that the Devil Rays craved. They chose Hamilton.

"We knew we would have to have pitching to win," LaMar said. "But we were picking so high in the draft that we made a concerted effort to lean toward position players. Our feeling there was that we might get pitching later on in the draft and that the attrition rate from a health standpoint of pitching made position players the better choice."

Hamilton was supposed to be the Devil Rays' biggest home run. Tampa Bay handed him a $4 million signing bonus and sent him to rookie ball, but Hamilton was too good for that entry-level competition, batting .347 with power in 56 games and finishing his first professional summer in low Class A. Following the season, *Baseball America* ranked him as baseball's number-13 prospect. He posted similar stats in 2000, hitting .302 with power and speed in the Class A South Atlantic League. This time *Baseball America* looked at Hamilton's pedigree, combined it with his precocious performances at age eighteen and nineteen, and named him the top prospect on the planet. Then the bottom dropped out. Hamilton got into a serious car accident. He plunged into a spiral of drug and alcohol abuse that wrecked his ability to play, earned him suspensions, and washed him completely out of baseball for three seasons, all of 2004 through 2006.

Scouting directors are hired and paid to avoid such mistakes. But drafting any supremely talented high school prospect is inherently risky. Often coddled by parents and coaches and lacking an authority figure who will speak the cold, hard truth, teenage superstars can lose their focus, drop the work habits that helped hone their skills, and flame out as prospects. And like a child actor given too much too soon, baseball players in similar situations can easily fall victim to all the temptations that come with fame at a young age. Talk to baseball men with any team, and they'll echo the glowing reports on Josh Hamilton. Sure, his precocious ability and young age carried risk as surely as it did huge upside. But the Devil Rays had no specific reason to believe that Hamilton would prove to be a cautionary tale rather than an organizational triumph.

As most baseball fans know now, Hamilton finally made the big leagues in 2007 and immediately played like a star. But his comeback began in Cincinnati; by then the Rays had given up. In something of a happy ending for Tampa Bay, Hamilton and the Rays would meet again under vastly different circumstances for each, in a memorable moment, years later.

What followed in the six years after the Hamilton and Pujols

whiffs, first under Jennings, then under his successors Cam Bonifay and Tim Wilken, was a decent run of later-round picks that
helped stock an eventual pennant-winning team (including James
Shields and Andy Sonnanstine, both part of the 2008 AL champion
Rays' starting rotation and the 2010 AL East–winning squad), as
well as the farm system. Still, the Devil Rays should have raked in
premium talent in the top rounds of the draft during LaMar's ten
years at the helm. During a seven-year span, they landed just five
players between rounds two and ten who have made notable contributions to the major league club or project as plus prospects:
Crawford (second round, 1999), Reid Brignac (second round,
2004), Wade Davis (third round, 2004), Jeremy Hellickson (fourth
round, 2005), and Fernando Perez (seventh round, 2004). The failure of the Hamilton pick in particular was a reminder that even
with the right process and the number-one overall pick, the draft remains a crapshoot, and soon the selection of Rocco Baldelli would
reinforce that point—though in retrospect bad omens followed him
from the start.

The Devil Rays loved the highly athletic high school outfielder
and A student from Rhode Island as a prospect and potential franchise cornerstone. A few of the more rabid prospect hounds
in baseball even mentioned him and Joe DiMaggio in the same
breath, somewhat for their common jersey numbers and heritage,
but yes, also for the raw talent. The Devil Rays sent Bill Livesey, the
special assistant to the GM who'd briefly served as director of
player development, to New England to watch Baldelli play. In his
second game watching the center fielder, Baldelli laid out for a line
drive and tore an oblique muscle. With Baldelli shut down for four
months, most other teams were chased off the scent. Just a couple
weeks before the draft, Baldelli returned to action, and Tampa Bay
sent an area scout to see him. That second look, combined with the
information they'd gathered earlier, convinced Jennings and eight
more talent evaluators to fly to Providence and work Baldelli out.

"We had to rent a van, there were so many of us," Jennings recalled. "We worked this kid out, and he was the same guy we re-

membered. He's crushing the ball all over the ballpark. The first at-bat he grounds out and runs a 3.97 or so to first base—some crazy number. We get back on the plane and set up our draft right away."

The Devil Rays spent the number-six pick of the 2000 draft on Baldelli. They thought they had a great prospect, so they were going to look past the injury that knocked him out for four months. Tearing a muscle while diving for a ball could be seen as a onetime event, so perhaps the Devil Rays shouldn't be faulted for what followed. But injuries and various maladies became Baldelli's kryptonite. His list of setbacks included a torn ACL, Tommy John surgery, chronic hamstring problems, and eventually a diagnosis of mitochondrial fatigue syndrome. He showed flashes of greatness when healthy and was a highly respected teammate who served as a source of inspiration in the 2008 playoffs, overcoming his mitochondrial condition and blasting a pair of homers as a part-time player. Still, given the early DiMaggio hype, the Devil Rays had to wonder what would have happened had Baldelli been able to stay on the field. He played in just 509 major league games, then retired just after his twenty-eighth birthday. Despite a token comeback in late 2010, Baldelli looked unlikely to ever again make a significant impact in the major leagues.

However, even considering Hamilton and Baldelli, the two biggest draft flops of LaMar's tenure were caused by the most indefensible excuse of all, the dirtiest word for any rebuilding team: *signability*.

In 2001, the Devil Rays owned the number-three pick in the draft. The consensus top two were, in some order, Minnesota catching phenom Joe Mauer and USC right-hander Mark Prior. The third-best player in the draft was widely believed to be Georgia Tech slugger Mark Teixeira. MLB strongly urged teams to adhere to a slotting system, with the maximum recommended signing bonus for each slot in the draft predetermined. A few months before the draft, Jennings and area scout Danny Hall went to see Teixeira. Was there any reason, Jennings asked, that he would *not* sign with the Devil Rays? No sir, Teixeira replied. Jennings left the meeting confident he would get his man. At the end of Georgia Tech's season, Jonathan Bonifay, another Devil Rays scout (and son of future scouting director Cam Bonifay), called Jennings. A third party had passed along the message that Teixeira wouldn't sign with the D-Rays if they drafted him. Livid, Jennings called the office of Scott Boras, the superagent who represented Teixeira. After a brief and heated chat, Boras told Jennings he'd have Teixeira see him for another face-to-face meeting. The young slugger had indeed changed his mind. His dad was whispering in his ear, as were other advisers, and Teixeira no longer wanted to play for Tampa Bay.

On the eve of the draft, LaMar called Boras in a last-ditch effort to sway Teixeira's camp in the Devil Rays' direction. To everyone's surprise, Boras told LaMar that yes, his client would sign with Tampa Bay. LaMar then held a closed-door meeting with Naimoli. The Devil Rays had fallen well short of attendance targets and other revenue projections put forth by Naimoli and his partners. They'd made matters exponentially worse by blowing tens of millions of dollars on Roberto Hernandez, Wilson Alvarez, and the aging bashers who comprised the infamous Hit Show. If the Devil Rays couldn't be disciplined about spending on major league talent, they were going to hold the line on the draft—never mind that elite prospects are the lifeblood of rebuilding teams, even more so for expansion teams. Besides, Naimoli fumed once the two men exited the meeting, if Teixeira's so unsure about playing in Tampa Bay, we don't want him anyway. Between the Teixeira camp's flip-flopping and contract demands that scared the D-Rays away, the team decided to pass.

With Teixeira out of the picture, the Devil Rays went to their fallback plan with the number-three pick: Dewon Brazelton, a right-handed pitcher from Middle Tennessee State. Brazelton's stuff was impressive; Jennings rated his changeup the best of any pitcher in the draft, an off-speed pitch held with a split-finger grip. Brazelton set win and strikeout records in college, and an ERA record with the U.S. national team. But red flags abounded. Brazelton's lack of a quality breaking pitch made him vulnerable against good right-handed hitters. He also had a history of injuries, including Tommy John surgery as well as knee surgery in high school; the latter had messed up his leg so badly that he couldn't run between starts and struggled with conditioning. Brazelton's biggest deficiency, though, was what baseball men call "makeup." Hailing from a small town in Tennessee, Brazelton was used to being the best player—by a wide margin—on every one of his teams; he bristled under the pressure of facing tougher competition. Even everyday needling from teammates, the kind of joking behavior found in every big league clubhouse, set him off. Brazelton was also burdened by personal tragedy: his twin brother, Fewon, was born with cerebral palsy, suffered through numerous other ailments, and finally died of pneumonia, a skin-and-bones ninety pounds when he passed in December 2002.

Brazelton struggled badly in his brief time in the majors, drawing boos from fans at the Trop and on at least one occasion from Naimoli too. His career ended in 2006 with an 8-25 record and a 6.38 ERA. The Devil Rays were so determined to draft on the cheap that they convinced Brazelton to accept his signing bonus spread over five years. Total amount: $2.5 million. Two picks later in the 2001 draft, the Texas Rangers picked Teixeira, paying him an identical $2.5 million bonus, but also giving him a $7 million major league contract. As with many other Boras clients, Teixeira ended up costing more but earning out many times over for his ball club. Just eight years into his major league career, he's already racked up more than 1,300 career hits and is closing in on 300 home runs, with four Gold Gloves and two All-Star appearances. For the additional cost of one year of Wilson Alvarez, Teixeira could have been a Devil Ray.

But LaMar, Jennings, and others noted that most major league teams don't think that way. They throw different baskets of cash at different organizational needs. Few teams actually take the time to crunch the numbers—gauge what percentage of draft picks pan out by round and by signing bonus, study how much pre-arbitration major league talent is worth for a team, and figure out the right formula for determining draft value. More often, the owner simply approves a certain number for a season's major league payroll, a certain number for international signings, and a certain number for the draft.

"Teams have a set signing budget," explained *Baseball America*'s John Manuel. "But you have to decide which players are worth stepping out for, worth paying the extra dollars. If your talent evaluators say that's the best guy for that spot, you have to take him, regardless of price tag. If he's as good as you think he's going to be, he'll be worth it anyway, especially when you consider those cost-controlled first few major league years. Taking a signability guy, unless you *really* believe in him, almost always is the wrong choice."

The D-Rays would eventually get all this right, remaining flexible in shuttling resources from player development to the big league roster and back, depending on need. They would smash league-recommended payment levels for certain prospects when they were confident they were getting a premium talent. They were nimble, creative, and open-minded in all their endeavors—*after* LaMar gave way to Andrew Friedman and the new management team.

LaMar didn't leave the cupboard entirely bare, however. In fact, he occasionally got lucky. In 2002, the Rays actually benefited from another team's cheapness when, with the number-one overall pick in the 2002 draft, the Pittsburgh Pirates took college right-hander Bryan Bullington. The Pirates proudly told the world they'd landed a future number-three starter that day, as if acquiring a pitcher with the upside of being a number-three starter was something to celebrate. (Bullington never met even that modest goal.) Ecstatic, Tampa Bay pounced on number-two pick B. J. Upton, who has since become a frontline player with the Rays.

Even LaMar's intransigence finally paid off: he gained a reputation among other GMs as being impossible to deal with because he would ask for more in return during trade talks than anyone else in the game. But after years of failed opportunities to stock the farm system with veteran-for-prospect trades, Tampa Bay acquired Scott

Kazmir, a hugely talented, hard-throwing lefty prospect who quickly became the best pitcher in franchise history. The main player going the other way in the four-player trade was Victor Zambrano, the Devil Rays' number-one starter at the time, who turned out to be anything but for the Mets. Zambrano made just three more starts that year before missing the rest of the season due to injury, and winning only ten more games for the rest of his career.

Despite the Kazmir heist, the end of LaMar's tenure in 2005 left the Devil Rays wishing they'd done more, especially with the stream of high first-round picks that came their way. First-rounders Evan Longoria and David Price followed in the Devil Rays' first two years under new management, giving the team a big lift. Still, cynics would later claim that any team could finish last for the better part of a decade, rack up a bunch of picks, and win—a position some of the game's brightest minds dispute.

"It's not as simple as that," said Dave Dombrowski, GM and architect of several successful, young teams, including the Montreal Expos of the 1990s, the two-time champion Florida Marlins, and the 2006 AL pennant–winning Detroit Tigers. "If you're consistently drafting high, you should have more hits than other clubs. But it's no guarantee. And if you don't, you should ask yourself, 'Why not? What are we doing wrong?'"

The problem was, the Devil Rays didn't ask themselves those questions. But as the transition from the Naimoli/LaMar era to Sternberg's new regime took place, they began to do exactly that. And fortunately for Tampa Bay denizens, they began to find and make their own advantages.

An example: in the franchise's first few years, the Devil Rays faced a problem that remains common around baseball—what one baseball ops executive called "stereo teaching." A pitcher coming up through the minor leagues might meet a pitching coach at A-ball who teaches the slider. At Double A, that same pitcher might be ordered to junk the slider and instead throw a curve. At Triple A, it's back to the slider. The different noises coming out of all those speakers can produce a player who hasn't mastered either pitch and isn't ready for the majors. Individual coaches, scouts, and roving instructors bring in their own expertise, with no guiding set of principles available to help convey a common message. Mitch Lukevics aimed to change all that. Lukevics ran the Yankees' farm system for eight years. During that time, he learned the importance of balancing a structured approach with granting autonomy to coaches and instructors. The goal, said Yankees senior VP of baseball ops Mark Newman, was to make sure the organization wasn't messing with top prospects' minds, while still allowing enough autonomy "for great teachers to innovate." When Lukevics signed on as the Rays' director of minor league operations, he aimed to create the equivalent of "the Yankee Way," a uniform, top-to-bottom approach that would produce topflight, major league–ready talent, the way he had with Derek Jeter, Mariano Rivera, Andy Pettitte, Jorge Posada, and other homegrown Yankees stars.

All those top-ten draft picks helped. So did a cadre of number crunchers. But the Rays needed more than raw talent, or even the ability to spot talent, to topple the Yankees and Red Sox. It took a player development system that could mold those draft picks, international signings, scrap-heap free agents, and trade targets into big league contributors. To that end, they employed two roving minor league instructors for the three biggest coaching specialties—two field coordinators, two hitting coordinators, two pitching coordinators—instead of the standard one per skill. "They're throwing more resources at the minor leagues, emphasizing it more, than anyone else," said *Baseball America* writer John Manuel.

The move to two pitching coordinators coincided with an organization-wide focus on developing young arms. Not that this was any kind of revolutionary strategy. But as the Devil Rays started to assemble young talent in the last days of Vince Naimoli and Chuck LaMar, most of that talent was on the position player side, especially in the outfield. The pitching cupboard was bare. In 2005, the final year for the old regime, the following pitchers made 130 of Tampa Bay's 162 starts: Mark Hendrickson, Doug Waechter, Seth McClung, Casey Fossum, Dewon Brazelton, Rob Bell, Tim Corcoran, John Webb, and a washed-up Hideo Nomo.

Once the Wall Street trio assumed control, the team's methodology changed. With LaMar in charge, Lukevics had watched old-fashioned pitching philosophies govern player development decisions. Some were excessively cautious, with no empirical evidence to back them up. When a pitcher recovers from an injury, for instance, the universal baseball rule is to make sure he rehabs by throwing long-toss from no more than 120 feet away. Somehow that untested practice became the norm for *all* long-toss for many old-fashioned teams, including the Devil Rays. That caution didn't extend to pitch counts, though: for years, Tampa Bay farmhands were allowed to rack up heavy workloads, both game by game and over the course of a season, leading to the usual litany of pitching injuries. Lukevics and his right-hand man, *Baseball Prospectus* alum Chaim Bloom, favored a more empirical approach. With Lukevics and Bloom running the farm system, the focus shifted to an evidence-based player development process, one the Rays hoped would produce a healthier and more productive crop of pitching prospects.

Xavier Hernandez embraced the Rays' new philosophy. Hired in 2002, the man most people call "X" spent three years as the pitching coach with Class A Charleston and two years at Double A Montgomery before landing at Triple A Durham in 2007. X found himself face-to-face with many of the best young players in the system, several of whom ended up on the Rays' pennant-winning squad of '08. One such pitcher was Jeff Niemann, the Rays' first-round pick in 2004. Many teams preach uniformity in their prospects' pitching and hitting mechanics. Hitches in swings are corrected, weird footfalls in pitchers are tweaked. The intentions are pure—get a hitter's bat through the zone quicker, prevent movements that might lead to a pitching injury. But X recognized that often the best approach was to leave well enough alone.

At six-foot-nine, 200-and-a-lot, Niemann faced the same prob-

lems most big pitchers face—having slight mechanical flaws magnified by the sheer size of his body. He was what X called a "jabber":
when Niemann took the ball out of his glove, there was no smooth
backstroke into his forward motion. X emphasized what Niemann
could do well, without overstressing what he didn't. "Technically
you want to clean that up, but really you can't. So you just have to
work around those flaws. You can be a jabber in back but still be
able to make a clean delivery out front. Pitching and delivery is all
about timing. As long as he had nice, smooth drive to the plate, it all
worked."

Pinpointing a pitcher's success, let alone a team full of pitchers,
creates a chicken-or-the-egg quandary. The increased focus on
pitching in the draft, starting late in LaMar's tenure and continuing
under Andrew Friedman and scouting director R. J. Harrison, improved the quality and quantity of arms in the Rays system. But
merely making more and better choices can't account for the massive difference in the caliber of pitchers who cracked and stuck on
the major league roster. Late-round picks such as James Shields
and Andy Sonnanstine joined higher-pedigree picks like Niemann,
David Price, and Wade Davis in turning the Rays' major league
pitching staff from the lowliest bunch in the majors to the back-
bone of one pennant-winning club and the foundation of future
contenders.

The Rays' new generation of pitchers wasn't merely good. It was
also extraordinarily healthy. From late 2005 to mid-2009, only one
pitcher at any level of the organization, left-hander Jacob McGee,
underwent Tommy John surgery; no team saw a lower rate during
that stretch. From May 2008 to August 2010, only one Rays starter,
Scott Kazmir, spent a single day on the disabled list, making Tampa
Bay's the healthiest pitching staff in baseball by a mile. (Niemann
and Davis went on the DL in August 2010 with minor injuries; both
returned quickly.) Meanwhile, the scarcity of healthy, homegrown
pitching drove other teams to load up on veterans well past their
prime, which in turn put them at greater risk for injury. Well past
their 1990s glory years for young pitcher development, the 2008

Braves turned to ancient names like John Smoltz and Tom Glavine and DL regulars like Mike Hampton to shore up a shallow staff. Those three wounded warriors combined with expected ace Tim Hudson to log a total of seven DL trips. All told, the Braves staff notched 467 DL days, costing the team $37.9 million in lost workdays.

Either the Rays were extraordinarily lucky in their ability to keep their starters upright and effective, or their scouts and player development staff found a way to produce starting pitchers who could take the ball every fifth day and succeed. Probably a little of both. Once the Rays pitchers caught up to (and passed) their hitters, the result was a farm system that earned annual plaudits from *Baseball America* as one of the best in the game. Lukevics, Bloom, Hernandez, and company parlayed a player development pipeline already improving by the end of the old regime into a feeder system for the holy grail of baseball accomplishments.

"Win right now *and* maintain long-term excellence," said Newman, the Yankees' head of baseball ops. "It is really, really hard to do both those things at the same time."

The Devil Rays showed that it would take a complete organizational overhaul—a new owner, a new GM, a new manager, a cadre of eager, young stat wizards, and a whole new way of thinking—to grow the seeds planted by the first Devil Rays regime into a winning baseball team.

They just needed the right people to lead the charge.

CHAPTER 5 THE TAKEOVER

With the prices of franchises, you've got to have
someone who understands the pocketbook, the brand,
and what it takes to grow it. Given all the needs, I need
someone with a broader set of skills.
—STUART STERNBERG

The most valuable skill an investor can possess is the ability to time the market. You can buy one hundred shares of Google, convinced the company's going to take over the world. But if a bear market attacks, even the best stocks will probably crash. Time your purchase right, though, and even a company with mediocre fundamentals and iffy prospects can make you rich. The same holds true for traders of commodities or any other investment. The best investing strategies can blow up in your face if the market doesn't cooperate.

Yet few investors have mastered the art of timing the market. Market tops tend to occur when conditions look perfect. In March 2000, Internet stocks seemed like a sure thing. Dot-coms with the flimsiest business models and no hope for profitability were racking up triple-digit gains, often in a matter of months or even weeks. Few investors can resist the greed that kicks in when such gains become possible. Market bottoms tend to occur when conditions look their worst. By October 2002, the NASDAQ had plummeted 78% from its peak two and a half years earlier. Few investors can resist the fear that takes hold when severe losses seem assured.

The same misconceptions prevail in baseball: dynasties look like they'll never end, perennial losers like they'll never turn it around. But where other prospective owners might have looked at the Tampa Bay Devil Rays and seen hopelessness, Stuart Sternberg saw a golden opportunity. The shrewdest equity investors understand that the stock market will often start to rebound several months, perhaps even a year or more, before the broader economy picks up and the hundreds of thousands of newly unemployed workers find new jobs. Sternberg could likewise close his eyes and imagine a Devil Rays franchise that could implement better business practices, connect to the community, and, with the help of new talent on and off the field, eventually field a winning ball club.

"We said, 'This is horrible,' and when I hear 'horrible,' I go 'ooooooh,'" Sternberg told *The New York Times*. "I'm a buy-low guy, and if you pay the right price for something, I don't care what it is, you can't go very wrong."

Sternberg bought a 48% share of the Devil Rays in May 2004 for $65 million, with Vince Naimoli retaining a 15% stake and a group of limited partners controlling 37%. Sternberg planned to wrest the title of managing partner from Naimoli in January 2007. Meanwhile, he watched Naimoli continue to alienate the team's fan base and the Tampa Bay business community, running the franchise on the cheap and further damaging its local and national reputation. Eager to start his planned overhaul, Sternberg paid Naimoli a reported bonus of at least $5 million to take control earlier, consummating the deal in October 2005.

The deal was a bargain, a price barely higher, when prorated, than the $130 million expansion fee Naimoli and his partners had paid ten years earlier. Just a few months after Sternberg took over, *Forbes* magazine valued the Devil Rays at $209 million, with $116 million in 2005 revenue and healthy operating income of $20.3 million (thirteenth-best in MLB, thanks mostly to Naimoli's penny-pinching and baseball's generous revenue-sharing program). Sternberg's camp later disputed the *Forbes* valuation, noting that the team was in fact losing money and that the magazine's figures didn't account for capital improvements, deferred salary compensation, and other expenses. During the 2005 season, then-manager Lou Piniella told *Sports Illustrated* that he could take the D-Rays to the playoffs, if only player payroll could be raised by $20 million. Matt Silverman read the article and shook his head. If payroll rose by $20 million, he said, the team would go bankrupt.

Still, given the typically steep inflation rates for pro sports franchise values, Sternberg was clearly buying low. Throw in the impressive stable of young talent that Chuck LaMar and seven years of high draft picks yielded and the Devil Rays had perfectly timed the bottom of the market.

Given Sternberg's track record, no one should have been surprised. His Wall Street career began in the late '70s, when he traded equity options part-time on the American Stock Exchange (a much smaller pond than the New York Stock Exchange) while majoring in finance at St. John's University in New York. He then landed a job at Spear, Leeds & Kellogg. The company was one of the leading market makers on Wall Street—despite its Jersey City headquarters. Market makers, also known as specialists, manage the sale of stocks on the floor of the exchange, matching up buyers and sellers at a fixed price, then taking a small cut off the top as commission. Specialists like SLK also buy stock when there's an imbalance between buyers and sellers and perform other needed trading services.

SLK started the 1970s with just fifty employees, then went on a buying spree. By 1978, when Sternberg was still at St. John's, SLK partner Jimmy Kellogg had overseen a series of acquisitions that added several longtime Wall Street specialist firms to SLK's arsenal. Kellogg retired that year, then died two years later, leaving behind trusts that allowed the company to continue its buying binge. By the early 1980s, SLK employed more than seven hundred people, including Sternberg. But the deregulation of commission rates, along with institutional trading in blocks of stocks far too big for specialists like SLK to handle, cast the company's future into doubt. A successful company alum named John Mulheren offered $350 million to acquire SLK in 1985. Had the buyout gone through, Sternberg's career might have turned out very differently.

Success on Wall Street, as in baseball, depends on a combination of skill and luck. Sternberg had both. After spurning the initial buyout offer, SLK then pondered a number of different liquidation events—methods the managing partners could use to cash out. The company first considered an initial public offering, following just-completed, successful IPOs by brokerage firms like Bear, Stearns and Morgan Stanley. SLK also pursued the options of either a leveraged buyout or a straight sale to a bigger company. Any of those moves would have been of little benefit to Sternberg, who was years away from becoming a senior partner who could get rich from a liquidation event. Instead, the company began a new era of growth, acquiring stock trade–clearing companies that helped SLK expand its reach. SLK then dodged several controversies, avoiding the pitfalls that beset numerous other Wall Street firms in the "anything goes" 1980s.

The company made several key moves in the 1990s, growing its electronic communication networks capabilities and program trading operations. Having dramatically grown the business and stayed independent all those years, SLK made itself into a prime buyout candidate. When Goldman Sachs finally offered $6.3 billion for the company in September 2000, SLK accepted. Sternberg was by then one of six senior partners who collectively owned a minority stake in SLK. Like Dallas Mavericks owner (and author of this book's foreword) Mark Cuban and his partner Todd Wagner selling Broadcast.com for $5.7 billion in Yahoo! stock at the top of the tech bubble, Sternberg and his partners landed the perfect price at the perfect time.

Scandals would soon rip through Wall Street, with SLK right in the middle of things. Business fell off sharply at Goldman's new SLK division as Wall Street entered a massive bear market that lasted two and a half years. None of this was Sternberg's problem: he'd sold right before things turned for the worse, getting paid in Goldman Sachs stock that would prove to be a gigantic winner in later years. The suddenly very wealthy Sternberg worked in Goldman's merchant banking division for two years before seizing on his next opportunity—a chance for him and his old SLK partners to buy into the Tampa Bay Devil Rays. Sternberg was a huge baseball fan who grew up in Brooklyn, cheered for the Mets, and named his first son after Sandy Koufax. Now he had an opportunity to own a major league franchise. It did take him a little while to warm up to the idea of the Devil Rays, though. His 2002 reaction to first learning that he could buy into baseball's perennial doormat was, he said, "Ewwww." But Sternberg would soon embrace the idea of buying a Devil Rays organization with precarious finances—and thus plenty of upside.

"Whatever needs to be done, we're going to do it," he vowed after completing the deal.

Sternberg's opportunistic approach would inform his decisions as the owner of a major league baseball club. The two lieutenants he would hire to run the club would employ the same "buy low, sell high" mentality. He didn't have to look far to find his first hire.

Matt Silverman graduated cum laude with an economics degree from Harvard in 1998, then caught on with Goldman Sachs. New talent working for the investment banking giant had to show ambition and ability if they hoped to advance. Silverman would show both. On top of his regular work coming up through Goldman's training program, Silverman started his own venture, cofounding a real estate software company that used the Web to aid large real estate transactions. The economy was growing fast in the late '90s, and software companies were on fire. Working as the company's CFO, Silverman saw huge potential for the start-up. But the bursting of the Internet bubble after the stock market's 2000 peak ended all hopes, and the company faded away.

Silverman's next big opportunity would come with Sternberg: the pair spent nine months working on mergers and acquisitions together in Goldman's merchant banking division, acquiring a total of ten companies, most of them relatively minor deals. In many ways, both men fit the Goldman profile. When Silverman talked about his work, he didn't reveal a single word that would give away any secrets. He wanted to learn from his new mentor and get better at his job. The best way to do that, he felt, was to measure his words and be a perpetual listener.

Working with mergers and acquisitions also forced Silverman to take an analytical approach to company valuation. He noted all the spending mistakes that struggling companies made and all the revenue-boosting methods that pumped up surging companies' balance sheets. Silverman had already gotten a firsthand look at how a good business idea could fail to pan out owing to circumstances beyond his control. Still in his mid-twenties, Silverman gained as much valuable experience and insight in a few short years as many others might in decades.

"He loves to learn," said Colorado Rockies president Keli McGregor, a few weeks before his untimely death in April 2010. "He's not going to interrupt a conversation—he'll take it in and listen first. Even as we sat here at Starbucks and reflected on their great [2008] season and where they were at, he was still very observant. He's got a great quality about him: if he doesn't know, he's not afraid to tell you he doesn't know."

After nine months working with Sternberg, Silverman was reassigned. Sternberg retired six months later. Silverman soon began looking for new endeavors. He'd become closer friends with Sternberg since his mentor's departure and went asking for advice: should he leave Goldman to pursue writing a book, loosely based on his relationship with his father and their love of baseball? Sternberg told him to follow his heart. Who knows, maybe one day they'd work together again. Maybe even on something big.

Such an opportunity would come sooner than he'd expect. While at Goldman, Silverman bonded with Sternberg over baseball, Silverman's own childhood having minted him as a big Cubs and Ryne Sandberg fan. A year after Sternberg left Goldman, Silverman got the call: Sternberg had a chance to buy controlling interest in the Tampa Bay Devil Rays. Would Silverman like to help put the deal together?

For Silverman, just twenty-six, it was the opportunity of a lifetime—a chance to blend the lessons he'd learned at Goldman with his childhood love, baseball. Still, he had to consider that most important of Wall Street concerns: opportunity cost. If he went down this road with Sternberg, he'd be shelving his new book project, not to mention the riches that could come with a successful return to investment banking if he went down that road. Still, working on a deal to buy a major league baseball team—and maybe stay on and build a career in baseball—was too much fun to pass up. He was in.

All three of the Rays' top decision-makers form a case study in the value of meshing passion with business acumen. Silverman had more than his share of alternate career opportunities. But so too would his running mate Andrew Friedman, a rising private equity star who also punted his Wall Street career and eventually rose to become the Rays' de facto GM. And a man of Sternberg's net worth could have chosen any number of business opportunities with greater profit potential. Not everyone gets a chance to do what they love. But "the Tampa Bay Three" would prove that pursuing that goal, even with risk and sacrifice involved, was usually well worth it.

The deal was done by May 2004. As Silverman had surmised, Sternberg asked that he stay on as an executive. Silverman started with the title of director of strategic planning but quickly graduated to vice president of planning and development. The tacit expectation, once he'd studied the industry and Sternberg had assumed control of the team from Naimoli, was that Silverman would eventually run the team's day-to-day business operations.

"Meeting Matt, the first thing you notice is that he's a pretty young guy," said Jeff Cogen, president of the Dallas Stars and former president of the Texas Rangers, who first met Silverman at the MLB owners' meetings in 2006, when Silverman was twenty-nine but looked younger. "That quickly dissipates after you spend ten minutes with the guy. Stu was impressed with Matt's prowess—he knew [Matt] could certainly do the New York banker thing. Then you talk to Matt and you see that Stu hit it on the button. Here's an incredibly cerebral, personable individual who really embraced his role in baseball."

With Silverman installed as the man to eventually head up the business, Sternberg needed someone else to run the baseball side. Overseeing sponsorships, driving new revenue streams, negotiating future stadium deals—these were tasks that could conceivably be handled by an outsider. But with the day approaching for Sternberg to wrest control of the Devil Rays from Naimoli, he would need someone with baseball acumen to make the big trades and player signings.

In the past, that person would probably have been an ex-player, maybe a former manager, longtime scout, or player development guru. Recently, that had started to change. The Boston Red Sox made Theo Epstein the youngest general manager in major league history when they hired him in November 2002. Epstein didn't remotely fit the role of a baseball lifer. For one thing, he hadn't lived much life, taking the GM job at age twenty-eight. He'd never played major league baseball, any other form of professional baseball, or even any college or high school ball. But he had accumulated some impressive baseball experience in a relatively short amount of time.

After earning his degree in American studies from Yale, Epstein started cramming for the job he'd long dreamed about. Starting as an intern with the San Diego Padres' public relations department, Epstein spent the next few years working insane hours, soaking up as much information as possible on subjects ranging from scouting to player arbitration, and earning a move to the Padres' baseball operations department and eventually a promotion to head of baseball ops. He did all that while also earning his law degree. When Padres president and CEO Larry Lucchino made the move to Boston, he remembered the only person in San Diego who would stay in the office as late as he did every night, hours after everyone else had gone home. Epstein's hire as Red Sox GM inspired an army of bright college graduates to try to follow the same path: take any job you can get in baseball, kill yourself for a few years, and maybe one day you too can be the man in charge—maybe even before your thirtieth birthday like Theo.

Just a few months after Epstein joined the Red Sox, veteran financial journalist Michael Lewis published *Moneyball*, the story of Oakland A's GM Billy Beane and the methods he used to win multiple division titles, slaying teams with much higher payrolls in the process. Beane was a top high school prospect who'd made it to the majors as a player. But as he later climbed the ranks of Oakland's front office and learned from incumbent GM Sandy Alderson, Beane realized that he would need to unlearn all the old saws that permeated decision-making in baseball. When Beane finally ascended to the role of A's GM, he embraced objective analysis over appeals to authority, hard evidence over tradition. He was a baseball insider who approached his job with an outsider's sensibilities.

Andrew Friedman had the same evidence-based background working in his favor when he first met Sternberg in 2003. But the introduction happened for simpler reasons. Working as an analyst for Bear Stearns, Friedman had become friendly with Silverman, a fellow Wall Street upstart who loved baseball. When Silverman signed on to assist in Sternberg's purchase of the Devil Rays, he recommended a meeting with Friedman. The three men met at a diner near Sternberg's home in Rye, New York. Sternberg and Friedman talked about Wall Street, baseball, and life, discovering they had much in common.

"He had the same thought process I did," Sternberg told the *St. Petersburg Times*. "He knows his stuff and he's a quick study. The bottom line is, ultimately, this is a results-driven business."

Friedman would prove his ability to deliver results, though he took a circuitous path to get there. Like Silverman, Friedman had dreamed of making a career in baseball. Unlike his buddy, he had enough playing ability to imagine a quicker path. Friedman played college ball at Tulane, manning the outfield for the Green Wave. He idolized Lenny Dykstra, writing the hard-nosed Mets and

Phillies star's number on the back of his cleats and adopting the same nickname, "Nails." Friedman didn't quite have Dykstra's ability, though, nor his longevity; a shoulder injury ended his collegiate career. Setting off for what he presumed would be a career on Wall Street, Friedman joined Bear Stearns in 1999, spending two years there as an entry-level analyst. It was at his next job, though, that Friedman would hone his deal-making skills (in stark contrast to Dykstra, whose own foray into investing would end in disaster).

Private equity is the lifeblood of many up-and-coming companies. Before a company's owners can monetize their business through an initial public offering or other means, they often need seed money—for research and development, to launch a new product, to hire key personnel, to build a death ray to dissuade would-be competitors, and so on. Private equity can take many forms, including venture capital, growth capital, and leveraged buyouts. In each case, the goal is to invest money in a company you believe has growth potential. Finding the right source for your investment is paramount, but so too is timing the investment correctly. The most successful private equity investors typically have a firm grasp of the quantitative factors needed to turn a profit. They also have excellent intuition, being able to spot broad market-, industry-, and company-specific trends well before they come into play. To become a successful private equity investor, you need to know how to make a deal.

When Wayne Clevinger first met Friedman, he saw the potential for all those qualities. Clevinger's firm, MidMark Capital, based in Morristown, New Jersey, is a small private equity shop that manages $300 million in funds. MidMark constantly searches for promising young junior associates. The typical path might see the company hire someone in his early to mid-twenties, keep him for a couple years, then wish him well as he heads off to get his MBA. It's a stepping-stone job for many Wall Street neophytes, though a few young associates will return from business school, then rise through the MidMark ranks. Within a few months, Clevinger realized that his new hire wasn't going to grad school to get his MBA, nor did he need to. Instead, MidMark would bump him up to senior associate in just two years, an unprecedented move by the company.

"He was the complete package," said Clevinger, MidMark's co-founder and managing director. "He had a winning smile and great personality. He was so damn bright, he actually appeared bored at times—he *was* bored. So we got him doing projects a junior partner would normally handle, and he handled them well. We wanted to make him a partner as quickly as possible."

Clevinger recalls the moment he knew Friedman was destined for big things. A couple of months into Friedman's tenure at Mid-Mark, Clevinger and most of the other partners and senior associates had to attend a black-tie affair. It was a delicate time to drop off the grid: MidMark was trying to nail down the purchase of a home health care company, but the two sides remained far apart on price. Clevinger left for the gala, frustrated by the lack of progress. He called Friedman, who was working late as usual. Did he want to take a shot at wrapping up the transaction, Clevinger wanted to know.

"I can wrap it up if you like," Friedman told his boss, "or do even better if you like." The young associate believed in his negotiating skills and had a handle on all the numbers. "It's your baby, full speed ahead," Clevinger said, eager to see what Friedman could do. Friedman closed the deal as promised. He also materially improved its terms, as promised.

Friedman's duties expanded rapidly. At any given time, Mid-Mark might have held fifteen companies in its portfolio. Friedman's job was to do the modeling for all of them—to project revenue and net income streams and break down best- and worst-case scenarios based on the dynamics of their particular industries. Crunching the numbers came easily to him. But taking the numbers and wielding them in negotiations? That, he loved. Friedman helped negotiate company purchase prices, lining up all manner of financing and using stock options and other incentives to convince a company's senior management to put their own skin in the game. He advised MidMark when to make a modest investment and when to go all-in on a company with big potential.

Sternberg kept in close contact with Friedman. Already working the kind of breakneck hours typical of a young Wall Street associate, Friedman toiled into the middle of the night on his own time, doing financial analysis to assist Sternberg's Devil Rays bid. When Sternberg and Silverman closed the deal to purchase the 48% stake in the Devil Rays, they wooed Friedman to join them. Friedman had no experience of any kind in a baseball front office. But it wasn't hard to see how his combination of analytical and people skills could translate to baseball. If he could forge a compromise with high-powered business execs, he could work out contracts that would benefit a baseball team and its players. If he could persuade a CEO to take a mutually beneficial risk, he could do the same with another team's general manager. If he could run complex mathematical models to gauge the value of a financing deal, he could weigh the merits of a baseball trade. That was the thinking anyway.

"A really smart, analytical GM is going to be better than one who is not as analytical," said Matt Finley, another managing director at MidMark. "If you have the ability to get to nuggets of truth, you have the ability to perform better than someone who manages by the seat of his pants. That's my belief in anything. Any complicated business can benefit from serious analysis, if there are enough data available."

Sternberg made his pitch: if he came to work for the Devil Rays and learned the ropes for a couple of years, when the ownership transfer was done Friedman could run—or at least co-run—the baseball side of the team. It was an offer that required guts to make, and guts to accept. The Oakland A's quantitative approach to winning on a budget had been compared to the methods used on Wall Street. But no one had successfully parlayed a career on Wall Street into the role of major league general manager before. Meanwhile, Friedman, like Silverman, would be leaving what could be a hugely lucrative career behind if he accepted Sternberg's offer. His decision was in many ways far more difficult than Silverman's: Friedman was working on multimillion-dollar deals every day, on his way to making partner at a successful private equity firm, while Silverman had willingly stepped away from the rat race to pursue other ventures.

Friedman went home to Houston to mull the decision with his family. His father told him to stay with MidMark. His girlfriend wanted to stay in New York rather than move to Florida. His mother had a different take.

"She told him, 'Andrew, you have to go with your heart on this,'" Clevinger recalled. "I thought, 'Oh boy, we're done.'"

Friedman took the job with the Devil Rays, with the nominal title of director of baseball development—though he and Silverman would soon gain promotions. When Sternberg seized control in October 2005, Silverman took over as the youngest team president in baseball, while Friedman became executive vice president of baseball operations, joining Jon Daniels of the Texas Rangers, another young gun plucked out of the business world, as the two newest members of "the Twenty-Something General Manager Club."

Baseball wouldn't have been ready for Silverman and Friedman five or ten years earlier. But the two men benefited from their own good timing. With the help of Dan Feinstein (a onetime video coordinator with the A's who was also featured in *Moneyball*), former Houston Astros general manager Gerry Hunsicker, and other baseball veterans, Friedman could assume the role of GM, knowing baseball had started to accept people with younger, nontraditional profiles in that role. With the help of skilled, handpicked sales, marketing, and operations people, Silverman could also settle in. Not only did Silverman and Friedman join the Devil Rays at just the right time, but they left their Wall Street careers behind right on time too. Friedman's first employer, Bear Stearns, would collapse during the Wall Street meltdown of 2008—the husk of a once-proud company was sold off to JPMorgan Chase. Silverman's former employer, Goldman Sachs, would remain very much intact, though it would become a symbol for Wall Street greed and impropriety, absorbing multiple accusations of everything from accounting irregularities to the U.S. subprime mortgage and European debt crises to an excessive coziness with the federal government that allegedly enabled the company to escape serious repercussions.

Silverman and Friedman experienced one of the biggest shifts from their old existence almost immediately. Neither would sign contracts, instead considering themselves, as Friedman said, "employees at will." Sternberg and his two young hires trusted each other. They sought to build an environment where everyone in the organization could do their job without fear of someone else micromanaging or undermining them—those types of bullying being hallmarks of the Naimoli era. Silverman and Friedman would thoroughly vet every hire, searching for people who not only were business- and baseball-savvy but were also self-starters; they meant to create a culture in which independent thought was rewarded rather than punished.

The organization had its first cathartic moment at Halloween 2005, immediately after operating control passed to Sternberg. Working under Vince Naimoli and his minions had felt like being the protagonist in *Office Space,* who fills out just enough TPS reports to avoid getting dressed down by each of his eight bosses. But under Sternberg, Silverman, and Friedman, a raucous Halloween party broke out instead, with the entire office staging a spirited costume contest. A group of staffers dressed as "the Ghosts of Devil Rays Past," honoring the unfortunate Tampa Bay legacies of Vinny Castilla, Wilson Alvarez, Paul Sorrento, Lou Piniella, and others. Chaim Bloom, a player development intern who would rise to become assistant director of minor league operations, stole the show, dressing as Greg Vaughn's regrettable four-year, $34 million contract and having everyone sign it for him.

"People had been beaten down by the Vince regime," said Phil Wallace, who spent two years as a special projects analyst with the Devil Rays, researching and assisting on multiple projects, including an eventual name, logo, and uniform change. "It was refreshing to let people do what they needed to do, to incentivize people for good work, and to have everyone actually enjoy coming to work every day. Sometimes it was just the little things. The first week or two [after Sternberg took over], they put up a suggestion box. It was the first time people were really allowed to express their opinions, *ever*."

Both Silverman on the business side and Friedman on the baseball side began delegating responsibilities, trusting others to perform their appointed tasks while the executives handled their own. They were following the example set by Sternberg, who spent most of his time in New York; he talked to Silverman often but otherwise let his people run the show. How that delegation took shape varied, though, as the differences between Silverman's and Friedman's personalities became evident.

Silverman looked the part of the Brooks Brothers–clad Wall Street graduate. He frequently went out into the community, eager to repair the damage done by Naimoli's combative approach, be it with the local Chamber of Commerce or at Little League field dedications. All the while, Silverman listened first and spoke second, without revealing too much information—typical of the close-to-the-vest style of a Goldman Sachs banker. The only thing missing was the Wall Street attitude. When Silverman joined Keli McGregor, Jeff Cogen, and other MLB presidents for league meetings, he carried himself differently from the rest.

"The egos in those rooms are not real open to suggestions and change," said Cogen. "But Matt wasn't like that. With him, it was more, 'Tell me why you do things this way.'"

Friedman could be equally guarded about information, despite his more gregarious personality. When he later went on to make trades, the media wouldn't find out beforehand because he hid his intentions like Phil Ivey at a final table. But Friedman also showed emotion. As Billy Beane did during A's games, Friedman often hit the treadmill during Devil Rays games to avoid getting too worked up over his team's play. He also maintained some of the habits formed during his youth. Friedman was not only baseball's first Wall Street–trained GM but the first to describe the concept of arbitrage in baseball while ejecting a stream of tobacco juice from his mouth.

Friedman was also the first GM to make video games a regular part of his stress management regimen. Soon after Sternberg took the reins, the organization spruced up Tropicana Field, adding fun features whenever possible. One section, "the Mountain Dew Extreme Zone," included a setup for stickball and an adjacent video game area. The most popular of those games was "RBI Baseball," complete with the old Nintendo console. When the season ended, someone got the idea to bring the game up to the Devil Rays' offices. It ended up in the baseball ops conference room. Friedman hadn't played the game since the 1980s, but like many baseball fans and gamers his age, he was still a sucker for its fun-and-easy format. Soon, nearly everyone in the front office was playing. They'd hold NCAA tournament–style brackets, bringing in as many as thirty-two office employees to battle for supremacy. Friedman and baseball operations director Dan Feinstein would usually be the last two standing. Friedman was once again working impossibly long hours (as he had on Wall Street), and "RBI Baseball" made for a great way to blow off steam.

He didn't like being interrupted, though. Sandy Dengler, Friedman's assistant and director of baseball administration, walked in one day while he was playing. "Dan O'Dowd is on the phone," she said. "Damn it!" Friedman yelled, slamming down the controller to take the call from the Colorado Rockies GM.

During the 2007 draft, Friedman's love for "RBI Baseball" and his supreme trust in his staff collided. The game had to be moved out of the conference room so that scouting director R. J. Harrison and a phalanx of scouts and cross-checkers could form their own war room. The Devil Rays took Vanderbilt pitcher David Price first overall, following Friedman's recommendation. Knowing Tampa Bay wouldn't pick again until number 65, Friedman snuck out to play some "RBI," getting fed frequent updates while reveling in eight-bit glory. He would return for the team's second pick, then duck in and out multiple times thereafter. By the middle to late rounds, though, he'd left the drafting to Harrison and the scouts. While teams threw darts at late-round lottery tickets, Friedman and Feinstein scooted down the hall to battle for the "RBI Baseball" championship of the world.

"He doesn't make you feel that you'd better toe the line and not goof off because he's the boss," said Josh Kalk, the team's baseball operations analyst. "Even when I hadn't been there very long, it felt like my opinion had some weight to it, that they valued it."

Outsiders agreed. The Devil Rays' willingness to divvy up responsibilities wouldn't just make employees feel more valued. With the role of GM or team president evolving into a job filled with complex analysis and far-flung decisions, farming out tasks was the logical and necessary next step to take.

"We're transitioning away from the GM as superhero," said Vince Gennaro, author of *Diamond Dollars: The Economics of Winning in Baseball*. "Today you have to have an infrastructure in place if you want to successfully run an organization."

Another important part of doing the job right is self-awareness. Sternberg, Silverman, and Friedman made a commitment from the start to track the effectiveness of their decision-making. Draft picks would need to be scrutinized several years out, to see how the scouting staff could have done better. Ditto for trades, business partnerships, ticket sales strategies, and other decisions. Making mistakes was acceptable. Failure to learn from those mistakes was not.

"We're constantly assessing what we're doing," Friedman said. "After we make decisions, we postmortem them at a later date. We keep copious notes on the variables we knew, everything we knew going in. Then we go back and look at it to review the process. It's something we're continuing to refine and will be in perpetuity. I hope to never get to the point where we're content, or we feel great about everything and go into autopilot mode."

Sternberg, Silverman, and Friedman knew they'd need to find unique individuals to fit into their nonhierarchical, self-reflective system. Finding a manager of that stripe would be especially difficult. Under Vince Naimoli and Chuck LaMar, the Devil Rays had tried first-timers and crusty old veterans alike in the manager's chair, only to find that they all held similar old-school beliefs about how to run a team. The new guard wanted someone different.

The club looked at Joe Girardi for the job. A World Series winner during the New York Yankees dynasty of the 1990s, Girardi had long been described as a future manager even while still playing. When he later landed a manager's job, he carried his detail-oriented approach to that role, wielding a folder with him every game that contained the minutest stats on every player and matchup. Girardi would become known by critics as something of an overmanager, someone with a firm grasp of the little things who would drill decisions down to the tiniest detail and occasionally fail to recognize the more obvious (and often correct) move. That reputation would be earned away from Tampa Bay, though; Girardi signed instead to manage the Florida Marlins, then later the Yankees (where he would win another World Series).

Through a combination of fate and foresight, the Devil Rays ended up with someone else, a manager who fit the organization's new culture perfectly. It would take a forward-thinking, unconventional mind to do the job, someone open-minded enough to deploy new, analysis-driven methods of making moves, but also caring and astute enough to get through to the young players the team was drafting and developing. It would take Joe Maddon.

CHAPTER 6 BROAD STREET JOE

His personality is like a spider. It goes in all different directions. He wants to be a complete man, which is something maybe we should all want.

—TREVER MILLER, former Rays relief pitcher, on Joe Maddon

There are only a few immutable rules in baseball. Never make the first out at home. Never share a bathroom stall with Jose Canseco. And never, under any circumstances, bring the winning run to the plate in the ninth inning if you don't have to.

So you can imagine the buzz that rippled through the stadium when Joe Maddon did just that on August 17, 2008. That night the Rays took a 7–2 lead over the Rangers into the bottom of the ninth in Arlington. Texas trimmed the lead to 7–3, then loaded the bases on a Michael Young walk. The potential tying run was now strolling to the plate in the form of none other than Josh Hamilton. Catcher Dioner Navarro squatted, then turned his head for a sign from the dugout. Navarro squinted, shrugged, then popped out of his squat. Joe Maddon was ordering an intentional walk.

The Rays and Rangers broadcast crews were dumbfounded. The fans too. A few in the stands might have recalled Diamondbacks manager Bob Brenly intentionally walking Barry Bonds with the bases loaded, but Bonds may have been the scariest hitter who ever lived. And it happened just once. This move was far rarer than any other rare baseball event, more unusual even than a perfect game or an unassisted triple play. Hamilton's free pass would mark just the fifth such intentional walk in a major league game since 1900. It was the first in the American League since 1901, the junior circuit's first season.

Going strictly by the numbers, Maddon's decision to walk Hamilton was debatable. Baseball analyst Tom Tango's research tells us that a team at bat with the bases loaded and two outs scores an average of 0.815 runs. Hamilton's intentional walk added another run to the Rangers' ledger, raising the situation's run expectancy in a typical situation to 1.815 runs. Caveats abound. Tango's research doesn't isolate the ninth inning, in which a team can and should opt to score as many runs as needed to win, which is not always the same thing as the most runs possible.

More important in Maddon's calculus was how likely Hamilton or Marlon Byrd, the on-deck hitter, were to produce a hit that would win, tie, or at least materially alter the outcome of the game. The entire 2008 season had been a big coming-out party for Hamilton, the Rangers' star center fielder. To that point, nobody in the majors had driven home more runs than Hamilton. Finally fulfilling the potential that had convinced Tampa Bay to make him the very first pick in the amateur draft nine years earlier, Hamilton had crushed homers at a breakneck pace and put on a jaw-dropping show in the Home Run Derby just a month earlier. The righty-swinging Byrd, Maddon figured, was a much lesser threat than left-handed powerhouse Hamilton, especially with righty-erasing relief pitcher Dan Wheeler ready and waiting. Even so, the gap probably wasn't as large as Maddon imagined. Hamilton was on his way to a monster year, but Byrd was no slouch himself. Even with Wheeler ready to enter the game, there was no guarantee that he'd retire Byrd and save the win for the Rays.

Maddon was violating one of baseball's unbreakable rules. If the move backfired and the Rangers won, Maddon would be berated for flouting the conventions of baseball, mocked for thinking he'd found new answers in a game that's remained stubbornly stagnant for a hundred years.

Of all the professions a person can pursue in this country, perhaps only one—president of the United States—engenders more criticism and second-guessing than that of baseball manager. But no matter how unpopular a policy he unveils or how spectacularly an initiative fails, the president gets at least four years. Not so for the manager of a major league baseball club. A few high-profile errors or one dramatic, disappointing season can send a skipper to the unemployment line—even if the thinking behind the manager's decisions was sound. In some cases, all it takes is one colossally bad result. One could surely debate the merits of Red Sox manager Grady Little's decision to leave a tiring Pedro Martinez in during the eighth inning of Game 7 in the 2003 American League Championship Series. But after Pedro blew Boston's 5–2 lead and the Red Sox eventually lost the game, Little got the ax. Maddon was among Boston's top candidates to replace Little. Luckily for the Rays, he didn't make the cut.

When you step through the door of the Third Base Luncheonette in Hazleton, Pennsylvania, the first thing you notice is the back wall. It's cotton-candy pink, adorned by a faded green Sealtest sign, the same sign that's marked that spot since Sealtest Dairy helped open the place in 1949. The Formica countertop shows the strain of tens of thousands of hoagie plates sliding across its surface. It winds its way through two seating areas, offering just enough space to feed the hungry souls who eat elbow to elbow on nineteen well-worn stools. Even the prices look like they come from the '50s: four bucks for a loaded hoagie that'll last you through the day. It's the kind of joint you'd expect to find in an old anthracite town that never lost the coal miners' mentality of a hundred years ago, where every street looks the same, decade after decade, except for the cars. Sitting on one of these stools, you half-expect Marty McFly to barge through the front door.

The second thing you notice is the familiarity that permeates the air—that, and the smell of sweet peppers. Clad in a white apron, owner Dave Mishinski tends the grill. He's cooked so much meat for so many years that he could do it with his eyes closed. Dave's wife, Tina, flits from patron to patron, pouring coffee, scribbling down orders, nodding at the old-timers as they belly up to the counter. On the other side of the counter, Tina's sister Charmaine tends to her own lot of hungry customers. When the lunch rush hits, they're joined by Autumn, Dave and Tina's daughter. She's home from college helping out at Third Base, barely old enough to drink but already a seasoned veteran in the family business. When afternoon deliveries pull Dave away from the grill, son Jake steps in, packing on extra onions one minute, extra cheese/no mayo the next. Dave's aunt Albina—Beanie to everyone who knows her—holds down the fort in back. She's Third Base's five-tool player, handling deliveries, sifting through paperwork, filling in on orders when needed. Well into her seventies, Beanie has spent three-quarters of her life at Third Base. This unassuming little luncheonette is run entirely by Joe Maddon's family. Dave and the rest of the Mishinski clan are Joe's cousins. Beanie is Joe's small-in-stature, large-in-influence mother.

When Joe was growing up, it didn't take Beanie long to realize she was raising an athlete. He was a terror at the plate in Little League. Later he was "Broad Street Joe," so named for the main drag in Hazleton and Maddon's admiration for Broadway Joe Namath; he donned flashy white cleats and the number 12 as the star quarterback at the Castle, the old high school turned middle school. He gravitated toward other sports-crazed kids. Joe, along with Jeff Jones and Willie Forte, became "the Three Amigos," three inseparable best friends who met as kids while playing against each other in baseball and football, then came of age as multi-sport stars at Hazleton High School.

In the '60's, there wasn't much for a young boy growing up in Hazleton to do other than play sports. And no one in town embraced them more heartily than Maddon, Jones, and Forte. By the time they reached high school, the three friends were at Maddon's house every day, eating Beanie's food, watching sports on TV, talking sports. During the school year, they played in baseball and football leagues, and later, basketball too. In the summertime, they'd run out in the morning armed with enough sports equipment to open a Foot Locker, not to return until sundown—a quick stop or two at Third Base for refueling aside.

Of course, many boys grew up in the '60s in small towns playing sports morning till night. But the Amigos' sports education started early. It was Maddon's midget football team that first stimulated his analytical mind, setting him on the road to becoming a major league manager.

"We were nine years old," recalled Forte, the defensive leader of his youth league and high school teams at middle linebacker, while Maddon led the offensive unit on those squads at quarterback. "Joe and I would design these football plays with eleven pennies on one side, eleven nickels or dimes on the other. This was 1963, and we were planning things like four–wide receiver sets, trip receivers on one side. We were asking questions normal kids at our age would never think to ask."

"Joe thought nothing of calling audibles, even when we were ten, eleven years old," recalled Jones. "Later on in junior high, coach would call a play, and Joe would say, 'I don't like the looks of that.' Just like that, the play would be changed. It usually worked too."

The boys' coaches, Richie Rabbitz and Jack Seiwell, offered inspiration. For four years, they followed Maddon and Forte through the youth football league ranks. The boys would meet for skull sessions at Joe's house, then bombard the coaches with questions—during games, at practice, and long after all the other kids went home. Rabbitz and Seiwell encouraged their star players' inquisitive nature. But the questions were so relentless, and so precocious for boys that age, that it was all the coaches could do to keep from cracking up laughing.

Rabbitz and Seiwell didn't just listen for the sake of humoring their young players. They implemented those cutting-edge strategies on the field. While other teams ran a few running plays and one or two passing plays featuring one wide receiver, Maddon was running a series of complicated passing sets before he hit puberty. On defense, Forte would call plays featuring a seven-man defensive line, an unheard-of scheme that put a man on every blocker and cleared the way for Forte to stop ball carriers in their tracks, often behind the line of scrimmage. From pennies and nickels, the boys created innovative, real-life plays that worked again and again. You could count the number of games Maddon and Forte lost from ages nine to thirteen on one hand.

"Other teams didn't know how to handle it," laughed Forte. "They resented us!"

The boys' gridiron success spilled over to their high school years. Boasting one of the smallest teams in the region (Forte grew to no more than five-foot-four, 170 pounds at middle linebacker, while Jones excelled as a five-foot-seven, 150-pound running back), underdog Hazleton High became a team of overachievers. As the starting quarterback, Maddon refined many of the same unorthodox plays dreamed up over pocket change, along with a few new ones. He also honed the leadership skills that would serve him well later in life.

"When I played with Joe, I fed off his relentlessly positive attitude," Jones said. "Sometimes we wouldn't pull it off, but he always kept that up, that was one of his greatest attributes. There might have been bigger or faster people than Joe. But you knew he was the quarterback, the captain of the baseball team—even when he wasn't the official captain. He gave you a sense of quiet confidence, a calming effect. That aspect of his personality, you can't train or coach that."

Hazleton High's football team rolled to an 8-2-1 record in the boys' senior season. Only a handful of seniors graduated from that team, setting up what appeared to be a strong veteran squad the next season. But the team sorely missed the Three Amigos. The year after Maddon, Forte, and Jones graduated, Hazleton High didn't win a single game.

Maddon's intellectual curiosity on the football field spread to other endeavors. He became a voracious reader, consuming great works of literature in his youth, then moving on to volumes on self-help psychology, philosophy, and other subjects as an adult. He excelled in school. He also poured countless hours into thinking about baseball. Hazleton was a couple of hours or more away from in New York, Philadelphia, and Baltimore. On the rare occasion that he got to travel to a big league game, he made the occasion count. At age ten, Maddon's coach took Joe and Willie to see the Mets (Forte's favorite team) face the Cardinals (Maddon's team).

"Bob Gibson was pitching," Forte recalled, "and Joe was watching every movement he made. He was enjoying the whole game, but you could tell he was just studying Gibson. Joe was like a sponge."

His father, Joe Sr., encouraged his love of sports every step of the way. Forte recalls the boys plopping down in front of the Maddons' TV to watch all the sporting greats of the '60s, Russell and Chamberlain, Unitas and Namath, Gibson and Aaron. The boys would give Joe Sr. the nickname "Howard Cosell," because he loved to call the action. "So what do ya say, Howard?" they'd ask him after a big play.

Joe Sr. worked as a plumber for C. Maddon & Sons Plumbing and Heating for sixty years, in the same four-family building on East Eleventh Street that housed the extended Maddon clan. Working alongside his father and three brothers, Joe Sr. handled all manner of backbreaking jobs: busted furnaces on ten-degree days, ankle-deep puddles in flooded kitchens, frantic calls in the middle of the night to fix any number of household mishaps. If the exhausting labor bothered him, he never showed it.

"He never had a bad word for anybody," Dave Mishinski recalled.

"He was the nicest, gentlest man you ever met," said Forte.

"They gravitated to him always, *always*," mused Beanie. "He had patience, lots of patience. They'd never know if he had a bad day. Joe's now the same way. He doesn't wear it on his face, nowhere."

If there was any risk of Joe (or Joey, as he was known as a kid) getting a swelled head from all the attention—star quarterback, captain of the baseball team—Beanie was there to make sure her son stayed grounded. The three Maddon kids outgrew their mom by sixth grade. Yet Beanie commanded respect, corralling Joey, Carmine, and Mark at home and calling out orders at Third Base. Ask any Maddon friend or family member about Joey's strongest influences and they'll all say the same thing: his patience, even temperament, and good humor come from his father. The drive and toughness that pushed him through thirty-one years of apprenticeship before landing his dream job with the Rays? That's all Beanie.

Beyond the impact of parents and loved ones, Hazleton had a way of making every kid fall into line when Maddon was growing up in the '50s and '60s. You learned the value of respecting your elders at home, then again in school. There were eyes on every boy and girl everywhere in town. Step out of line and word would get back to your parents before you walked through the door.

Sister Suzanne was the kind of doting, tough-love figure who played a big role in Maddon's development. A seventh-grade teacher at Mother of Grace parochial school, the kindly nun would play ball with the boys every recess. She claimed to be the person who taught Maddon how to play baseball, a slight exaggeration that no one had the heart to refute. Above all, she did teach him the value of respect—giving it and earning it.

"The last time somebody interviewed Joe," said Beanie, "they asked him, 'When a player does something wrong, do you ever point at them?' He said no. He never talked down to anyone. Because Sister Suzanne taught him, she said, 'Point your finger at somebody and three come back right at you.' And he remembers things like that. He never forgets. He doesn't forget where he's from."

If family, friends, neighbors, and baseball-teaching nuns weren't enough, Hazleton had one fail-safe method to keep kids in line, one word that would strike fear into the hearts of even the hardest cases.

"Kislyn," said Hazleton mayor Louis Barletta, who grew up playing Little League with Maddon. "It was a home for troubled kids. If you were sent to Kislyn, you did something bad. And our parents used that against us, to their benefit. And it worked, I'm telling ya. As soon as you heard the word 'Kislyn.' . . . There was a sign, with an arrow pointing down this road. You never even wanted to go down that road. It was worse than a haunted house." Neither Barletta nor Maddon nor anyone in that extended circle knew anyone who'd actually *been* to Kislyn. But they heard the stories.

Maddon's formative years in Hazleton taught him many lessons. He's more creative and open-minded in his decision-making thanks to his midget football days. He relates well to young players, following his father's example of patience and understanding. He draws from childhood friends, attentive nuns, and a hard-driving mother in shepherding an up-and-coming team. If Joe Maddon had grown up in a different place under different circumstances, Josh Hamilton gets his shot to win the game that August night for the Rangers.

However Maddon's intentional walk for the ages might play out, it didn't much matter to the Rays' skipper. Sure, a loss in that situation could have thrown the Rays off course. Criticism of his maybe-too-clever tactics would have exploded. But none of that mattered. Maddon makes decisions one way with one thing in mind: trust the process, don't sweat the results.

"You've got to go with what you think is the right thing in the moment, based on everything that's presented to you," Maddon told Yahoo!'s Gordon Edes after the game. "Of course, if it didn't work out, I would have been skewered, and that would have been fine."

Duck out of the Third Base Luncheonette, make a left on Ninth, then drive past the cemetery. Rising on the left is the Hazleton

Little League field. That's where the legend of Joey Maddon first blossomed.

"There's a huge water tank that sits beyond the fence in left-center field," said Fred Barletta. "That was the rite of passage, if you could hit the water tank. Joey hit 'em *on top of the water tank*. He was the Mantle, the Mays of Hazleton Little League."

Thirty-five years later, a sign on a white shack at the entrance to the field reads: THANK YOU TAMPA BAY RAYS MANAGER JOE MADDON FOR MAKING HAZLETON LITTLE LEAGUE PROUD.

For all his early baseball exploits, most of the people who knew him figured Maddon would take a shot at a football career. From his early success in punt, pass, and kick competitions to his precocious quarterback play in midget ball to his star turn at quarterback for Hazleton High, Maddon showed extraordinary football talent. Nearby Lafayette College agreed, recruiting him for football—but also baseball. Maddon didn't take long to decide between the two. Though he loved the physical challenge of football, he figured he'd have a better chance of walking straight in thirty years if he made baseball his career.

To have a shot at a lasting career, though, Maddon realized he'd need to change positions. A shortstop and pitcher in Little League and in high school, he knew he lacked both the agility to play short and the rocket arm to pitch at a high level. Still, Maddon loved analyzing a pitcher's mechanics and approach, be it Bob Gibson's or his own. He loved the chess match that went into every pitch. If he couldn't toe the rubber, Maddon figured, why not crouch behind the plate?

He hit well enough at Lafayette—.280/.351/.387 in a power-starved environment—but that wasn't enough to generate heavy attention from scouts.

Still, the California Angels were intrigued, especially after hearing the positive reports on Maddon's ability to call a game, and signed him as an undrafted free agent. From there, Maddon roamed the Single A landscape, playing in Salinas, Santa Clara, and Quad Cities. The bus rides were long, the accommodations spare, the pay just enough to get by. By conventional measures he struggled, never hitting enough to pressure the Angels into bumping him up the ladder. Only Maddon didn't see those bush league experiences as a failure.

"I met Joe at a Domino's Pizza on the Illinois side of Quad Cities, I remember it perfectly," said Forte. The two childhood friends hadn't seen each other in a while, Maddon embarking on his baseball journey while Forte pursued a music career that eventually led him to join the B Street Band, a Bruce Springsteen cover group that he's now fronted for more than thirty years.

"He told me he was quitting playing, that he would become a scout, or maybe a coach," Forte recalled. "He said, 'I love this game, I really have a feel for it,' even if it wasn't going to happen for him as a player. He found out he had a real desire for coaching, because parts of the game clicked for him. He had a good relationship with other players since he's soft-spoken and has such an easy demeanor. But he also loved the intricacies of the game. To get on a school bus, driving all over with twenty players—being in A-ball was pretty rough back then. You had to be either crazy or so in love with the game you couldn't leave if you wanted to be an A-ball coach."

Maddon wasn't thinking about long bus rides, crummy per diems, or doubleheaders in the sweltering summer heat of the Midwest. The wheels were already turning in his head. He was visualizing ways for batters to make better contact, for pitchers to make smoother hip rotations, for the Angels to do a better job of developing future major leaguers. Maddon approached the Angels about staying on after his playing days ended, and the organization agreed. Thus began a three-decade journey up the ranks.

If the lessons handed down from his father hadn't adequately taught him the value of patience and a positive attitude, those first few years navigating baseball's backwaters surely did. After a brief stint as a scout, Maddon became manager of the rookie-league Idaho Falls team at age twenty-seven. From a distance, it looked like an inauspicious debut, with the team going 27-43 on the year. But just as he had in his playing days—and would in his future major league managing days—Maddon wasn't stressing over lumpy results. Sure, he wanted to win, just as he wished he'd hit .350 at A-ball. But learning the intricacies of the game remained his biggest focus.

The wins and losses didn't improve much as the years ticked by. Trekking from Idaho Falls to Salem, from Peoria to Midland, Maddon never once earned a winning record in six years of minor league managing. Others saw past the losses, though. Outmanned in his first year at Salem, Maddon still guided his team into the playoffs with a 34-36 record, then rolled through the postseason, winning the league championship and Manager of the Year Award in the process.

Moreover, a minor league manager's success is defined—by smart teams anyway—as much by the players he elevates and the lessons he instills as by his record. The Angels liked the way players responded to Maddon's mentorship, how Maddon interacted with coaches and instructors, and how he prepared for a game. They routed talented but raw prospects to Maddon's teams, sending steady, productive minor league lifers elsewhere. That long-standing practice let Maddon manage the team's most promising young talents, while hurting the records of the teams he managed. It was a huge vote of confidence for a young manager on the rise.

"Preston Gomez was my right-hand man, one of the most astute baseball people I've ever met," said Mike Port, the Angels' director of player development from 1978 to 1984 and general manager for the ensuing seven years. "Preston did not volunteer compliments lightly. In 1986, he went to see Joe's Midland club play, in Double A. He came back and said, 'I'm going to tell you right now, this man will manage in the major leagues.' In the thirty-some years I worked with Preston, only one other time did he say that, and that was about [former Milwaukee Brewers and Oakland A's manager] Ken Macha. So he was two for two."

Port had spent several days in Idaho Falls a few years earlier with Gomez and minor league pitching instructor and Hall of Famer Warren Spahn, when Maddon was a twenty-seven-year-old rookie manager. The three men were struck by Maddon's skill at running workouts. But there was more.

"There was a definite care and concern for his players, for the people he was working with," Port recalled. "We found several of our young Latin American players had no experience with banking. They'd cash their checks and keep their money under mattresses. Joe took the initiative, he said, 'Let me help you with this.' Other people might have said, 'That's their problem.' But Joe's got a certain interest in people, a certain bent toward being helpful."

Maddon quickly became known throughout the organization as a progressive thinker. In his early minor league days, he harped on the value of rest and nutrition, mental preparation and handling pressure, at a time when such topics were rarely discussed in baseball spheres. When technology became more prevalent a few years later, Maddon was an early adopter of all the latest gadgets, especially when they helped him gather and organize information.

Bill Bavasi, former general manager for the Angels and Seattle Mariners, started his career with the Angels in 1978, just as Maddon was winding down his playing days. One tight-budget year required Bavasi to tell Maddon he'd get a modest raise, far less than Bavasi felt Maddon deserved. Momentarily perturbed, Maddon's eyes lit up when he saw the gift Bavasi bought him as a token of thanks and appreciation: a Sharp organizer, an early predecessor to the modern PDA that ran about $500 in those days—big bucks for Bavasi on his $15,000-a-year salary, much less Maddon's more modest wages. Maddon embraced the new device, using it to organize the growing number of his tasks and to take copious notes on player performance. Years later, when the Angels began allotting funds for portable computer purchases, Bavasi pushed for Maddon to get one of those rudimentary, ten-pound behemoths. Everyone who'd worked with Maddon knew no one would appreciate a portable computer more, make better use of it, or be more willing to lug it around everywhere he went.

Later in his career, Maddon latched on to newer devices, wielding them with the confidence and enthusiasm of a tech-savvy teenager. He became one of the earliest adopters of customized, small-ball pitching machines. If hitters could track a tennis ball going up to 140 miles per hour, the idea went, they'd have an easier time following a 90-mile-per-hour baseball in game situations. Maddon took the concept and tweaked it. He set the machines to lower heights so as to challenge hitters' plane of vision. More challenging still, he began marking tennis balls with red and black marks. If hitters could call out "red" or "black" on high-speed pitches, they might gain a better approach to hitting that could yield better pitch selection, more favorable hitters' counts, and more chances to drive the ball to all fields. Years later, star Rays third baseman Evan Longoria would prove to be a whiz at this exercise, amazing onlookers with his ability to call out pitches on their way to the plate. Did his incredible natural batting eye make Longoria a superstar hitter, or did the machines hone his pitch selection? Mostly the former—but Maddon liked to think a little of the latter too.

Meanwhile, Maddon kept finding new ways to inspire players. His seven-year run as minor league hitting instructor coincided with a big influx of organizational talent—future major league All-Stars Tim Salmon and Jim Edmonds ranked among his top pupils. One of Maddon's favorite methods in those days was to give out motivational T-shirts.

"His most famous one was, I GOT LOUD," said Bavasi. "It had a ball on it, screaming as it flew through the air, because it'd been hit so hard. What he was trying to do was get guys to forget their statistics and focus on hitting balls hard. If you hit the ball hard and made an out, no problem. When he came to your town, if you got loud, if you hit the ball on the nose a bunch of times, he'd give you this T-shirt. Guys really liked it."

Maddon moved on to become minor league field coordinator for the Angels, then director of player development. In 1994, he finally got the call: he was headed to the big leagues to serve as the Angels' bullpen coach. In the next twelve years, he would add the titles of first-base coach and dugout/bench coach to his résumé. By 2005,

Maddon had covered nearly every position in a major league organization other than general manager and batboy.

Ask him about the thirty-one years he spent in the Angels system and Maddon credits all those stops for helping him accumulate
the knowledge and experience he'd later need to become a big
league manager. But he saves the biggest accolades for the people
who worked alongside him and mentored him on the way. Marcel
Lachemann taught him how to handle a pitching staff, everything
from knowing when to yank a starter to finding the right reliever for
the right situation. Rick Down and Ben Hines influenced his
already developed thoughts on hitting. Bobby Knoop and Larry
Bowa taught him the subtler points of defense, how shallow to play
outfielders in given situations, when to move fielders over, and
when to play an occasional, aggressive shift. Terry Collins, Maddon
said, was one of the brightest managers he ever met, passing along
both tactical advice and suggestions for how to handle the twenty-
five players who walk through the clubhouse every day.

Gene Mauch, Maddon said, was the first person to make a big
impact on him. Mauch managed the Angels from 1981 to 1982 and
again from 1985 to 1987, while Maddon was first cutting his teeth
as a minor league manager. Whenever an organizational meeting
would come up, Maddon would gravitate toward Mauch, soaking
up whatever bits of wisdom the longtime skipper could offer.

"Gene, for me, was the guy that you never thought he was
wrong," Maddon recalled. "Whatever he said, you took it as gospel
and it had to be right. I'm kind of inquisitive by nature, but with
him, I never—if Gene Mauch said it, it has to be so. And he had a
presence about him that I thought was spectacular. He wasn't a
loud, boisterous man at all. He'd throw a spread once in a while, but
Gene was pretty much a communicator. The way he ran a game,
and his thought process and his simplicity, I always thought he had
more common sense than any person I had met to that point in
baseball."

But nobody clicked better with Maddon than Mike Scioscia.
When Scioscia took over as the Angels' manager in 2000, he and

Maddon quickly found common ground. Scioscia grew up in Morton, Pennsylvania, just ninety-eight miles from Hazleton. They liked the same music. Laughed at the same jokes. They agreed 95% of the time and engaged in lively debates the other 5%.

"I really didn't know Joe [before that]," Scioscia said. "But even during those first conversations with him, you just saw that he has a very gifted baseball mind. He's really a visionary. He's about as progressive as anyone I've ever been around in the game of baseball."

More than three decades spent climbing the ladder helped Maddon craft a unique viewpoint as a manager. He took the best that each of his mentors and peers had to offer, melded that knowledge with the kind of thick skin that only places like Idaho Falls and Peoria can impart, and became a manager who wasn't afraid to fail. Unlike other baseball lifers who took a similar road to the majors, Maddon didn't settle for conventional wisdom. He believed in his own instincts and brought new coaching methods to the fore. When he finally got his shot, Maddon became a near-overnight success—thirty-one years in the making. Trust the process, Maddon told himself, and success will never be a surprise.

When the Rays invited Maddon to interview for their manager job, they didn't yet know they'd be sitting face-to-face with a field manager version of themselves. Andrew Friedman, Matt Silverman, and Stuart Sternberg all relied heavily on process-based analysis in their previous roles on Wall Street. They were just getting started in running the Rays' daily operations, yet already they were using rigorous tools to analyze every aspect of the organization, from marketing and sales to stadium operations to player free agency. The team's brain trust would be equally thorough when hiring their first manager.

The Rays' scouting report on Maddon pointed to a promising profile. After three-plus decades in the Angels' organization and a few short stints as interim manager of the major league club, Maddon had built an army of supporters and fans within that organization, many of whom lobbied for their man to land a full-time manager's gig. Those recommendations, combined with Maddon's interviewing style, had nearly landed him a job with the 2004 Boston Red Sox.

If you're into what-if scenarios, consider this: What if Joe Maddon, not Terry Francona, had gotten the Red Sox job after Grady Little's 2003 ouster? Would Terry Francona have won a World Series (or two) elsewhere? Would Maddon have matched Francona's accomplishments at the helm of a deep, powerful team? For Rays fans, the bigger question is this: Would the Rays' stable of young talent have come together, gone from worst to first, and become one of the most feared up-and-coming teams in a generation under a manager *not* named Joe Maddon?

Friedman and company had no need to ponder such hypotheticals, not after hiring Maddon on November 15, 2005. A few years earlier, Michael Lewis's best-seller *Moneyball* suggested that a baseball manager should serve as a sort of middle manager, cheerfully taking instructions and loyally implementing the strategies cooked up by the smart guys upstairs. Maddon would be damned if he was going to spend thirty-one years toiling away for his shot at the big job, only to serve as a mindless vessel for his bosses. Fortunately, Friedman also saw the manager's role as being much broader and more interactive than the Art Howe caricature portrayed in *Moneyball*.

"When we sat down with Joe and went through the interview process, it was apparent that his thought process was similar to ours in a lot of respects, in terms of being very inquisitive and trying to view things differently than maybe is conventional," said Friedman. "He fit in exactly with what we were looking for. And we view him as part of the management team. That was something that was important to us in hiring a manager."

In Maddon, Friedman and the Rays brass found a manager who was both an extension of themselves and an independent thinker. From the start, Maddon's creativity and bold decision-making shone through. He once had speedy outfielder B. J. Upton steal second and third base in the sixth inning of a game against the Indians—*while trailing 9–0*. He took the super-utility role to new levels with Ben Zobrist, slotting the switch-hitter at seven different positions in 2009, against the strong objections of several local media members. Zobrist put up MVP-caliber numbers that year, both offensively and with the glove. Under Maddon, the Rays tossed out old conventions about righty versus righty and lefty versus lefty matchups. Facing starting pitcher Mike Mussina, a right-hander who fared better against left-handed hitters, Maddon stuffed his lineup with eight righty swingers. The Rays took a similar tack against righty Tim Wakefield, even ordering switch-hitters to bat right-handed against the knuckleballer.

Maddon faced perhaps the most scrutiny in his handling of Rays bullpens. He often eschewed the traditional closer role, opting instead to use his best relief pitchers in the highest-leverage situations. When J. P. Howell served as the Rays' nominal closer, it wasn't unusual to see him come into, say, a tie game with the bases loaded in the eighth inning—a far cry from the cushy two- or three-run lead, bases-empty, start-of-the-ninth chances given to most closers.

Even starting pitchers occasionally entered the bullpen mix. In a span of two and a half weeks during the summer of 2010, the Rays sent James Shields and then Matt Garza into the late innings of close games, as relief pitchers. In a June game against the Marlins, Maddon tapped Shields to hold the line in the tenth inning. He summoned Garza in the ninth inning of a game against the Red Sox. In both cases, the manager's hyper-aggressive style of relief usage had prompted the move. Against Florida, Maddon had burned most of his pen earlier in the game, trotting out four different relievers to cover a single inning. Rather than go to one of his two weakest relievers in the tenth inning, he sent out Shields. Against Boston, the Rays had worked top bullpen arms Joaquin Benoit and Rafael Soriano hard in the prior few days, leaving a spent bullpen that needed a lift. Beyond mere situational matchups, though, Maddon and pitching coach Jim Hickey used a strategy that was achingly simple, yet rarely deployed by other teams: starting pitchers usually throw off a bullpen mound halfway between two starts to keep their arms strong and limber and avoid atrophy. Rather than have Shields and Garza waste those pitches against imaginary hitters, the Rays sent both straight into the fire. The strategy worked: Shields pitched a scoreless tenth for the win against the Fish, while Garza slammed the door in the ninth against the Sox.

"You talk about 'thinking outside of the box,' I think that expression was made for Joe," said Scioscia. "Joe would've been an incredible engineer if he wasn't in baseball, because he has that type of mind. He could look at parts of an organization, parts of a team, and in imaginative ways, just based on sound common sense, make an organization better, make people better, make a team better."

Not all of the Rays' unorthodox moves are Maddon's creations. In fact, many of the team's tactics start as data points on a graph pieced together by James Click, Erik Neander, or another front-office number cruncher. Yet that too counts among the advantages the Rays derive from having Maddon at the helm. The manager craves information and is receptive to new ideas. If anything, Maddon can be more skeptical of old baseball traditions than the new ways of looking at the game.

"He's absolutely the most willing to do something that's out of the ordinary," said Hickey. "A lot of managers will do things simply to cover their butt. If it doesn't go right, well, 'I did what I was supposed to do.' But Joe is absolutely willing to totally go against that. Rightfully so too. A lot of the things that are in 'the book' are antiquated and no longer fit today's game."

A delicate blend of hands-on experience and data application goes into every decision the Rays make, and Maddon's decisions are no exception. Before a game, you might see him exchanging player acquisition possibilities with Andrew Friedman, poring over reams of data sent in by Click and Neander, digesting copious reports from advance scouts, spitballing ideas with his pitching and hitting coaches on how to snap players out of slumps, and batting around scenarios with various players.

It's in that last area, interacting with players, that Maddon receives the most glowing reviews. Soon after taking the manager's job with the Rays, Maddon posted a series of motivational and philosophical quotes throughout the clubhouse for players to read—a natural progression from his "I Got Loud" catchphrase as a minor league instructor.

RULES CANNOT TAKE THE PLACE OF CHARACTER.
— ALAN GREENSPAN

INTEGRITY HAS NO NEED OF RULES.
— ALBERT CAMUS

DISCIPLINE YOURSELF SO NO ELSE HAS TO.
— JOHN WOODEN

To inspire his players and bring them together, Maddon has concocted slogans for every season. His most famous creation has been the "9 = 8" mantra of 2008—a way of urging nine players to play hard for nine innings every game so that the Rays can become one of eight teams to make the postseason. To reward them, he's arranged for teamwide shipments of Ed Hardy T-shirts, the de rigueur choice for young ballplayers. To keep them loose, he's created themes for different road trips, including a Johnny Cash theme for which he himself, a trendy, glasses-sporting wine aficionado, added jet-black hair dye to his look. To promote team unity, he joined the likes of B. J. Upton, Jonny Gomes, and others in sporting a Mohawk haircut—a "Ray-hawk," as it was called during those heady stretch-run days of the 2008 season.

All of Maddon's interactions with his players, he said, are rooted in positive reinforcement.

"It's just how I was raised," said Maddon. "My parents and my father's side of the family in particular were just a bunch of hard-working men that never had a bad day. Also psychologically—I mean, I read a lot, and I've been influenced somewhat by what I've read. I know one thing—the negative method of teaching, for me, it never worked."

Some outside observers have scratched their heads over Maddon's methods. They didn't know what to make of his practice of serving chips, salsa, and beer in his daily meetings with the media. And was he too focused on outside pursuits like fine wines? Was he getting too close to his much-younger players? And what about those funky, horn-rimmed glasses? If the Rays' youth movement had failed, Maddon would have drawn harsh criticism for his unorthodox ways.

His old friend and colleague Bavasi said that Maddon doesn't do any of those things to be purposely quirky. His girlfriend bought him the glasses, so he wore them. He likes fine wines, so he drinks them. He reads self-help psychology books and sees the value in motivational quotes, so he shares some of those quotes on the clubhouse wall.

"I remember, in 2007, you'd hear people say, if Joe's off-the-wall approach doesn't work pretty quick, he's out of there," Bavasi recalled. "But Joe's never going to sit there and think, 'What do I have to do to keep my job?' He sticks to his plan, he's never scared, he doesn't waver on things because of nerves. Everything he does is to make sure that a player gets the most out of his ability and that the team gets the most out of him." (Memo to CEOs and small-business owners out there: hire this guy, or at least someone who thinks like him.)

For a team that seeks to quantify and improve as many parts of the organization as possible, it's not clear whether Maddon's efforts to reach his players somehow translate into more wins on the field or whether they're merely intangible niceties. What is clear is this: if Maddon didn't earn his players' trust, they'd tune out his motivational efforts or just laugh him off the plane the first time he showed up wearing a jumpsuit or a cowboy hat for a team flight.

Veteran Rays outfielder Gabe Kapler once took a year off from playing in the middle of his career to manage in the low minors. If he goes back into managing when his playing days are over, Kapler said, he'll try to emulate many of Maddon's best traits.

"I don't know if you can duplicate it, but his energy," said Kapler, "and his ability to look you in the eye and smile and make you feel comfortable. I don't think there are a lot of managers out there like that."

"When I first got here, I was filled with emotions, wondering what the big leagues were supposed to feel like, what I was doing right or wrong," recalled Fernando Perez, an outfielder for the Rays who's also a published poet and *New York Times* blogger. "Joe just told us: 'Don't do anything different than what you've been doing all along,' that we should just enjoy it. He didn't just put me at ease, Joe was able to do that with an entire group of people. As a writer concerned with poetry, when you can do so many things with just a few words of rhetoric, that's amazing to me."

When a manager connects with his players and earns the trust of management, he starts earning increased job security. Silverman notes that many managers would have been looking over their shoulders after two losing seasons like the Rays had in Maddon's first two years at the helm. But the front office preached patience, liked how the team's player development was going, and liked the job Maddon was doing with his young charges. When the Rays notched their first winning season, first playoff berth, first division title, and first AL pennant in 2008, Maddon earned more security, eventually inking a contract extension to keep him with the Rays through 2012.

When self-confidence, an even-keeled personality, a nose for analysis, and job security come together, you get coaches and managers willing to make decisions that fly in the face of conventional wisdom. The masses hated New England Patriots coach Bill Belichick's 2009 decision to go for it on fourth-and-2 from his own 28-yard line with 2:08 to go against the archrival Colts. But Belichick firmly believed that the surest way to beat the Colts and Peyton Manning was to get one more first down, thus keeping the ball out of Manning's hands. The decision was disastrous. The Colts stopped the Patriots on fourth down, then quickly drove for the winning touchdown on a short field. The loss was tough. But the Patriots' coach didn't second-guess himself (not publicly anyway). Trust the process, the three-time Super Bowl champion coach believed, and the results will take care of themselves.

Moments after the kid from Hazleton ordered a bases-loaded intentional walk, standing a century's worth of baseball wisdom on its head, Dan Wheeler struck out Marlon Byrd to win the game. This was merely a bonus in a season full of happy endings.

CHAPTER 7 THE EXORCISM

Tampa Bay Devil Rays officials announced Monday that the team will be shortening its name to the Tampa Bay Rays, that their updated uniforms will feature a blue-and-white color scheme accented by orange rays of sunshine, and that they are now a minor-league hockey team in the Florida Panthers system.
—The Onion

David Pinto was in trouble. He'd dealt with high-pressure situations before, compiling cutting-edge data for STATS Inc., doing research for ESPN's *Baseball Tonight,* and scraping to make a living with Baseball Musings, one of the first baseball blogs ever to gain traction with readers. But never before had the president of a major league team sent him a letter accusing him of a grave misdeed.

Dear Mr. Pinto:

November 8, 2007 was a landmark day for our organization. On that day, we shed the "devil" from our name and became the Tampa Bay Rays. Our organization introduced a new logo, colors and uniforms to accompany the name change. A bright yellow sunburst now adorns our jerseys. Replacing the devil ray fish, this sunburst icon invokes the magnificence of life in the Sunshine State.

. . . It has been brought to my attention that you . . . recently used our former team name.

The note, sent by Rays president Matt Silverman, detailed to Pinto the steps taken by the team to rid itself of its old name. The newly christened Rays spent thousands of man-hours and big bucks brainstorming over a new name and logo. They fined any employee for using the old Devil Rays name, with the proceeds going to charity. Now, thanks to the team's elaborate network of spies, they'd nailed Pinto in the act. The penalty for this egregious act? One dollar. Pinto paid the fine, times ten.

The Rays hit several other baseball writers with fines that off-season, drumming up publicity for their "Drop the Devil" campaign. It was a rare display of cheeky humor in an industry where those in charge often take themselves too seriously. But Silverman and the rest of the front office had bigger ideas than just drawing a few chuckles. For eight seasons, the Tampa Bay Devil Rays were the butt of everyone's jokes, poisoned by the mishaps of Vince Naimoli. The franchise made better decisions after Naimoli's ouster, but kept losing. Other teams' fans saw the name change as a con, as window-dressing for a team that still stunk. Erasing all of this team's bad karma would require more than a little fine-tuning. It would take massive changes in Tampa Bay's on-field performance . . . and a full-blown exorcism.

"It gave everyone an excuse to start fresh and separate themselves from the Devil Rays and everything associated with the name," Silverman said.

The new regime's quest to change the team's brand and reputation began more than two years before the official name change. One of Silverman's first hires would be the man in charge of ramping up customer service and fan entertainment at the Trop.

Darcy Raymond worked as a brand manager for Procter & Gamble, then as a marketing VP for Mamma.com, a search engine company based in Raymond's hometown of Montreal. Mamma's business model was to build a meta-search product that could combine ten to twelve engines at a time. The idea was better than the execution, though. Mamma's core product wasn't very good, and the company was being run by twenty-somethings with limited business experience. The firm had reeled in $27 million in venture capital at the height of the dot-com boom in 1999, failed to cash out before the bubble burst, then struggled. By hiring Raymond, Mamma's brass hoped it could find someone who would drive traffic to the site, which could eventually lead to that most elusive of Internet start-up goals: real profits. The hire proved to be a bad fit.

"He was spending money and driving traffic to the site," said Jeremy Wiseman, Mamma's former director of business development. "But the CEO didn't understand that if you spend $1 million on marketing, you won't get it back, at least not for a long time. Darcy's approach was right for consumer goods, but a Web search company was a different model. We didn't have the patience to try and build a brand. A baseball team could be more conducive to that type of brand-building. In baseball you're trying to sell tickets, but also to go beyond that, to build a brand, get some buzz behind it, and build for the long term."

Raymond left Mamma, eventually landing at Harvard Business School. When he and classmate Brian Auld graduated in 2005, both went looking for new career paths. Auld had worked as a teacher at East Palo Alto Charter School, a K-8 school that gained renown for its teaching standards in a community that was rife with unemployment and vastly different from the neighboring enclaves of Palo Alto and Menlo Park. This time, he opted for a different direction, signing on with the Devil Rays. Auld quickly reached out to Raymond, inviting him to do some marketing consulting for the team. Auld would ascend to the role of senior vice president of business operations, while Raymond eventually took over as VP of branding and fan experience.

Raymond's experience at P&G would guide the rebranding of

the Devil Rays. He urged the team to emphasize the elements that get people excited about the game. Get people looking forward to the day in February when pitchers and catchers would report by marketing the team during the off-season. Play up the game's history and its heroes. Appeal to its status as a piece of Americana. Even raise the stakes for catching a ball hit into the stands: the D-Rays installed a new policy that enabled any fan who caught a home run hit by a Rays player to get it autographed before leaving the ballpark—a unique promotion.

Raymond stressed getting multiple generations into the ball-park. Unlike their division rivals in New York, Boston, Baltimore, and even Toronto, the Devil Rays hadn't been around long enough to convert a generation of kids into avid fans and adult season-ticket-holders. He played up the upstart team's growth, how it could become better than its bigger rivals and convert fans of the Yankees, Red Sox, and other teams who'd moved to the area. The D-Rays strived to make the team an attraction for the whole region—by becoming more involved with local charities and building ball fields in poor neighborhoods.

Those somewhat nebulous goals began to yield tangible results. The team invested some $20 million in the first two years after the takeover, making upgrades ranging from fixing the aging bathrooms and interior paint job to installing a 10,000-gallon "touch tank" beyond the outfield wall where fans could pet cow-nose rays. Where Naimoli-bullied ushers once used Gestapo tactics on anyone in the stands who so much as nibbled on an unapproved sandwich, employees now stopped hassling fans with outside food. The D-Rays sent employees to Disney World to observe the nearby theme park's customer service methods. Silverman also hired Tom Hoof away from the marketing department of Disney's Wide World of Sports complex, installing him as the team's new VP of marketing and community relations. From there, the team started RAYS (Ready At Your Service) University, a mandatory program designed to encourage friendlier customer assistance during games. Ushers got raises, had their traditional uniforms replaced with team jerseys, were re-branded as "fan hosts," and received financial bonuses for out-standing performance.

Meanwhile, Silverman and company kept generating little pub-licity stunts that built goodwill and grew into (minor) national sto-ries. In February 2007, blogger Manny Stiles decided to auction off his baseball fandom to the highest bidder. Stiles had never rooted for any particular team, and the proceeds of the eBay auction would go to pediatric AIDS research. The popular sports blog Deadspin jumped on the story. "What Would It Take to Get You to Blog About the Devil Rays for a Year?" the headline read. The auction topped out at $535, the high bidder winning the right to have Stiles blog about whatever team that mystery person commanded.

Following the auction bid by bid on his blog, Stiles wondered aloud who that person might be. "I don't know yet. I am at work and have no access to my personal e-mail. The winning bidder is lo-cated within the vicinity of Tampa, FL. Uh oh . . . I don't think that means they are *definitely* a Devil Rays fan, but??? I guess I'm getting what I asked for!!! hurray!"

The winning bidder was indeed a Devil Rays fan—Matt Silver-man. Tampa Bay's team president bought his team its own blogger and donated another $1,000 to AIDS research for good measure.

"We have to say, this is the most proactive move we've seen the Devil Rays organization make," wrote Deadspin's Will Leitch. "We now have a new favorite baseball exec . . . though we're not masochistic enough to follow the Devil Rays any closer because of it."

Leitch's snub notwithstanding, the changes—big and small, sys-tematic and spur-of-the-moment—worked. The D-Rays won six fewer games under Sternberg and Silverman in 2006 than they'd won under Naimoli in 2005. Yet attendance jumped 20% in that 2006 season. And despite the new policy of allowing outside food in the stadium, concession sales actually rose on a per-fan basis; the team negotiated new deals with vendors and also found ways to keep fans in the stadium and engaged for longer periods on game day. Nationally, the team began to earn some modicum of respect—

in the form of a few flattering profiles and less abuse—even as the losses kept piling up through 2007.

Still, the team had only begun its drive to lure more fans to the ballpark and raise its profile. When Sternberg took over, employees began carrying Rays Rewards Cards around town. Stroll through downtown St. Pete on a random Tuesday afternoon wearing a Devil Rays cap and you could end up with a Rewards Card, redeemable for free game tickets. In 2006, the team rarely found fans decked out in D-Rays gear, gave away just a few cards, and quickly nixed the promotion. Locals weren't quite ready to embrace the team to the point that they'd dramatically alter their dress habits. By 2010, though, the entire Tampa Bay region was swarming with men, women, and children walking around in Rays caps, T-shirts, and jerseys. As it turned out, fans just needed time to get to love the new Rays. The 2008 season would bring seismic changes on the field and off, driving much of that transformation in fans' attitudes.

Changing the team's name, logo, and brand was one of Silverman's first, and biggest, mandates after the franchise sale. Rebranding any company can take a long time, hog the schedules of entire divisions, and cost some bucks too. Jumping through Major League Baseball's hoops and getting the "Devil" out of Tampa Bay would prove even tougher. Becoming the "Devil Rays" in the first place had seemed an almost random occurrence that required a long series of random events.

Whenever a major league team wants to design a new logo, plus the uniforms and various marks to go with it, that team must go through Anne Occi, MLB's VP of design services. In 1995, Occi flew to Tampa Bay to meet with then-prospective owners vying for an expansion team. Occi thought the team's name should involve some derivation of Rays. The cartilaginous fish were abundant in Florida, so much so that the Florida aquarium in downtown Tampa featured a big statue of a giant ray right out front. Occi's choice echoed the locals' preference: a "name the team" contest had been held, and Sting Rays was the name that drew the largest number of submissions. After further discussions, all parties agreed on a name: Tampa Bay Sting Rays.

Unfortunately, a team in the Hawaii Winter Baseball League, the Maui Stingrays, got there first. Major League Baseball has extremely strict rules when it comes to trademarks. When Denver won its own expansion franchise, everyone was thrilled with the team's name: the Colorado Rockies. Everyone except an apparel company called "Rockies Jeans." No one had noticed. The fledgling baseball team struck a deal where it could sell clothes stamped with "Colorado Rockies" . . . but nothing that carried only the word "Rockies" on it. After that incident, baseball wanted absolutely no confusion or ambiguity in its trademark deals. If Tampa Bay's new team wanted to call itself the Sting Rays, it would have to buy the name from the tiny franchise in Hawaii. The cost? A pittance: $35,000. *Less* than a pittance. Naimoli, ever the stubborn skinflint, flatly declined. He liked the name, Major League Baseball liked the name, the marketing people like the name, and the community liked the name. But he sure as hell wasn't paying for it.

Occi didn't like the idea of simply dubbing the team the Rays, arguing it was too short and weak a name. Ultimately, all parties instead agreed on Devil Rays as a compromise. The next step was to pick the team's logo and color scheme. The '90s saw a move toward a bunch of new designs and colors. Several teams, for instance, adopted teal as a component of their uniforms. Occi wanted something even bolder: a rainbow grading pattern featuring teal, light blue, dark blue, shades of green and yellow, and . . . it was a mess, the kind of logo that even the most ironic, retro-loving hipster would struggle to wear today. When the new name and logo were unveiled, the community nearly rioted. Religious types objected to the satanic reference. Most critics simply thought the name was dumb. One restaurant on Kennedy Boulevard, a major east-west artery in Tampa, put up a big lettered sign, the kind you would normally see outside a high school or hotel. The sign read:

THE EXORCISM

DEVIL RAYS?
TERRIBLE NAME
COME ON VINCE
WE CAN DO BETTER

Naimoli was furious that people didn't like the name. He ordered the team to conduct a phone poll, where people could vote on one of two names: Devil Rays or Manta Rays. The team was pulling hard for Devil Rays to prevail, having already printed boxes full of jerseys with the name and logo on it. Naimoli tried to hedge his bets even before the votes were tallied. Newspaper ads told readers that if the Manta Rays name came out ahead, they should make sure to buy up all the existing Devil Rays gear, since they would become collector items. When the poll started, Manta Rays surged to a big lead. But in the ensuing few days, Devil Rays started to catch up—or so the team claimed. As soon as the vote supposedly got close to 50–50, the team stopped the count. Tampa Bay Devil Rays it would be.

By the time Phil Wallace joined the Devil Rays as special projects analyst in the fall of 2005, the team was working on its second logo, having taken the nearly unprecedented step of scrapping its first one after just three seasons. Darcy Raymond was charged with leading the effort to change it yet again, while also finding a new team name. Right before opening day 2006, Raymond got sucked into overseeing ushers and other customer service matters. That left Wallace, less than two years out of Columbia undergrad with a degree in political science, to shepherd the project. The D-Rays hired the global branding consultancy Interbrand to lead the effort on their behalf. Despite Interbrand's big reach and strong reputation, the firm didn't mesh well with MLB's specific demands. The D-Rays quickly dropped Interbrand and hired Frederick & Froberg, a small New Jersey firm that had worked with the Pittsburgh Pirates and San Diego Padres and other projects and learned to deal with the league's quirks. The lag time for approving and implementing a new MLB logo was huge, so much so that a hard deadline was given: get this done in a few weeks (by late May 2006) or we won't be able to unveil the new identity by November 2007, as planned.

The team flipped through reams of other ideas: Aces, Bandits, Cannons, Dukes, and Stripes. Sternberg's favorite was the Nine, a takeoff on the Mudville Nine. Though Tampa Bay Nine offered the path of least resistance, Sternberg preferred the Florida Nine, as he hoped to become Florida's team (excepting south Florida, Marlins territory). Combine Tampa Bay with Orlando, Gainesville, Jacksonville, and Tallahassee and he'd control one of the five biggest media markets in Major League Baseball. But the Nine faced trademark conflicts, and the Florida name never got off the ground owing to objections from the league and the Marlins.

Back at the drawing board, the team leaned on both Occi and Frederick & Froberg, hoping to find a workable idea in a short time frame. Sternberg and Silverman visited MLB headquarters and laid out their case. They wanted a design that was timeless and traditional, a look that could hold its own with longtime marks like the New York and Boston logos found on the road uniforms of the Yankees and Red Sox. That is, they wanted the polar opposite of what the Devil Rays had worn on that first opening day.

"They wanted to go from a fish to a feeling, to 'this is where I want to be,'" said Occi, who headed Adidas USA's marketing department before joining Major League Baseball more than two decades ago. "They felt that a ray of sunshine represented everything good about Florida, the happiness, fun, and warmth."

To shift from fish to feeling, the team turned to Bill Frederick, Frederick & Froberg's cofounder and partner. It took several tries for Frederick to find a new logo and mark that would last. The initial designs blasted the sun out in a way that was too flashy for Sternberg's taste. The final version featured a more subtle ray of sunlight beaming from the jersey. The color scheme also took a while to finalize before everyone agreed on navy blue, gold for the sun ray, and some light blue. Just as the NHL's Mighty Ducks of

Anaheim, some years earlier, had called on Frederick to chase away the ghost of Emilio Estevez, the Rays asked him to help them rid themselves of the Devil for good.

A year after Tampa Bay staged its exorcism, the Rays claimed the American League pennant.

The newly renamed and newly successful Rays became more aggressive in pushing their product. Sales and marketing expenses jumped 17% in 2008 and continued to rise thereafter. Monetizing the team's success on the field played a big role in driving that increased spending. But so did the Rays' awareness of their weaknesses, and those of the market in which they played. Attendance soared 31% in 2008 as fans started turning out to see the eventual AL champs. But per-game attendance remained weak relative to the rest of the league: just 22,370 fans per game, twelfth out of the fourteen American League teams.

There were plenty of reasons for those low figures. The Rays were still a relatively new team, with only a decade of history in their favor, versus generations of history for rival teams that had converted wave after wave of fathers and sons and mothers and daughters into fans. Tropicana Field was in an awkward location in South St. Petersburg, making the Rays the major league club with the smallest percentage of fans within a thirty-minute drive of the ballpark. The Trop was one of the oldest nonlandmark ballparks in the game, meaning it benefited from neither the nostalgic draw of Wrigley Field or Fenway Park nor the novelty effect of new stadiums. The national and local economies tanked. Public transit was nearly nonexistent. Roaming packs of rabid unicorns attacked fans in the bleachers. Whatever the relative legitimacy of those excuses, the net effect was the same: the Rays needed to do more than put a baseball team on the field, even a *great* team, to pack the Trop.

One of the Rays' most visible moves was to bring in big-name acts for postgame concerts. That was hardly a new idea; game-and-concert pairings went back a few years for several teams. But the

Rays expanded the idea, holding more frequent concerts, with a wide range of acts for many different tastes. The Commodores, Kool & the Gang, the Beach Boys, John Fogerty, and Hall and Oates attracted an older set. Ludacris, Daughtry, and Nelly roped in younger music fans. The Rays scheduled most of the concerts against lesser teams, aiming to maximize attendance with the Royals or Orioles in town and worrying less about turnout versus the Yankees or Red Sox. They hosted more concerts in the 2008 through 2010 seasons than any team in baseball.

"We try to select acts with mass appeal," said senior marketing director Brian Killingsworth in an interview with the *Tampa Tribune*. "We are getting a lot of calls from other teams asking how we do it. A lot of teams are starting to follow us now. We were not the first, but we are among the strongest."

The concerts worked. The Rays drew an average of 32,697 fans for its eight concert games in 2008, versus the season's per-game average of a little over 22,000. In 2009, the nine concerts lured 33,350 a game, versus 23,000 and change for the year. Through August 2010, an average crowd of 28,497 had seen the Rays' ten concert games, compared with fewer than 23,000 a game for the year. The concerts mostly occurred on Saturday nights, with a few Friday night shows, both bigger-drawing days for the Rays and other teams. Even after controlling for day of the week, though, the concerts proved a boon to attendance and concession sales. It didn't hurt that the Rays played exceptionally well during those games, as Tampa Bay reeled off a 23-4 record for concert games in 2008, 2009, and the first five months of 2010. Casual fans could go to a Rays-Tigers game in the thick of the 2008 pennant race, watch the home team win, then bop to LL Cool J's greatest hits with more than 36,000 others. After a fun Saturday night like that, those casual fans might start showing up for Tuesday and Wednesday night games too.

"I think it's great," said *Diamond Dollars'* Vince Gennaro. "Having a baseball game break out during another event is a very good, potentially profitable idea." The profits were rarely huge, as staging a concert cost tens of thousands of dollars. But the ancillary benefits made the endeavor worthwhile, even more so during the most successful concert nights, which drew 35,000-plus.

The success of the concerts made Sternberg and Silverman realize that they could make money through a variety of nonbaseball activities. A few other pro sports teams had started subsidiaries designed to draw in more revenue, expand into alternative event hosting, and manage investment in other enterprises. The rival Red Sox expanded in 2004 with Fenway Sports Group, a spin-off company with investments in NASCAR, minor league baseball, concert promotions, a Red Sox–centric travel venture, and Fanfoto, a firm specializing in photography at sporting events. In 2008, *Fast Company* reported that Fenway Sports Group was raking in more than $200 million a year.

In the summer of 2009, the Rays followed suit, founding Sunburst Entertainment Group. The new company allowed the Rays to better operate other ventures without getting them mixed in with the activities and balance sheets of the baseball team. Sunburst would be run by existing Rays executives, including Michael Kalt, the team's senior vice president of development and business affairs. Kalt had served as New York City Hall's point man for Yankee Stadium and was also a driving force behind the construction of the Mets' Citi Field and the renovation of the Rays' spring training complex in Port Charlotte. Kalt, John Higgins, Brian Auld, and Silverman now lead the company, which has taken on a large and diverse set of projects in its brief existence.

In 2009, the Rays acquired a 50% stake in the Florida Tuskers, an Orlando-based team in the United Football League. They hoped to tap into the state's rabid football following and (ideally) someday push Tuskers games to Tropicana Field. When and if the Rays eventually land a new ballpark, they could bring in football games, soccer matches, lacrosse tournaments, and other events, creating a 365-days-a-year model (or close to it anyway) for capturing revenue. Sunburst eventually sold its share of the Tuskers, realizing the UFL's limited potential wasn't worth its while. But the company continued to push for other deals, including luring more concerts, charity events, high school baseball tournaments, NCAA tournament basketball games, and even Cirque du Soleil. Thanks to Sunburst, the Trop now hosts a college football bowl game as well, the Beef 'O' Brady's Bowl St. Petersburg (hey, the name wasn't Sunburst's choice).

Sunburst also started offering consulting services. Local companies had peppered Rays execs with questions, asking how they were able to transform the team's reputation in the community—given the damage done by years of losing and especially the mishaps of the Naimoli era—beyond simply winning more games. Becoming sports and entertainment consultants became the next logical step for the group.

"We've always wanted to be more than a sports team," Auld said.

They always wanted to be more than a Tampa Bay sports team too. Leveraging a connection via Disney marketing whiz turned Rays executive Tom Hoof, the team played a regular-season series at the Disney Wide World of Sports Complex in Orlando in 2007. The idea to shift one series a year to Orlando came about a year earlier, while the Rays were shopping for a new spring training home. The Disney fields were unavailable in March, since the Atlanta Braves trained there. But the Rays still saw untapped potential in the central Florida hub just one hundred miles from the Trop. Impress fans in Orlando and neighboring communities—the thinking went—and they'll venture down to St. Pete more often, as well as buy team merchandise and follow the Rays on their TVs and radios and computers.

"Becoming a regional club is key to our success," said Silverman. "If we're able to take advantage of the entire region, that's three million, four million, even five million people. We'd become one of the bigger midmarket teams and hopefully have the resources for us to do what we need to do: stay competitive."

Silverman's lofty goals will take time, if they're achievable at all. Part of the challenge involves seducing media organizations outside Tampa Bay to follow the team. The *Orlando Sentinel* doesn't cover the Rays despite their relative proximity to Orlando; compare that lack of interest with New England, where media outlets from the Canadian border down through Connecticut cover the Red Sox.

Still, management presses on. Having expanded their efforts to the northeast, the Rays have also sought to extend their reach south of Tampa Bay. In 2009, they got their wish, moving spring training games from Progress Energy Park in downtown St. Pete an hour and a half farther down the coast to Port Charlotte. A newly completed $27 million renovation of Charlotte Sports Park, combined with the Rays' success in 2008, sent spring training ticket sales through the roof. The team went from 300 season-ticket-holders for spring training games in St. Pete to 3,000 in Port Charlotte, selling out every seat in the Rays' first year there. The Rays have looked for other ways, however small, to expand their reach. Management quickly realized that legions of baseball aficionados in Hazleton, Pennsylvania (population 23,329), had ditched the nearby Yankees, Phillies, and Orioles to root for their native son, Joe Maddon. The Tampa Bay Rays radio network soon expanded to Hazleton, where fans can now catch every game while sitting on their porches on peaceful Pennsylvania summer nights.

For all the talk of branding efforts, regional outreach, and high-minded subsidiaries, few companies of any stripe put more effort into giveaways and promotions than Major League Baseball teams—and the Rays try harder than most. In 2009, the team needed to capitalize on its amazing postseason run but faced a nasty headwind from a struggling local economy. Nearly every home date on that year's schedule featured some kind of fan enticement. There were bobbleheads of course, with four different players getting immortalized. There was a Carlos Peña robot, a Japanese baseball–style rattle drum in honor of second baseman Akinori Iwamura, replicas of the AL championship trophy, and that league-leading lineup of concerts. And yes, the infamous cowbells.

The Rays cowbell started as a goofy little idea from Sternberg. Like just about everyone else who'd seen it, Sternberg fell hard for a *Saturday Night Live* sketch featuring a spoof of rock band

Blue Öyster Cult. In the sketch, a disheveled, bell-bottomed Will Ferrell jumped into the middle of the band's hit song "Don't Fear the Reaper" and began banging away on a cowbell. Christopher Walken, playing fictional music producer Bruce Dickinson, ordered the band to stop the music, then demanded, "More cowbell." It was a silly little premise that somehow evolved into a ubiquitous catchphrase, plastered on tens of thousands of T-shirts. Sternberg liked the sketch and decided to take it one step further: distribute cowbells to fans, get them to make noise throughout the game, and maybe the Rays could gain a home-field advantage.

The plan worked. Players and journalists from other cities complained that the cowbells were bush-league distractions. This only encouraged fans more. Giving out doodads and talking in grand terms about branding were all well and good. But the cowbell became a Rays trademark that—much like the Angels' Rally Monkey and the Mets' inability to avoid shooting themselves in the foot—came to define the franchise. Creating that kind of avidity for a product or ritual is the stuff Harvard Business School grads dream of.

"It's crazy what's happened," said Cary Strukel, a Rays season-ticket-holder who dons a Rays jersey, bright blue wig, strands of beads, and Viking horns for every game. During one fifteen-minute conversation, a half-dozen passersby stopped to pose for pictures with Strukel, the interested parties ranging from small children to halter top–wearing blondes. With no prompting from the team, he evolved into an unofficial Rays mascot, going by the handle "Cowbell Kid" and firing up the right-field stands during every game. "It's kind of a hang-loose, kinda crazy, fun atmosphere. I'm trying to turn right field into WWE wrestling."

The Rays continued to harness their inner Barnum & Bailey during the 2010 season. That year brought "Senior Prom for Senior Citizens" night, an idea stemming from an MLB commercial in which Evan Longoria jokingly suggested the idea to Johnny Damon. It also featured "Baseball Nightclub," a Friday night promotion aimed at attracting college kids and twenty-somethings to the Trop with postgame festivities that included dance music, T-shirts for women that say I HEART LONGORIA, and fireworks . . . yes, indoor fireworks.

"You're really coming to see a show," Darcy Raymond told *The New York Times*. "To some people, the traditionalist, it may be sensory overload. If you're not into a sensory experience, the Trop is not for you. We're a new-school team."

Outsiders have noticed the Rays' efforts. In 2010, ESPN.com named the Rays the sixth-most fan-friendly team among all MLB, NBA, NFL, and NHL teams, and the second-friendliest in baseball alone (behind the Angels).

Despite the accolades and clanging cowbells, steep challenges remain. Attendance rose just 3% in 2009 following the Rays' AL pennant, then fell slightly in 2010, even as the team nabbed the best record in the American League. The Rays must find ways to draw fans to their outdated ballpark, even as negotiations press on with local politicians on a new stadium.

Still, the picture grew much brighter than it had been during Naimoli's heyday. The most memorable marketing moment of that era occurred during the 2002 season. Outfielder Jason Tyner had batted .280 the year before, with 31 stolen bases. Never mind that Tyner also hit zero home runs that year and graded out as one of the worst everyday players in the game. The pre-exorcism Devil Rays were woefully short on talent, let alone young talent. So in '02, the team scheduled a Jason Tyner Bobblehead Day. Ten thousand tiny Tyners were handcrafted in China. But by the time the June 2 promotion rolled around, Tyner was toiling away in Triple A Durham, on his way to a disastrous split season in which he hit just .214 with three extra-base hits in the big leagues. Jason Tyner Bobblehead Day, featured prominently in the Devil Rays' promotional materials, was axed.

And what of the 10,000 bobbleheads? After sitting in storage for a while, the bobbleheads ended up at the Pinellas County Education Foundation. They ended up in the hands of Enterprise Village, a county educational program that teaches grade school kids about business and commerce. If the present-day Rays ever lose their way, they can always pay a visit to Enterprise Village, plop down in a room full of eager students, and learn the wrong way to promote a baseball team. Tiny Jason Tyner will no doubt nod his head in spirited agreement.

CHAPTER 8 ARBITRAGE

I am purely market-driven. I love players I think that I can get for less than they are worth. It's positive arbitrage, the valuation asymmetry in the game.
—Andrew Friedman

How does a team go from the worst record in the majors one season to an American League pennant—and one of the biggest year-to-year turnarounds ever—the next?

By losing. On purpose.

The 2007 Tampa Bay Devil Rays weren't the 1919 Black Sox. No shady mobsters convinced players to throw games. Joe Maddon did everything he could to squeeze every last win from the roster he was given. No one made a grand announcement during spring training that the D-Rays would lose 96 games. But Andrew Friedman knew his team wasn't ready to compete. Not with most of its best talent either still in the minors or not quite ready to perform well in the majors. And certainly not in the American League East, baseball's toughest division and the single biggest hurdle for any team to overcome in any major American sport.

So the Devil Rays hatched a plan. Rather than conducting exhaustive searches for talent or spending millions of dollars on players who could help the team win a few more games, the D-Rays would let nature take its course.

"Winning 66 or 71 games didn't make a dramatic difference to us," said Friedman. "It was about putting ourselves in a position to win 92-plus."

Just not immediately.

The team that jogged onto the turf at Tropicana Field in 2007 wasn't all bad. The offense that year was actually decent, finishing eighth in their league in runs scored and fourth in weighted on-base average (a catchall stat that runs along a similar scale to regular on-base percentage but also takes into account slugging percentage and other factors). Two players, first baseman Carlos Peña and center fielder B. J. Upton, enjoyed career years, ranking among the top performers in the majors at their respective positions.

But oh, that pitching. And ouch, that defense.

The Devil Rays posted a 5.53 team ERA in 2007, by far the worst mark in the majors. James Shields and Scott Kazmir formed an effective (and young) tandem at the top of the rotation. But the other six pitchers who started games that year put up impossibly ugly numbers. Jae Weong Seo allowed 104 base runners and 11 home runs in 52 innings, for an 8.13 ERA. Casey Fossum got belted for 109 hits and 15 bombs in 76 innings, logging a 7.70 ERA. Edwin Jackson, owner of the *lowest* ERA among all starters not named Shields or Kazmir, went 5-15, giving up 195 hits and 88 walks in 161 innings and 5.76 earned runs per nine innings. You could see the Devil Rays at least trying to cobble together a decent rotation. Jackson was a highly touted right-hander acquired in a trade from the Dodgers. J. P. Howell was a first-round pick of the Royals who Friedman hoped would bounce back after falling out of favor in Kansas City. Andy Sonnanstine was already a success story, having battled his way to the majors on the strength of pinpoint control and being projected as a fourth or fifth starter who could keep his team in games.

The bullpen—showing hardly a glimmer of promise—was another story. As shaky as the starting pitchers were, the relievers were far worse, their 6.16 ERA dwarfing the largesse of any other team. The numbers failed to tell the full story. The pitchers deployed to handle the bullpen's workload that season were the living embodiment of baseball dumpster-diving. The motley crew included a cavalcade of undrafted free agents, minor league lifers, and pitchers years past not-all-that-impressive peaks. Two of the relievers hadn't thrown a single major league pitch the year before. The results would have been hilarious if they weren't so sad.

There was the 21–4 loss to the Yankees that still haunts Shawn Camp's dreams. Camp threw 1⅓ innings and surrendered five runs on nine hits; his sixth inning went home run, strikeout looking, double, ground-rule double, home run, single, ground-rule double. There was the 12–11 loss to the Blue Jays, which saw Tampa Bay blow an early 8–1 lead and an 11–6 lead heading to the bottom of the ninth. The 14–8 loss to the Marlins might have been the topper. The best D-Rays reliever that night was shortstop Josh Wilson, who pitched a scoreless ninth after the three guys before him yielded eight runs in two innings.

There were only two plausible explanations for not only the bullpen's results in 2007 but also the lack of ability among the club's relief corps: either Andrew Friedman and his staff were the worst assemblers of bullpen talent in decades, or the Devil Rays had no interest in paying more than the minimum for their pen that year, figuring a few extra wins saved wouldn't make a difference and their resources would best be saved for when the team was ready to contend.

As bad as Tampa Bay's pitching was in '07, a more pervasive problem infected that team, one that made run prevention nearly impossible and needed to be fixed before the Devil Rays could ever hope to win: the defense was historically awful. The D-Rays ranked last or nearly last in the majors in every fielding category. Going by old-time stats, their .980 fielding percentage tied for second-worst in baseball. More advanced stats painted an even uglier picture. Mitchel Lichtman's "ultimate zone rating" figured the Devil Rays' defense cost the team 47.5 runs (nearly five wins) that year, the second-worst mark in MLB. John Dewan's "plus/minus" system tabbed the D-Rays at −107, meaning that Tampa Bay made 107 fewer defensive plays than an average team—the worst mark by any team from 2006 through 2008.

But no metric was crueler to the Devil Rays than "defensive efficiency rating," a statistic invented by Bill James that measures the percentage of balls in play turned into outs. *Baseball Prospectus* tracks the stat all the way to 1954—and no team had ever been worse than the 2007 D-Rays. In 2007, Tampa Bay converted just 65.6% of balls in play into outs; looked at another way, opponents hit a stratospheric .344 when putting the ball in play against Rays pitching.

Though the extent of the defensive meltdown was a surprise, the Devil Rays knew going in that 2007 would be a down year for them. The team's double-play combination alone was the source of much tsuris for D-Rays fans. The team installed Brendan Harris at shortstop, thus handing the most important position on the diamond to an infielder with limited range. Josh Wilson, who also played some shortstop, was even worse. Ty Wigginton, a bruising 230-pounder who made up for his decent power with stone hands and even less range, manned second base. Still, Wigginton was a far sight better than the man he replaced. Though enlightened teams knew that errors and fielding percentage were lousy ways to measure defensive aptitude, even the most hard-core stathead had to acknowledge that B. J. Upton's 12 errors in 48 games at second base were not going to get it done. Upton, an ex-shortstop and ex–third baseman, finally wound up in center field.

Like the abominable bullpen, the Devil Rays' defensively challenged middle infielders were mere placeholders, low-priced players plugged in while the front office continued to search for talent that could make up part of the next—the first—Tampa Bay contender. If those players happened to perform even worse than expected, that wasn't necessarily a bad thing. Tampa Bay had spent the first eight years of its existence losing unintentionally, resulting in a slew of high draft picks. Though the team might've won a few more games with slightly better players in '07, Friedman didn't much mind when the D-Rays' worst record in the majors landed them the number-one overall pick in the 2008 draft.

"It wasn't about constructing an optimal twenty-five-man roster," Friedman said of the '07 season. "A move we didn't make in 2007 allowed us to make certain moves in the off-season."

The lousy defense's huge impact on the pitchers' '07 results confirmed the convictions of the Devil Rays' brain trust. They had already delved into defensive analysis before the '07 meltdown. The baseball operations department was jammed with number crunchers who for years had followed the impact of defense on run prevention and on wins and losses. James Click, the team's manager of baseball research and development, invented an advanced defensive stat of his own, two years before the team hired him: park-adjusted defensive efficiency, or PADE. If bad defense could so profoundly wreck a season, they realized, what would happen if Tampa Bay trotted out a lineup full of good, even great defenders?

Friedman would later say, "We certainly appreciated how defense and pitching were intertwined." But there was more to it than that. When the A's, Red Sox, and a handful of other teams went searching for undervalued baseball commodities, they stumbled upon on-base percentage—especially players who produced high OBPs by dint of hefty walk rates. Load your roster with a bunch of players who knew how to take ball four and you'd score more runs, wear down opposing pitchers more quickly, and, best of all, do all of that without busting the payroll.

In the rush to acquire on-base machines, though, defense hadn't merely been overlooked. It had been shoved aside. Big, hulking sluggers like Adam Dunn, once knocked for their high-strikeout counts, became nearly deified in sabermetric circles for their combination of power and patience. But for all the good 40 homers and 100 walks a season could do, Dunn would give much of that value back in the outfield with his suspect range and poor instincts. And he wasn't alone. The prototypical "toolsy" player who could run, cover a lot of ground, and catch the ball—and perhaps struggle some to get on base—had become passé in some quarters.

This was surprising, given the game's history. "The best player in a nine is he who makes the most good plays in a match," sportswriter Henry Chadwick wrote about defense—*in 1870*. Many of the most famous plays in baseball history featured glove work, from Willie Mays's over-the-shoulder catch off Vic Wertz 450 feet from home plate in the 1954 World Series to Bill Buckner's agonizing misplay of Mookie Wilson's slow roller in Game 6 of the '86 Series. Yet thanks to souped-up home run totals and a newfound appreciation for ninety-foot jogs to first base, many teams' interest in defense, at least temporarily, had gone the way of the bullpen cart.

"Five years ago, defense was still a pretty nebulous subject," said Steve Moyer, president of Baseball Info Solutions. BIS produces pitch-by-pitch, spray-chart hit location and pitch-charting data, which help teams isolate the effects of pitching and defense and evaluate pitchers and fielders accordingly. The changes Moyer saw from 2005 to 2010 in teams' attitudes toward the value of defense were, he said, "huge. People didn't talk about it at all before."

An increasingly available stream of play-by-play information started to change all that. Suddenly, analysts could see what happened with every batted ball, which fielders were in position to field them, and how they fared when they tried. Many teams still ignored the advanced defensive stats, preferring to trust scouts' eyes instead. A few clubs dipped their toes into the water, at least glancing at a few numbers when making personnel decisions.

But no team embraced defensive analysis as early, or as devotedly, as the D-Rays. Rather than relying on others' work, they built their own database, incorporating everything from scouting information to minor league and major league stats for everyone in the organization—and other teams too. Using existing advanced statistics from Lichtman, Dewan, Tom Tango, *Baseball Prospectus*, and other leading analysts, they created their own proprietary measures for hitting, base running, pitching, and defense. What they found convinced them that they could vastly improve the ball club, very quickly, with just a few well-placed moves.

"If you look at statistics like [wins above replacement] over the past few years, and then specifically at the spread between offensive and defensive contributions, you find that players would get penalized for having higher defensive value," said *Diamond Dollars'* Vince Gennaro. "The undervaluation of defense was just waiting to be exploited."

If the Devil Rays were going to exploit market inefficiencies and compete on a small budget, they could take comfort in knowing that other teams in similar situations had succeeded before them. The A's, Twins, and Marlins had all won with low payrolls, using a variety of approaches ranging from old-school talent evaluation to advanced analytical systems. The D-Rays would take a different tack, drawing on years of lessons learned by Friedman on Wall Street. At the heart of that approach was a practice known as arbitrage. Arbitrage refers to any financial transaction in which you simultaneously buy one thing and sell another. The thing you're buying is cheaper than the thing you're selling, thus netting you a profit. An arbitrageur can complete such a transaction using any number of financial instruments, including stocks, bonds, derivatives, commodities, and currencies. He always believes he has better information than the other guy and can thus make the best trades—of equities, of gold . . . or of cleanup hitters.

"The idea is, I buy a widget, sell a wodget, and I don't care what happens long-term," said Felix Salmon, a finance blogger for Reuters. "I'm betting the price of widgets will converge on wodgets, then I've made money and I unwind my trade."

That term, *arbitrage,* has come to take on the broader meaning—especially in nonfinancial circles—of simply acquiring an asset for less than it's worth, especially when coupled with selling an asset for more than it's worth. Every team strives to make these kinds of advantageous moves; the Devil Rays had to be pathological about it. When you take over a team that's finished last almost every season and you're the laughingstock of the league, one good move isn't going to cut it. Friedman knew he'd have to harness all the bright analytical scouting minds he'd assembled, combine them with his own deal-making ability, and spend several years arbitraging toward a brighter future. And the challenge was doubly daunting given the competition from Boston and New York.

If you're the Yankees, you're not as motivated to trawl for cheap talent or invest precious time and effort cobbling together minor trades. Nor are you likely to entertain offers for superstar players, Salmon noted, even if they are overvalued and such a trade could pay off a few years down the road. "They're trying to win the World Series every fucking year. If you're the Yankees, you would never sell Derek Jeter, no matter what you were offered."

In a sense, acquiring a baseball player at a discount, then holding on to him as his value appreciates, was a familiar process to someone with Friedman's private equity background. The best time for a private equity investor to grab a piece of a company is often when it's just getting off the ground. Likewise, the best time to invest in a player is often before he's played a single major league game. At that stage, he's likely to improve and will cost much less than when he's a proven commodity—and far less than when he racks up six years of major league service time and becomes eligible for free agency. In both cases, the ideal holding period should be only as long as the asset maintains the right price-to-earnings ratio, whether those earnings take the form of dollars or wins. You might hold a little longer if shares of that company are throwing off dividends, or your player is helping you win championships.

If all of this sounds familiar, it should. Successful baseball executives have always excelled at identifying when to buy and when to sell players, even if no general manager in the game's history has ever wielded a Wall Street background quite like Friedman's. But where Friedman implemented a new-school approach in Tampa Bay, his methods also resembled those of one of baseball's old-time greats, Branch Rickey. One of Rickey's favorite expressions was,

"Trade a player a year too early rather than a year too late." Tampa Bay's disastrous 2007 season set the stage for a blockbuster trade, one so daring it would leave critics wondering if the Devil Rays had traded a player *five* years too early.

The 2007 season had just ended when Friedman first approached Twins GM Bill Smith with a question: would he be interested in Delmon Young?

Had Smith hung up the phone at that moment, Friedman wouldn't have blamed him. Few prospects in recent history had been more vilified than Young. When things didn't go his way, the number-one overall pick of the 2003 draft might melt down. Playing at Double A Montgomery in 2005, Young found himself on the losing end of a 13–0 game. After being called out on strikes for the third time that game, Young lashed out at the home plate umpire, earning an ejection. He got in the ump's face, bumping him with his chest, then yelling at him some more in the runway leading to the clubhouse after the game. The dustup drew a three-game suspension. It would prove to be a mere warm-up act.

Promoted to Triple A Durham the next season, Young would be teamed once again with Elijah Dukes, another skilled outfielder with the talents of a future major league star. But while Young was pegged as a good kid and solid teammate who occasionally lost his temper, Dukes was a deeply troubled individual. He fathered five kids by four women from 2003 to 2006 alone. He would later be accused of impregnating a seventeen-year-old foster child living with one of his relatives. Dukes cemented his reputation as a big bowl of crazy in April 2007, when he barged into the middle school classroom where his wife taught. Fearing for her life, she ran to the principal, who banned Dukes from the building. She had reason to be afraid: Dukes had sent a photo of a handgun to her cell phone and, she said, left her a threatening voice mail. "You dead, dawg," the message said. "I ain't even bullshittin'. Your kids too."

"Everyone in the clubhouse agreed, you had to keep one eye on

Dukes and one eye on your own stuff," said *Baseball America* writer John Manuel, who covered most of Dukes's games in Durham. "They knew that if Dukes wanted to fuck with you, there was nothing you could do about it, because he was so physical."

Before "You dead, dawg" became a snarky Internet meme, Dukes's influence poisoned the Durham clubhouse and infected his teammates. Though Young had lost his cool a few times coming up through the minors, none of those events compared to what happened on April 26, 2006. Playing in a game against Pawtucket, Young took a called third strike. No chest bump this time, but he did stare at the umpire, refusing to leave the batter's box for a couple of seconds. What happened next became an Internet sensation for all the wrong reasons. The center-field camera caught Young, as he finally walked back to the bench, flinging his bat backward. The bat whipped toward the ump, then whacked him in the chest and arm. Young apologized the next day for the incident, but the damage was done. He got off lightly with just a fifty-game suspension.

For all the animus that incident provoked, Young's youth, talent, and production still made him a hot commodity. He'd won the Southern League MVP in 2005, despite playing barely more than half the season at Double A; *Baseball America* named him its Minor League Player of the Year. The publication also chose him as its number-one prospect in 2006; he was the number-three prospect in 2004, 2005, and 2007. In his first full major league season, Young played in all 162 games, hit .288, and drove in 93 runs, all while turning twenty-two just before the end of the season. Players like Young, with a rare combination of youth, low salary, raw talent, and potential, almost never get traded. But where others saw a future superstar, Friedman saw an overvalued commodity. As a rookie in '07, Young struck out 127 times and drew just 26 walks. He didn't hit for the kind of power that the Devil Rays hoped to see, and despite impressive athleticism, he was a terrible defensive player with lousy instincts. Bat flings and chest bumps aside, the D-Rays saw a player whose perceived value might exceed his actual value.

Young might eventually blossom into a franchise player. But the newly dubbed Rays saw a chance to cash in that potential for a top-line starting pitcher, while making a quantum leap defensively at the same time. On November 28, 2007, the Rays dealt Young, Brendan Harris, and minor league outfielder Jason Pridie to the Twins. In return, they acquired right-handed starting pitcher Matt Garza, shortstop Jason Bartlett, and minor league pitcher Eduardo Morlan. The deal caught the baseball world by surprise. Rarely did two teams execute this kind of "challenge" trade, with two potential stars changing teams so early in their major league careers.

For Friedman and the Rays, this was a unique opportunity, one that transcended the usual protocols for low-revenue, rebuilding teams. Young's attitude issues aside, the Rays were overloaded with young outfielders. What they sorely lacked were young starting pitchers with ace potential. Garza came with makeup questions of his own, with observers wondering if he could handle adversity, given the mound blowups he'd flashed over the years after giving up big hits. But Garza's upside, combined with Bartlett's slick glove, gave the Rays a chance to dramatically upgrade their run prevention with a single deal. The trade was so promising that rival executives cursed it.

"We were pissed!" said Jed Hoyer, former assistant GM for the Red Sox who became the man in charge in San Diego. "We'd always liked Garza, even with the makeup issues, and we had tried to get Bartlett also. Young for Garza you could start to understand, but then for them to get Bartlett too?"

Bumping Young out of the lineup gave the defense its first boost. The next one came by subtracting Brendan Harris (12 runs worse than the average shortstop in 2007, prorated over 150 games) and replacing him at shortstop with the fine-fielding Bartlett. (The Twins have fared well since doing the deal too, with Young enjoying his best season in 2010 and a slew of talented, homegrown players—plus a new, revenue-rich stadium—making Minnesota a perennial contender.)

The biggest changes to the Rays' defense would come from players already in the organization. Soon after opening day, the Rays called up third baseman and first-round draft pick Evan Longoria. Combining a potent bat with the best glove in the league at third base, Longoria became an instant star. Installing Longoria in the lineup shifted Akinori Iwamura to second base. Iwamura won six Gold Gloves playing third base in Japan but had virtually no experience playing second base at any professional level. Still, the Rays must have seen something they liked, and Iwamura teamed with Bartlett to form the best double-play combination in team history. Other, more subtle changes also helped. After they had jerked him across multiple positions coming up through the farm system and early in his big league career, the Rays finally slotted B. J. Upton in center field on opening day and left him there. The result was an 11-run defensive improvement there too.

Few people saw it coming, but the Rays were about to become a huge threat to the AL East hierarchy.

"We were annoyed by [the Young-Garza/Bartlett trade], but we didn't think they were that close to being competitive—we didn't think the bullpen was good enough," mused Hoyer. "We'd always had this two-team division, and you knew the wild card could come out of our division every year. All of a sudden, that changed completely. It continues to this day, where you know one of the three best teams in baseball is not going to make the playoffs."

The Rays would answer their rivals' doubts—and their own fears—about their bullpen by finding value in unlikely places. Tampa Bay made twenty-two trades between the end of the 2005 season and opening day 2008, several of them for relief pitchers. Very few of those trades looked like much at the time. But several of the players became key cogs by the time the Rays fielded their first winning team in 2008.

On June 20, 2006, Tampa Bay shipped outfielder Joey Gathright and throw-in middle infielder Fernando Cortez to Kansas City for left-handed starting pitcher J. P. Howell. A first-round pick by the Royals out of the University of Texas, Howell immediately dominated in professional ball, fanning 138 hitters in his first 128 minor league innings. Promoted to the majors on June 11, 2005, Howell excelled in his first big league start, tossing five innings of one-run ball against Arizona and striking out 8 batters. The rest of the season was awful. In his next 68 innings, Howell struck out 46 batters, walked 37, and surrendered 69 hits and 9 home runs. He finished with a 6.19 ERA. When a baseball player slumps, there's a tendency for teams to fixate on the negatives. Those who watched Howell that year couldn't help but notice his slight frame. Listed at 6 feet, 175 pounds, he looked closer to 5' 10" and 160. Where successful undersized pitchers like Pedro Martinez used whiplike actions to generate velocity on their fastball, Howell's heater topped out below 90 miles per hour and never averaged even 87 miles per hour for a full season. The Royals couldn't help but wonder if their number-one draft pick had been something of a mirage, able to get by with mediocre stuff against feckless minor league competition, but overmatched against the big boys in the majors.

The Devil Rays chose to focus on Howell's positives. They noted the larger sample size of success in college and in the minors, compared to fifteen shaky starts for a twenty-three-year-old rookie in the majors. They saw flashes of impressive results, including his first start of the season, and also his second-to-last, in which he struck out seven Twins in five hitless innings. Sure, he couldn't dent a slice of bread with his fastball. But his curveball was a dazzler. When Howell was on, he could spot his big curve anywhere he wanted in the strike zone, freezing not only left-handed hitters but also righties, thus fulfilling the crucial requirement that a pitcher have an out pitch against opposite-sided batters.

Following the trade, Howell pitched at Triple A, earning a promotion to Tampa Bay. Yet again, he appeared to struggle, posting a 5.10 ERA in '06 and an unfathomable 7.59 mark in 2007. Still, the Rays remained patient. Howell had flashed excellent strikeout-to-walk ratios both seasons, a sign of good command. His fielding-independent numbers again pointed to a pitcher whose true ability suggested he could put up a much stronger ERA around 4.00 with some better fortune. Still, management contributed to Howell's fortune in 2008, shifting him to the bullpen . . . and everything came together: 89.1 innings, lots of strikeouts, very few home runs, great clutch performance, and a 2.22 ERA. He duplicated his success in 2009, this time as the team's nominal closer. By changing Howell's job description and the defense behind him—and showing the patience of Job—Tampa Bay had essentially created one of the best relief pitchers on the planet. It was a lesson in how changing circumstances can help people get the most out of their abilities, in baseball as in business.

"I couldn't really handle those days off in between starts," Howell said. "It was pretty bad. But once I knew I had to be ready every day, everything started to change."

The hits kept coming. At the 2007 trade deadline, Tampa Bay dealt Seth McClung, a huge right-handed pitcher with a blazing fastball, to the Milwaukee Brewers for Australian reliever Grant Balfour. As if his name wasn't unfortunate enough for a pitcher, Balfour's career was plagued by shaky control that often earned him return trips to the minor leagues. Making matters worse was an array of injuries that would have prompted many pitchers to retire: five stints on the disabled list, with forearm, elbow, and shoulder injuries and surgeries. He lost the entire 2005 season and most of 2006. When Balfour was traded to the Rays, he was almost thirty, and it had been some time since he'd done anything promising in the majors.

But Friedman trusted his scouts—who saw Balfour regain his velocity after multiple injuries—and his cadre of analysts, who pointed to Balfour's long track record of minor league success (more than a strikeout per inning) and suggested that some dormant skills might be on the verge of busting out. Friedman knew that Balfour's upside far exceeded the minimal risk that came with a contract for just over the league minimum. Called up May 31, Balfour joined Howell in forming one of the most devastating bullpen combinations in the game that year. All told, he fanned 82 batters in 58.1 regular-season innings, with a 1.54 ERA.

Balfour's signature moment that season came in Game 1 of the American League Division Series, the first playoff game in franchise history. With the bases loaded and two outs in a key spot, Balfour and White Sox shortstop Orlando Cabrera began yelling at each other, with Cabrera kicking dirt toward the mound and taunting Balfour to throw the ball over the plate. A fiery and animated competitor even in meaningless games, Balfour blew a fastball by Cabrera for strike three, pointed at him, then shouted, "Sit the fuck down!" The moment became so iconic that Rays blog DRaysBay quickly crafted a T-shirt with Balfour's silhouette and the inscription "STFD." Led by Balfour and Howell, the 2008 bullpen lopped more than two and a half runs off its ERA, dropping down to 3.55, fifth-best in the majors after finishing dead last a year earlier.

For all the success enjoyed by bullpen castoffs and other low-priced talent on the 2008 Rays, a commonly voiced knock was that management owed its success to a string of high draft picks, most of them made by the previous administration. There was something to this. The Rays picked in the top ten every year from 1999 through 2008. The list of first-rounders included several players who contributed to the '08 AL pennant winners, either directly or indirectly: Evan Longoria, the number-three overall pick in 2006, won 2008 Rookie of the Year honors; David Price, the top pick of the 2007 draft, moonlighted as a fire-breathing closer in the '08 playoffs before moving on to become a top starter in later seasons; and Delmon Young, the top pick of the '03 draft, was parlayed by the Rays into Matt Garza and Jason Bartlett. Still, with Longoria and Price the only players to go directly from top draft picks to the '08 team, and only Longoria spending the bulk of the season on the major league roster, it was clear that other factors played a bigger role in forging that team.

The biggest of those factors: Friedman's uncanny knack for striking a deal in his favor.

"Andrew had a natural negotiating ability that was well beyond his years," said Wayne Clevinger, managing director at Friedman's old private equity firm, MidMark Capital. "Half of life is negotiating, and he had a great gift for it. He had a feel for what could be done and what couldn't. After that you could sense that there wasn't too much you could give him that he couldn't handle. The more balls he had in the air, the more invigorated he was."

The single most important task on a general manager's to-do list is the identification of talent that can push a team toward a championship. Many teams never make it past that first step. They overrate their own prospects, go after free agents well past their prime, and fail to spot statistical warning signs. The result is a string of losing seasons, followed by a stack of pink slips. Make it past that initial talent-vetting stage and you still need to sign your building-block players for a price and amount of time that fits the team's needs, with enough money left over to address other needs. The Yankees could paper over player-evaluation mistakes by flexing their financial muscle on high-priced superstars. The Rays had no such wiggle room.

When Friedman left Wall Street for Tampa Bay in 2004, few players on the major league roster matched the profile of a worthy long-term keeper. Carl Crawford was an exception. A two-sport star from Houston, Crawford was just starting to convert his raw tools into major league skills. In '04, Crawford's third season with the Devil Rays, he hit .296, led the league in stolen bases and triples, and made his first All-Star Game. Advanced defensive metrics, though still in their infancy, suggested that Crawford was also an elite defender (an evaluation generally shared by scouts).

When Friedman signed on, he joined the D-Rays as director of player development. Nominally, Chuck LaMar remained the team's GM and the man in charge of baseball operations. But from the start, Sternberg groomed Friedman to take the reins so that when the ownership change was complete, a capable new GM would already be in place. Until then, the D-Rays would separate into two cliques: LaMar and the old guard on one side, Friedman and a small but growing generation of business and baseball minds on the other. When the time came to explore long-term contract possibilities with Crawford, it was Friedman, not LaMar, who took charge.

When Major League Baseball adopted free agency in the mid-1970s, it created a system in which players' earning power would change dramatically over the course of their careers. The explosion of revenue over the ensuing three decades accelerated the skyrocketing of player salaries. More and more, teams' incentives grew to acquire as many contributing players as possible with less than three years of service time. Why? Because nearly all of those players could (and still can today) be paid the major league minimum, as they were not yet eligible for salary arbitration and were still years away from free agency. As the revenue gaps between richer teams like the Yankees and poorer teams like the Devil Rays widened, many lower-revenue clubs began aggressively trading players before they reached free agency. Why risk losing a premium player for nothing more than the potential for compensation draft picks, when a proactive team could trade their free-agent-to-be for bigger hauls of young talent?

Friedman sought a different course. Crawford turned twenty-three near the end of his 2004 breakout season. Studies done by Bill James and other analysts confirmed that baseball players tend to peak in their mid- to late twenties. If Crawford didn't sign a long-term contract, the D-Rays risked losing him at the height of his powers, just after his twenty-seventh birthday—or even earlier, if they traded him. To capture Crawford's best seasons without breaking the bank, Friedman needed to find the right balance of risk and reward for both parties.

For Crawford, the best time to sign a lucrative contract would be immediately. Still a full year from becoming eligible for arbitration, and four years away from free agency, he risked losing major earning power if his performance tanked or he suffered a major injury before those milestones were reached. The Devil Rays could offer Crawford a big enough contract to leave him financially set for life. In exchange for that security, Tampa Bay would have a long-term commitment that could net the team a healthy profit if Crawford developed as everyone hoped he would. This wasn't an entirely new concept. In the 1990s, John Hart, then the Cleveland Indians' general manager, popularized the practice of offering long-term deals to players on the brink of arbitration, thus assuring financial security for young stars Kenny Lofton, Albert Belle, and Jim Thome—and, more to the point for Hart, cost certainty for their employer.

What made the Devil Rays' approach different was their affinity for club options.

A baseball player can sign a contract with three different types of options tacked on. A player option gives the player the right to opt out of the deal and test the free-agent waters, a move he'll almost certainly make if he's coming off a successful season and feels he can make more on the open market. A mutual option requires both parties to sign off, a scenario that almost never plays out that way: if a player's likely to make more in free agency, he'll opt out, and if the player struggles or gets hurt, the team is likely to let him go. But with a club option, the team wields all the power. Got a 40–home run hitter? Keep him. Did he turn into Mario Mendoza? Happy trails. As the stewards of a franchise that would probably always struggle with limited revenue streams, Sternberg and Friedman were as aggressive as possible in tacking club options on to long-term deals. Doing so gave them the possibility of risk-free profit at minimal cost. Baseball arbitrage.

The two sides consummated the deal in April 2005. Crawford would earn $15.25 million from 2005 through 2008, the four years before what would have been his free agency date. The contract then called for an $8.25 million salary in 2009, Crawford's would-be first post–free agency season, and another $10 million in 2010 (with a chance to earn up to $11.5 million based on various escalator clauses). If Crawford maxed out his earnings, he would make $35 million over six years—one pre-arbitration season, three arbitration-eligible seasons, and two (would-be) free agency years. No one knew for sure how Crawford's career would play out, and the D-Rays would be exposed if their promising young left fielder suffered a career-ending injury or an irreversible performance decline.

Still, the potential was there for the Devil Rays to make a gigantic profit. Which is exactly what they did.

Baseball analysis website FanGraphs shows every player's earned value on a year-by-year basis, based on a formula that measures a player's batting and defense (or a pitcher's pitching), then scales it against the going rate for free-agent talent in a given season. Through the first four years of the contract, Crawford's performance added up to $55.7 million in value—nearly four times what he was paid in those seasons. In 2009, Crawford's production netted 5.5 wins for Tampa Bay, worth $24.9 million on the open market—triple his salary for the year. By late June 2010, Crawford's earned value had easily surpassed that season's salary too. All told, Crawford produced $108.9 million worth of value for the Rays over the life of his contract, compared with the deal's maximum value of $35 million.

Friedman's next big coup came in January 2008, when the Rays signed starting pitcher James Shields to a long-term contract. Having already seen some of Crawford's profit potential pay off, Friedman took an even more aggressive approach with Shields. After just 52 major league starts (including an impressive 12-8 record and a 3.85 ERA on an awful 2007 team), Shields had shown the Rays enough to earn his own multi-year offer. From 2008 through 2011, Shields would be paid $11.25 million, already a potentially huge bargain for a Rays team that believed it had found a top-tier starter.

But the kicker would come at the end of those four seasons, with the Rays tacking on not one, not two, but *three* club options. No team in baseball had so completely embraced the idea of club options or lobbied for that much latitude at the end of a deal. But Shields had one less year of service time under his belt than Crawford did at the time of his signing. As a pitcher, Shields was also a riskier investment. The higher attrition rate carried by pitchers compared with position players was a concern. Even more worrying was the 2002 shoulder surgery Shields had to remove a benign tumor; the procedure dropped the velocity on his fastball and left him wondering if he'd ever pitch again. But Shields had proved himself since then, developing one of the deadliest changeups in the game. If anything, those drawbacks gave the Rays more negotiating leverage. The deal to date has been a big success. Three years into the contract, Shields has been worth $44.4 million (market value) despite an erratic 2010 season. If he serves the contract's entire seven-year term, including the club's three option seasons, his maximum total salary would be $44 million. Less than halfway into the deal, the Rays have already made their money back.

Still, offering contracts to players who are two-plus years, or a year and change, into their major league careers? Big deal. At no point in a player's professional career is his future so uncertain as when he's toiling in the minor leagues. The vast majority of minor leaguers never even sniff the majors, and the tiniest percentage of them actually achieve some degree of success thereafter. For any player, even a "can't-miss" prospect, getting the call to the show means a big celebration (and a sigh of relief). What if a team could convince a top prospect, on the cusp of making the majors, to trade in that uncertainty for an eight- or nine-year contract? What teenager or early-twenties up-and-comer, the idea went, wouldn't want to lock up tens of millions of dollars before playing his first big league game?

In 2004, soon after settling into his new role in baseball, Friedman approached B. J. Upton with that very idea: waive your arbitration rights and forgo free agency for a little while, and we'll make you an instant multimillionaire. Upton had already received a $4.6 million signing bonus, to be paid over five years, as the number-two overall pick in the 2002 draft. He was also baseball's number-two prospect, as rated by *Baseball America*. But he was just nineteen years old, having just arrived at Triple A. Plenty of uncertainty lay ahead.

As it had done with Crawford, the new regime spearheaded the discussions while Chuck LaMar watched from a distance. "I thought it was an innovative idea, well thought out," LaMar said. "You take a risk. But you save money if it works out. And you give lifetime security to a young man who knows that if he plays well, he'll have another big contract coming. B. J. Upton was exactly the type of player they wanted to try to sign."

Upton turned down the D-Rays' overtures. Still, Friedman wasn't about to abandon the idea of targeting a top prospect for a long-term deal. He just needed to find the next suitable candidate. Someone like Evan Longoria.

In sizing up the possibility of inking Longoria to a multi-year contract, Friedman seized on the practices he developed in his private equity days. When investing in a company, he had to assess not only that firm's operations but also the quality and risk tolerance of management, the current trends within its industry, and the state of the broader economy. Likewise with a potential Longoria deal, Friedman had to consider a lot more than the quality of the player. The success of the Crawford contract and similar deals across baseball offered a sound precedent. The Rays' revenue streams—outside of the estimated $70 million to $80 million a year they would pocket in revenue shared via MLB Advanced Media and other leaguewide ventures, as well as from richer teams—remained tight. And then there was the matter of Longoria's agent.

Paul Cohen, an agent for Los Angeles–based TWC Sports whose client list included Yankees second baseman Robinson Cano, Braves pitcher Tim Hudson, and Rockies shortstop Troy Tulowitzki, also repped Tulowitzki's former Long Beach State teammate Longoria. After tearing up Double A for most of the 2007 season, Longoria's numbers tailed off slightly in Triple A as he hit .269/.398/.490 with 29 strikeouts in 31 games. Cohen had just locked down a six-year, $31 million contract for Tulowitzki—the biggest contract of all time for a player with one-plus seasons of major league service time—with a $15 million club option at the end. Would his other high-profile Long Beach State Dirtbag client, *Baseball America*'s number-two prospect for 2008, be willing to consider an even longer deal, coming off *zero* seasons of service time?

"Evan said, 'If I can get financial security for my family, in line with other multi-year contracts, I'd have interest in doing that,'" Cohen recalled. "'If I have a health or performance issue, what happens to me and my family?'"

Cohen discussed multiple scenarios with his client. What would happen if he went year to year instead of signing a long-term contract and then hit .300 with 40 homers every season? What about .250 with 10 homers? Cohen then explained how the Rays might handle Longoria's service time. If he didn't sign a deal, the Rays might be reluctant to bring him up to the majors until they were sure they could contend. That way they could save money now by waiting longer to get to salary arbitration and, eventually, free agency. On the other hand, if he did sign, the Rays would be more likely to promote him as soon as they felt he was ready and there was an open spot. Longoria considered all the what-ifs. Like most of Cohen's clients in his twenty-plus years as an agent, he didn't come from a wealthy family. And while the $3 million signing bonus he got for signing after the '06 draft could keep him going for a while, Longoria understood the potentially short shelf life of a professional athlete.

Finally, Cohen proffered one last thought. "I told him what it would look like in the media, from an intellectual standpoint, if he signed the deal and became a star. I told him, if media perception was important, don't do it."

Longoria decided the positives outweighed the negatives. No player had ever agreed to a contract quite like the one the Rays were proposing. He would be the first. When Willy Aybar got hurt a few days into the 2008 season, the Rays called up Longoria to play third base, knowing they no longer had to artificially hold back his service time. Six games into his big league career, both sides made it official: Longoria had signed a six-year deal for $17.5 million. As with Shields's deal, the Rays tacked on three club options at the end, making the total package a potential *nine-year* contract worth about $48 million.

Three years into the deal, Longoria had fulfilled Cohen's prophecy: he became a star, triggering criticism and even some mockery for signing the contract he did. According to FanGraphs' win values, he earned nearly $85 million for Tampa Bay through 2010, with six years to go on the deal if the Rays trigger all three options—which, barring some cataclysmic event, they surely will. Longoria won Rookie of the Year in 2008, made the All-Star team in his first three seasons, and emerged as an MVP candidate. In his annual "MLB Trade Value" column, which considers a player's ability, age, and contract status, then ranks the top fifty players in baseball based on who'd have the most value in trade, FanGraphs' Dave Cameron ranked Longoria as the single most valuable commodity in the game in *each* of his first three MLB seasons.

"Yes, I know, he only has a half-season of major league experience," Cameron wrote in 2008, "and we have to be careful drawing too many conclusions from sample sizes that don't include more than 300 major league at-bats. However, the value of his abilities is so great, and his contract is so ridiculously awesome for Tampa, that the positives more than outweigh the negatives and make him the guy I wouldn't trade for any other one player in the game."

Friedman defended the deal, noting that Longoria was owed $20.5 million (including a potential 2014 buyout) after six games in the big leagues. Still, it was clear the Rays had made out like bandits.

"I might just have to retire his jersey if I keep doing this list going forward, because unless he gets hurt or takes a big step back, it's hard to see anyone passing him for the next five years," Cameron wrote about Longoria in his 2009 trade value column.

"His on-field value puts him in the discussion with the best players in the game, but his contract is just so unbelievably team-friendly that no one else comes close to his overall value to their club. He's going to be paid like a league-average back-end starting pitcher through a potential Hall-of-Fame prime. Agents, this is the template of what not to do with your best client going forward."

CHAPTER 9 WORST TO FIRST

*We were in last place, all of a sudden we were in first.
That's crazy. You know how cool that is? It's like we
were the Bad News Bears.*
—CARLOS PEÑA

The Tampa Bay Devil Rays spent eight years in baseball hell. Under Vince Naimoli, the club took up residence in the American League East's basement and repelled fans with a poorly maintained stadium, belligerence toward the local community, and general indifference toward public opinion.

The D-Rays then spent two years in baseball purgatory. New management blew up every major element of the previous regime. Marketing efforts became more focused, more creative, more successful. A new generation of number crunchers began studying ways for the team to find new, stealthy talent sources. But the results on the field still stunk: two more last-place finishes and 197 more losses.

In 2008, everything changed.

The most noticeable difference was in the team's name. After ten years' bearing the likeness and moniker of a large, batlike fish known as the devil ray, the team dropped the "Devil" from its name. They were now called the Tampa Bay Rays, complete with new uniforms and a new logo. Now the players needed only look at their own chests to see the changes the Rays had made. That off-season brought more than branding changes and cosmetic adjustments, though. After two years of evaluating the organization's talent, Andrew Friedman and his staff spent the winter reshaping the roster.

Delmon Young, the mercurial former number-one overall draft pick, was gone. So was starting shortstop Brendan Harris, designated hitter Greg Norton, and most of the bench. The bullpen exodus was more dramatic: four of the team's top six relievers from 2007 weren't invited back for the '08 season. New faces were everywhere. Veteran Cliff Floyd was already making new friends, on his way to filling the role of team leader and elder statesman that management hoped he'd embrace. Willy Aybar and Eric Hinske would join Floyd as newcomers in the opening day lineup. Matt Garza ascended to the starting rotation. The recast bullpen featured seasoned pickups like Troy Percival and Trever Miller, with incumbents J. P. Howell and Grant Balfour thrust into higher-leverage roles. The Rays' perennial youth movement remained in full swing: college superstar and number-one pick Evan Longoria looked primed to grab the starting third-base job ahead of schedule.

No one knew if this new cast of characters would make the team markedly *better*. But there was no doubt that the 2008 Rays were *different*.

"People ask all the time what our expectations were," said Friedman. "We don't get caught up in those things because we're so caught up in the process. We believe, with the right process, good things will happen. I felt like we would score more runs than we allowed. What that meant, we weren't really sure."

There was another change in the Rays' approach, though it was so subtle that most pundits and fans scarcely noticed. Traditionally, rebuilding teams tend to stockpile assets. They trade veterans for prospects and take fliers on cheap, unwanted talent, hoping to hit the lottery. They rarely sign major league free agents. Spending significant money on a veteran free agent and potentially giving up a compensatory draft pick rarely makes sense for a team coming off a last-place finish. Yet the Rays spent the 2007–2008 off-season making the kinds of moves you'd expect from a contender.

This new approach made sense from multiple angles. Even the most patient ball club, stacked with promising young talent, can't simply wave a wand and go from cellar dwellers to champions. Losing teams eventually need to make the kinds of moves you'd expect from a contender, thus making them more likely to become contenders themselves. For the Rays, this wouldn't involve handing $100 million contracts to free agents so much as acquiring veteran talent that could help fill in whatever gaps remained once the team's young core had been assembled and push them closer to a playoff berth. There were off-field considerations too. In "Is Alex Rodriguez Overpaid?"—a chapter from the 2006 book *Baseball Between the Numbers*—Nate Silver showed that each additional win earns a ball club about $1.2 million in additional ticket, concessions, merchandising, and other revenue. So even if the Rays merely bumped their win total from 66 in 2007 to 71 in 2008, they would stand to add $6 million (or more after accounting for inflation) to their top line.

The Rays announced two more signings about a week before spring training. Trevor Miller signed a one-year, $1.6 million deal to serve as the team's lefty relief specialist, while journeyman outfielder Eric Hinske, a former Rookie of the Year, took an $800,000 deal to compete for a share of the right-field job. Rounding out the off-season moves was a little-noticed trade: the Rays shipped spare arm Jeff Ridgway to the Braves for two utility infielders, Chase Fontaine and Willy Aybar. Fontaine and Ridgway didn't pan out. Aybar also seemed destined to fail. In 2007, Aybar had spent three months rehabbing from substance abuse, then broke the hamate bone in his right hand, collectively costing him that entire season. In January 2008, the Rays made the deal to acquire him; a few weeks later, he was arrested on domestic violence charges in the Dominican Republic. Clearly the Rays saw *something* in Aybar— why deal with all that drama otherwise?

To see the utility of the Aybar trade—or any of the other deals—

you needed to take a step back. The on-field results, when Aybar made it onto the field, were impressive. He'd shown a solid bat (.384 on-base percentage in 383 plate appearances) and the versatility to play several positions in his first two seasons with the Dodgers and Braves. Yes, his life and career had gone into a tailspin. But with an asking price of nearly nil, the Rays saw a lot more potential reward than risk in the deal.

Nearly a decade of high draft picks, followed by two years of well-placed trades and pickups, had stocked the Rays' roster. The team had blazing speed and defense in Carl Crawford and B. J. Upton. Carlos Peña had grown into one of the deadliest power hitters in the game. The starting rotation boasted five promising arms, all twenty-six years old or younger. The supporting cast—the bottom of the order, bullpen, and bench—had been completely revamped, yielding a balanced team with no glaring weaknesses. The baseball world didn't realize it yet, but Friedman and his advisers had taken a bunch of talented young players and turned them into a team. The Rays' payroll would rise from just over $24 million in 2007 (lowest in the majors) to just shy of $44 million in 2008 (still the lowest in the AL, second-lowest in the majors). Despite the modest price—three times less than the Red Sox's $133 million payroll and nearly five times less than the $207 million the Yankees spent—all the pieces now fit.

"Our emphasis changed," Friedman said. "We felt like we had the talent on hand to aggressively move this thing forward. We identified certain areas we were going to attack so that we'd be in a position to achieve success, whether in 2008 or 2009. We were more focused on the construction of a twenty-five-man roster than we ever had been."

Maddon liked the look of his team enough to predict an 81-win season, a modest outlook at first blush, but still a 15-game improvement over 2007's result if it happened. *Baseball Prospectus's* PECOTA forecasting system was more optimistic, predicting an 88-win season for the Rays. Still, only Scott Kazmir had the nerve to call a playoff appearance for the Rays.

Despite all the optimism coming out of spring training, the Rays started the 2008 regular season looking like the same old Rays. After scoring an impressive 6–2 win on opening day against the Orioles, Tampa Bay lost 10 of its next 16 games. Fan interest, as usual, was minimal. The Rays drew 36,048 fans for their home opener against the Mariners. The next night, they sold just 12,106 tickets. Weekend series, normally significantly bigger draws, weren't much better. The Rays drew only 48,189 fans to the first home weekend series of the season against Baltimore, averaging just over 16,000 a game.

After taking two out of three against the O's to draw back to .500, the Rays hosted the Yankees for a two-game set, April 14–15. The Bombers smoked Rays starter Andy Sonnanstine for seven runs in 3⅓ innings. Tampa Bay stormed back, scoring five in the bottom of the seventh—only to see the Yankees take the lead right back in the eighth and hold on for an 8–7 win. The next day, Edwin Jackson took his turn as the Yankees' punching bag by ceding five runs. Final score: 5–3 Yankees, and a series sweep by New York.

The two losses dropped the Rays to 6-8. Worse, attendance was again sorely lacking. Home of the Yankees' spring training, Tampa is packed with New York fans, some of whom would eagerly make the drive over the Howard Frankland Bridge and see their team beat up on their St. Pete–dwelling neighbors. But the boosts in attendance for series against the Yankees and Red Sox still left wide swaths of empty seats. In just their seventh and eighth home games of the year, a two-game set against the Yanks, the Rays drew fewer than 20,000 fans per contest.

One bright spot did emerge from that series, though: Evan Longoria belted his first major league homer, in his third major league game. The Rays had started the season with super-utilityman Willy Aybar at third base, before a quick injury brought Longoria up April 12. The third overall pick in the 2006 amateur draft, Longoria had already established himself as one of the sport's premier prospects. Still, most observers figured it would be a while before he cracked the big leagues. Little did they know, but Longoria and his agent had already laid the framework for the nine-year contract that would become the talk of baseball—and the foundation for a new era of winning Rays teams.

The ink was barely dry on that deal before Longoria began carving up the American League. The second homer of his big league career was a solo shot that launched a comeback win over Toronto on April 22. Two days later, Longoria doubled, tripled, walked, and cracked a sacrifice fly in four trips to the plate, pacing another victory over the Jays. By the end of his first month in the majors, Longoria was hitting .273 with a .388 on-base percentage and .527 slugging percentage, while playing stellar defense at third. The Rays had added another star to what suddenly looked like a loaded roster.

"There was really no identity with the Rays before," said Dan Wheeler, a member of the 2008 Rays bullpen in his second stint with the team. "They were searching for something. They went young and they went old and then they went young. And then when these new guys stepped in, they picked the people they felt were going to be the future of this team—the Carl Crawfords, the B. J. Uptons, and the Evan Longorias. That's what we had [in 2008]."

The Rays reeled off six straight wins in late April, sweeping the Jays and Red Sox at home. The team was getting contributions from its marquee players, but also from the supporting cast. Facing Boston in the opener of a three-game series, the Rays sent the game to extra innings. In the bottom of the eleventh, little-used reserve Nathan Haynes came up with men on first and second and nobody out.

The Book, baseball's catchall name for the long-held strategies that most managers follow, called for a bunt in that situation. Moving the lead runner to third base with one out would give the Rays a chance to win the game via a sacrifice fly, a well-placed grounder, a wild pitch, a passed ball—a number of ways that weren't a hit. But Joe Maddon, as usual, threw the Book in the crapper. He knew that run expectancy charts, which track the probability of a given number of runs scoring in different base/out situations, made a successful bunt the slightly superior option in a situation where a team needed only one run. But Maddon also knew that sacrifices are no sure thing: a player can bunt a ball right at a fielder, setting up a force play; he can pop a bunt attempt in the air, leading to an out where no runner advances; or he can simply fail twice in a row, setting up a two-strike count and lowering the likelihood that the batter will produce a hit. Weighing all those factors, as well as Boston's need to draw their corner infielders in to protect against a bunt, Maddon ordered Haynes to swing away. The lefty-swinging outfielder lashed a single to right, knocking in Carl Crawford with the winning run in a 5–4 victory.

"My first year here I put out a T-shirt: TELL ME WHAT YOU THINK, NOT WHAT YOU'VE HEARD," said Maddon, whose more adventurous against-the-Book decisions included issuing the infamous bases-loaded intentional walk to Josh Hamilton, sending a runner while down 9–0, using unusually aggressive defensive shifts, and starting same-hand hitters against a handful of quirky pitchers. "So much of this stuff has been regurgitated for years. I love the basics of baseball, but when it comes down to moving it forward, why not utilize all the new technology involved, whether it's video equipment or whether it's numerically or statistically speaking. If you choose to not do that, you're going to get left behind."

Haynes's game-winner marked just the fourth RBI of his career, one of only 10 hits he'd collect all season. He wasn't the Rays' last unlikely hero in '08.

After finishing April at 15-12, just a game out of first place, the Rays hit a rough patch at the start of May. At Fenway Park for their first road series of the year against the Red Sox, Tampa Bay ran into a buzz saw. Boston outscored the Rays 26–10 in a three-game sweep. A split in the subsequent series against the Jays left Tampa Bay two games over .500, a respectable pace in most divisions but one that had the Rays three and a half games out of first place in the murderous AL East.

Just when it seemed they were again headed for also-ran status, the Rays reeled off their second six-game winning streak of the season. The streak's capper came in a rematch against the Yankees. Starting pitchers Edwin Jackson and Chien-Ming Wang traded punches for seven innings, with the Rays heading to the eighth up 1–0 after a five-hit, no-run performance by Jackson. Dan Wheeler retired the Yankees in order in the eighth, setting up Troy Percival for the ninth-inning save chance. With one out in the ninth, Hideki Matsui took Percival deep, tying the score at 1–1 and sending the game to extra innings.

Most of the player moves the Rays made heading into 2008 worked out well, with a few paying massive, unexpected dividends. The two-year, $8 million deal the Rays gave Percival was the only significant failure, given the gap between performance and pay. For the Yankees or Red Sox, eating an $8 million contract amounts to a rounding error. Percival's pitching failures and injuries would knock him out of the bullpen stopper role before the end of the '08 season. It also served as a useful reminder of one of sabermetrics' better-known truisms: pay for performance, not for the overrated concept of a "proven closer."

J. P. Howell, another quiet but effective Rays pickup by the new regime, faced the minimum six Yankees batters, surrendering one walk before wiping out that base runner on a first-pitch double play by Matsui. The winning hit came from an even stealthier Rays trade pickup, though. The front office had kept tabs on Gabe Gross, a reserve outfielder for the Brewers who would soon be out of a job when Mike Cameron returned from his suspension. With the suspension about to expire, the Rays knew they could grab Gross cheap, since the Brewers would have nowhere left to stash him. On April 22, Tampa Bay dealt minor league pitcher Josh Butler for Gross. The Rays would install him later in the season as the left-handed portion of a right-field platoon, where Gross combined competent offense with an excellent glove. On this day, Gross would replace Eric Hinske in right late in the game, then come up in the eleventh to face Mariano Rivera, the greatest reliever in base-ball history. Gross's solid single to center scored pinch runner Jonny Gomes, giving the Rays a dramatic 2–1 win.

The May 13 victory was one of the Rays' 11 walk-off wins in '08, tied for most in the majors. It also made Tampa Bay a first-place team.

"It's tough to look at a guy after a loss," said Howell, who saw more losing than most MLB players in his first three seasons with the lowly Royals and Devil Rays. "I don't want to say you want to punch the guy, but you kinda do. You get sick of looking at people after a while. Being cool to each other is much easier when you're winning. Once we figured out how to stop losing games in the seventh, eighth, and ninth innings, we knew we could be really good."

The Rays won 9 of their next 15 games, setting up a showdown against the Central-leading White Sox at the Trop. Rays starter James Shields was his usual self in the opener, giving up just one run in six strong innings, with six strikeouts and just one walk allowed.

The problem for Shields was lack of run support. The teams remained tied at 1–1 going into the bottom of the ninth, when Cliff Floyd led off against White Sox reliever Scott Linebrink. Two months into the season, Floyd had cemented his role as a team leader, a smiling presence who, like Maddon, found a way to relate to the club's many young players. Floyd also brought ample experience to one of baseball's youngest rosters. His brush with pennant races dated to 1994, when he was a twenty-one-year-old rookie playing for the Montreal Expos. Like the Rays, the Expos had suffered through years of futility, then built a deep stable of young talent. Floyd just had to hope the Rays' 2008 Cinderella run would have a happier ending for this new band of twenty-somethings than 1994 did for the upstart Expos, when a players' strike ended the season in August—and with it the Expos' best chance at a World Series.

On a 1-1 pitch from Linebrink, Floyd blasted a shot over the wall in right-center to win the game for the Rays. His teammates were so overjoyed by the win, and by Floyd being the man who won it, that their welcoming party at home plate became an emblem of the team's magical season: Aki Iwamura crouched and pointing at home plate; Jonny Gomes clutching his hat with his left hand, looking like he's about to giddily bash Floyd with it; B. J. Upton gleefully leaping above his teammates from the back of the scrum. The image, captured by a *St. Petersburg Times* photographer, would become ubiquitous in the Tampa Bay area, doubling as desktop wallpaper, blown-up posters, even a giant cutout at Tropicana Field.

At 35-22, the Rays were off to their best start in franchise history. But the team's recent hot streak had done little to give it any cushion in the standings—the Rays led the loaded AL East by just a single game as they embarked on a nine-game road trip. That's when it all threatened to come apart.

On their return trip to Fenway Park, the Rays' offense vanished. They scored just six runs in three games against the Red Sox and suffered their second straight sweep in Boston.

This wasn't just any old sweep, though. The history of confrontations between the two teams dated back several years. The fourth pitch Red Sox starter Pedro Martinez threw on August 29, 2000, whacked Devil Rays outfielder Gerald Williams on the left hand. That set off a bench-clearing brawl. All told, the game included eight ejected Tampa Bay players, four hit batters, and two Boston players sent to the hospital. Among the players *not* ejected was Pedro Martinez, who tossed a one-hit shutout and afterward vowed revenge for Williams's charge. Over the years, the bad feelings and the rivalry endured, even as the faces changed and the Red Sox continued to dominate the Rays.

Now, with the Rays playing winning baseball for the first time in franchise history and the two teams battling for first place, tensions ran even higher than usual. There were whispers of bubbling on-field hostilities between players; even Stuart Sternberg privately sneered at Red Sox owner John Henry, the two men having both made their fortunes on Wall Street, only to butt heads in their shared quest to topple the Yankees and establish dominance in the AL East. The Rays had grown frustrated after dropping the first two games of the series, doubly so when Red Sox outfielder Coco Crisp slid hard into Akinori Iwamura as retaliation for a sprained thumb caused by Rays shortstop Jason Bartlett earlier blocking second base with his knee on a Crisp stolen base attempt. The incident prompted Maddon to turn to the Red Sox dugout and yell something to Crisp, then accuse him after the game of trying to hurt Iwamura.

Tempers erupted in the second inning of the series' final game. James Shields hit Crisp on the right hip, prompting him to charge the mound. Both benches emptied, and the fight turned ugly on the ground. The first player into the pile, unsurprisingly, was the team's eccentric enforcer, Gomes. After Dioner Navarro tackled Crisp before he could get to Shields, Gomes pounced on Crisp and landed several punches.

The fighting Rays' reputation grew, but their first-place lead disappeared: the club found itself a game and a half behind Boston after the Red Sox completed the sweep. A split of the next six games against the Rangers and Angels dropped Tampa Bay two games behind the first-place Sox. Never before had any Rays team gone this deep into a season with legitimate playoff aspirations, and players were necessarily approaching each game with more intensity than they'd shown during their all-too-recent losing days. When the Rays' fortunes turned against them after that first burst of success, losing became doubly hard to swallow.

Simmering tempers boiled over again just three days later, on a 94-degree Sunday in Arlington. The Rangers led 1–0 in the bottom of the fourth when Ramon Vazquez singled with one out. That brought up number-nine hitter German Duran. A light-hitting, fringe prospect rookie with just two extra-base hits in the first 26 games of his big league career, Duran didn't seem like much of a threat—until he blasted Matt Garza's 3-2 pitch over the center-field wall, 400-plus feet away.

A big, strong right-hander from California, Garza had long toed the line between spirited competitor and hothead. When the Rays shipped off Delmon Young in the trade that sent back Garza, they were dealing one player with a checkered reputation for another. The Rays soon learned that Garza is nothing more complicated than a perfectionist. From the moment he settles into his clubhouse chair before a start, he's wired as tightly as any pitcher in the game, Tupac Shakur blasting through his earbuds, the rest of the world far away. When he fails, the world knows he cares: even when he's on his game, Garza has a habit of twirling around in a blur after giving up a long fly ball, then cursing himself if the ball clears the fence. When Duran's homer sailed over the center-field wall on this day, Garza came unglued—he stalked around the mound, swore loudly, and had trouble settling down.

This time, Navarro was having none of it. The catcher had watched Garza dominate at times, only to lose his concentration and get knocked around. Garza knew, Navarro knew, everyone knew that the right-hander was too good to be giving up bombs to the likes of German Duran. Navarro walked to the mound, and told Garza to quit complaining and get his head in the game. Talking quickly escalated into yelling, and both players shoved their gloves in each other's face. Pitching coach Jim Hickey separated the two. But at inning's end, the confrontation got worse and the two players went jaw to jaw, spilling into the dugout tunnel before Maddon, Hickey, and others split them up.

"It was a younger brother against older brother fight," said Navarro. "It was in the heat of battle, we were in the pennant race, we were playing well, and Garza, he's a really competitive guy, and I'm a really competitive guy, and I think we just got carried away at the moment."

Maddon rarely berates players, preferring the same positive reinforcement he got from his favorite managers and coaches growing up and his most revered role models as a young minor league manager. When he does get on a player, it is never in public. Still, Maddon didn't admonish Navarro, nor did anyone else on the coaching staff. Instead, Maddon and the coaches brought Garza into the manager's office for a talk. No one was taking sides. But the prevailing message was clear: if Garza could just learn to settle himself, he could become one of the best pitchers in the game.

"With him, you can see it coming, you can see the smoke coming out of his ears," said Hickey. "So we did a lot of behind-the-scenes type of work. Nothing big, just conversations, just saying, 'Listen, next time this happens, this is what you need to do. Let's just be realistic about our expectations, control what we can control.' I love the energy, love the emotion. It's just a waste when it's expended in a negative way, a nonproductive way. We would always say, if we can just take the energy and the emotion and just channel it toward productivity, this guy is gonna be off the charts."

Garza downplayed the incident. "Just heat of passion," he said after the game. "We're both competitors. Whatever happened, we'll just keep it here and we'll fix it. This is a great bunch of guys, and everybody is on each other's side. We can fix it."

Call it a direct result of the confrontation or just a happy coincidence, but Garza's season instantly turned for the better following his showdown with Navarro. Here again, the Rays brain trust wouldn't be able to conclusively quantify the impact of an attitude adjustment. Still, Garza's numbers through that June 8 game and his numbers afterward were markedly different.

	ERA	WALKS PER 9 INNINGS	STRIKEOUTS PER 9 INNINGS	INNINGS/ START
Opening day–June 8	4.38	3.7	5.0	5.6
Rest of the season	3.37	2.5	6.9	6.5

"It was the single biggest improvement in a pitcher out there on the mound, mentally and emotionally, that I have ever seen in that short of a period of time," raved Hickey.

The Rays split the final 6 games of their road trip before heading home for a 9-game home stand and the start of 15 straight games against National League opponents. American League teams have dominated interleague play for years, and Tampa Bay took 12 out of 18 games against NL opponents. The team's interleague success included another showdown against a first-place team from Chicago, in this case the Cubs. The Rays swept the three-game set, with a big assist from the bullpen: Rays relievers allowed just two runs in 11 innings. For Stuart Sternberg and Matt Silverman, the team's attendance was even more encouraging: nearly 98,000 fans swarmed the Trop for the three-game series. The prevalence of Chicago transplants in the region surely helped, but these were still heady numbers for a midweek series, doubly so given the team's long history of attendance woes.

The Rays started July with a seven-game winning streak, including another Tropicana Field sweep of the Red Sox. Tampa Bay's record was a jaw-dropping 55-32 through July 6, when the Rays were up five games in the East. But the team's fortunes would quickly turn for the worse. The Rays lost their last seven games before the All-Star break, dropping back to second place. Their July 10 loss typified the streak. The Indians outscored the Rays 13–2 and out-hit them 15–5 in that game. The Rays' hitters went 0-for-6 with runners in scoring position, while their pitchers ceded four home runs. For a team that trusted the process and didn't overreact to small sample sizes, the streak was frustrating, but not a source of panic. The Rays knew that clutch hitting tends to regulate by season's end, that the line drives they were hitting would eventually fall in, and that other teams' seeing-eye singles would eventually fall into their own gloves. It was only a matter of time before their luck would turn.

In their first game after the break, Jays starter A. J. Burnett shut out Tampa Bay for six innings at the Trop as Toronto claimed a 1–0 lead. After two quick outs, Hinske worked a walk. That brought Ben Zobrist to the plate. Coming up through the minors, Zobrist gained a reputation as a slap hitter with a good batting eye. The most optimistic scenarios had him grabbing a starting middle infielder job for a few years and holding his own. More likely, he'd stick around for a short while as a utility infielder, then fade into baseball oblivion. Such was the probable fate of a baseball player who hit just 23 homers in 1,642 minor league plate appearances.

But Zobrist had begun a transformation in the off-season. This wasn't some suspicious training regimen that turned a 150-pound weakling into Jose Canseco in four winter months. Instead, Zobrist teamed up with Jaime Cevallos, an aspiring hitting instructor. Cevallos recorded footage of Zobrist swinging the bat, broke it down from a variety of angles, then delivered a succinct message: swing harder. For years, coaches and instructors had taught Zobrist that the best way for him to establish a career in the big leagues was to become a spray hitter, slapping singles to all fields. Cevallos wanted Zobrist to change his approach, use more weight transfer, and try to crush the ball. Zobrist still couldn't find his way into the everyday lineup. But he was proving to be a valuable utilityman with serious power.

Still, Zobrist's reputation as a banjo hitter preceded him. Hoping to make quick work of the Rays' number-nine hitter, Burnett's first pitch to Zobrist was a hit-me-if-you-can fastball. Zobrist whacked it deep down the right-field line. Gone. Game-winning, two-run homer. The Rays reclaimed first place with that swing. They wouldn't give up their lead for the rest of the season.

"I didn't have much time to think about it," said Zobrist, referring to both the Rays' Cinderella season and his own breakthrough year, in which he cranked 12 homers in just 198 part-time at-bats, with a .505 slugging percentage. "I just continued to work on my swing and find a way to stay in the big leagues. I think a lot of us younger guys didn't really realize how difficult it was to do what we were doing. It was just *happening*."

The Rays' return to first place did little to put Maddon at ease. The Rays' skipper had become known as a manager who was willing and able to speak frankly with any player who needed to strategize or just vent—that was the influence of his late father, Joe Sr. But Maddon could also grow frustrated when he felt a player wasn't giving his all, and that reaction occasionally led to a heated confrontation or disciplinary action—that side of his personality came from his tough mother, Beanie. As the hot summer wore on, Maddon began to sense complacency among a few players. Few players could push Maddon's buttons more than B. J. Upton.

Many of the reasons Upton drove Maddon crazy were not Upton's fault. Here was the type of tools-oozing player who gave scouts palpitations. Upton had, at various times in his career, shown an ability to hit for power (24 home runs in 2007) and for average (a career-high .300 in 2007 and multiple .300-plus performances in the minor leagues); run (he'd topped 40 stolen bases in three different minor league seasons); field (the Rays, confident in Upton's instincts and speed, played him shallower than any other center fielder); and throw (he'd finish second in MLB with 16 assists in 2008, prompting runners to stop testing his arm the following season). He'd shown himself to be a thoughtful, intelligent player who picked his spots well, at the plate, in the field, and on the base paths—all this before his twenty-fourth birthday.

But Upton had also shown an occasional tendency to lose his focus. On routine grounders and pop-ups, he would, from time to time, jog halfheartedly to first base. This wasn't a terrible offense. Maddon wasn't the type of manager to preach hustle just for show. Players have been jogging to first base for about as long as there's been a first base. Still, when Upton failed to run out a ground ball in an August 5 game against the Indians, Maddon benched his center fielder for the next game. The manager harbored great expectations for his young star and treated him accordingly when his concentration lapsed—the way a teacher might treat a star pupil who tries to coast through an exam. Asked why he'd benched Upton, the manager didn't mince words.

"When it comes down to individual effort, it takes absolutely zero talent, zero, to try hard and play hard every day," Maddon told reporters. "I'm okay with physical mistakes, with mental mistakes, I'm accepting of all that. The part that I'm not accepting of is the part that you can control. And that's your effort. You just can't pick and choose when you put your effort out there. It has to be all the time."

The timing was classic Maddon. The Rays *won* the Upton nonhustle game, their sixth win in seven contests. But the manager had gone against the grain in his handling of the team all season long, offering words of encouragement after losses, then sternly lecturing players for failing to execute after a win. When Upton again failed to run out a ground ball in the sixth inning of an August 15 game against Texas, Maddon again yanked him from the lineup—in a 7–0 win.

While Maddon sought to keep his team's emotions in check, Friedman searched for ways to improve the roster. The Rays' GM had scanned the trade market in search of reinforcements, but ended up not completing any deals before the July 31 nonwaiver deadline. Friedman thought he had a deal for slugging Pirates outfielder Jason Bay. But just a few minutes before the deadline, the rival Red Sox swooped in, pulling off a huge three-way trade that shipped Manny Ramirez out of town and brought in Bay to replace him. (That the deal didn't happen for Tampa Bay would prove to be a blessing: the Rays reportedly would have given up rising young right-hander Jeff Niemann and shortstop prospect Reid Brignac in the trade, two players with the mix of talent and available service time that a low-payroll team like Tampa Bay could ill afford to lose.)

If the Rays were going to upgrade their roster down the stretch, they'd do it with the kinds of moves that had defined the season to date: claims of free talent and reinforcements from the loaded farm system. Like hedge fund managers planning against multiple contingencies, Friedman and his cohorts hoped they'd have an in-house answer for any pennant race challenge.

Still, anyone who says they could have predicted what happened on the ninth of September would be lying.

Back in April, the Rays had claimed a fringe first baseman named Dan Johnson off waivers from Oakland. Johnson had enjoyed a decent 2007 season with the A's before quickly falling out of favor in '08. The Rays didn't have any big plans for him; they were just looking for a little minor league depth. There was a decent chance he might not see a single at-bat for the Rays—until the entire fairy-tale season threatened to unravel.

The Rays dropped six of their first seven games in September, sending shock waves through the clubhouse and roiling giddy fans who'd been bracing for a celebration. The losing streak was especially shocking given the timing: the Rays had closed out August with five straight wins, capped by a three-game sweep of the Orioles that saw Tampa Bay score 34 runs, pack Tropicana Field for the final two games of the series, and stretch their lead in the AL East to five and a half games. But in a span of eight games, the Red Sox sliced that lead to just a half-game. The most heartbreaking loss came in Toronto: on September 7, the Rays trailed the Jays 3–0 for most of the game, dramatically rallied for three runs in the ninth to send the game to extra innings, scored a single run in the 13th to set up a possible win, only to watch Troy Percival serve up a game-winning, walk-off grand slam to veteran catcher Gregg Zaun. It got worse from there as first Toronto, then Boston, shut out the Rays. Tampa Bay was now missing Upton and Longoria, owing to injuries, and heading into the second game of a three-game set at Fenway Park. One more loss and the Rays would relinquish first place in the division. Skeptics started to wonder if the team could even hang on to win the wild card.

Battered and bruised, the Rays called up Johnson to start September 9 against the Sox. Even Mother Nature seemed to conspire against Tampa Bay, though. Trying to fly from Scranton, Pennsylvania—where his Durham Bulls were playing in the International League championship series—Johnson watched as stormy weather grounded nearly every plane scheduled to leave the airport. Granted some free time during the delay, Johnson bought shoes at the airport, since he'd packed just a couple of T-shirts for Durham's short trip. He finally boarded an afternoon flight due to arrive in Boston at 4:30, only to have it get in around 6:30, just thirty minutes before game time. From Logan Airport, Johnson negotiated his way to Fenway, arriving in the locker room just before the game's opening pitch.

The Rays clung to a 3–2 lead until the bottom of the eighth. After setting down the first two Red Sox hitters, Wheeler walked

Kevin Youkilis. One walk wouldn't convince Maddon to pull Wheeler from the game. The Rays had already used Balfour, and no other right-hander could approach Wheeler's strong track record against righty hitters. He was staying in the game to face Jason Bay. On the third pitch of the at-bat, Bay launched the ball high and deep over the Green Monster for a two-run homer—4–3 Red Sox. With one swing of the bat, the Rays had gone from being on the verge of opening up a one-and-a-half-game lead on Boston to giving up first place for the first time since before the All-Star break. Bad teams aren't used to heartbreakers; their hearts are usually broken slowly and steadily over the course of the season, until avoiding 100 losses becomes the only reasonable goal. As Bay's homer sailed into the night, Wheeler and his teammates experienced the kind of pain that few of them had known in their major league careers.

The Rays had one more chance. By season's end, Tampa Bay would rack up 45 come-from-behind wins, third-most in the majors. The odds seemed long this time, though. Trotting in from the bullpen was Red Sox closer Jonathan Papelbon, so unhittable that Boston fans were already comparing him to Yankees legend Mariano Rivera. Papelbon was also the only player in baseball who required two different songs to mark his appearance: "Wild Thing," the 1965 classic by the Troggs that was also the anthem for Charlie Sheen's Rick Vaughn character in the movie *Major League*, and "I'm Shipping Up to Boston," a 2005 anthem by Celtic punk band the Dropkick Murphys. If you were an opponent and had to sit through 39,928 Bostonians singing "Sweet Caroline" miserably off-key in the eighth inning, followed by Papelbon's two-song coronation in the ninth, that usually meant two things: (1) you were going to lose the game; (2) you would concoct ways to burn down Fenway Park and get away with it.

Leading off the ninth for the Rays was the one player who seemed least likely to do anything against Papelbon: the all-day-traveling, late-arriving, ice-cold nobody, Dan Johnson. On the plus side, Johnson had been a star at Triple A Durham, hitting a robust

.307/.424/.556 with 25 homers in just 394 at-bats. Still, Johnson's harrowing travel itinerary didn't seem to bode well for a pressure-packed matchup against one of the best closers in baseball. His passive approach seemed to confirm it. Through the first five pitches of the at-bat, Johnson never once took the bat off his shoulder.

In retrospect, this was precisely the point. The Rays liked Johnson largely for his batting eye—a trademark of Oakland's early *Moneyball* teams, as well as every successful Yankees club since their 1990s dynasty and every successful Red Sox squad since Boston started its own run in 2003. Johnson needed a few looks at Papelbon's offerings before he could pick a pitch he liked. The hope was for that pitch to come on what was now a 3-2 count. Papelbon threw a fastball. Johnson connected. High, deep, and gone, into the stands behind the bullpens in right-center field. Tie ball game.

Every team talks about the virtues of depth. But as Johnson jubilantly rounded the bases and a stunned Fenway crowd looked on, it became clear that the Rays weren't just any team. The Rays would go on to win that night against the Red Sox, then surge to an AL East title. They carried those winning ways into the playoffs, knocking off the White Sox in the League Division Series, then taking out the Red Sox in the League Championship Series. Well before their historic pennant run, they'd done more due diligence than any other Rays team had. They scoured every organization looking for relievers to layer on top of relievers, knowing you could never have enough choices in the bullpen—insurance policies they were happy to have when Percival didn't pan out. They agonized over utilitymen, choreographed minor leaguers' paths to the big leagues, checked and double-checked every contingency they could possibly imagine.

The Rays had even picked up a discarded left-handed hitter to stash in the minor leagues for five months, a journeyman with just enough pop in his bat to give him a fighting chance, in the unlikely event he'd ever make it to the plate in a big spot during the 2008 season. In 100 more tries against Papelbon in that spot, Johnson might never hit another home run—a testament to the good fortune that helped the Rays during their unlikely run from worst to first. The late, great baseball architect Branch Rickey had a ready-made response whenever someone noted the way his teams always seemed to catch a break. Luck, he said, is the residue of design. Or in the Rays' case: trust the process.

CHAPTER 10 MYSTERY MEN

We have to find [the next big thing]. And if we do, I promise you we're not going to talk about it.
—ANDREW FRIEDMAN

Two days before the start of the 2008 World Series, a curious email arrived in Josh Kalk's in-box. The sender was James Click, manager of baseball research and development for the Tampa Bay Rays. Kalk had read Click's writing for analysis site *Baseball Prospectus* years earlier, but the two men had never met. Why, he wondered, was Click emailing him now, two days before the Rays would play in their first World Series in franchise history?

"What can you tell me about Moyer's release point?" Click wanted to know. "It looks like his curve is being released from a higher spot than his fastball."

That Click wanted more information on Phillies starting pitcher Jamie Moyer was no surprise, given that the Rays were about to face the veteran lefty on baseball's biggest stage. What was surprising was that Click would seek outside counsel to build a scouting report. The Rays employed the usual cadre of advance scouts, who'd seen Moyer pitch and could relay vital information on his arsenal of soft tosses. They also held a dizzying array of statistics on their upcoming opponent, courtesy of the proprietary database Click had built and now managed. That database contained reams of information on thousands of players at the professional and amateur levels and was unmatched by all but a few other major league clubs. If any team was going to be well prepared, it was the Rays.

A telltale marker of any successful company, though, is recognizing its own weaknesses and seeking to resolve them. For the Rays, one chink in their armor was PITCHf/x analysis. Developed by Sportvision, a company founded by former News Corporation and Fox Sports executives, PITCHf/x debuted in 2006 as a system that pegs the location and velocity of a pitched baseball, as well as arm angle and pitch type. Though a few baseball analysts had dabbled in PITCHf/x–based analysis, Click knew that no one could do it better than Kalk. A physicist and math professor at remote Bluefield State College in West Virginia, Kalk quickly gained a reputation as someone who truly understood how PITCHf/x works and how to leverage it for real-life situations through his personal blog posts and work for *The Hardball Times*. If Jamie Moyer was tipping his pitches, even in the most subtle way, Kalk would be able to spot it.

He told Click that his hunch was correct, that Moyer's release point on his curveball was indeed slightly higher than the spot from which he delivered his fastball—but not enough for hitters to notice. That was the entire extent of the conversation. Armed with their usual scouting information, as well as Kalk's analysis, the Rays faced Moyer and the Phillies in Game 3 of the World Series . . . and didn't do a heck of a lot against the forty-four-year-old warhorse, scoring just one run through six innings before touching Moyer for two more in the seventh. The Phillies went on to win the World Series in five games. Kalk wasn't paid a cent for his feedback, nor did he know if he'd ever hear back from the Rays. But a few months later, again out of nowhere, another email arrived from Click. "Can you come down next week for an interview?"

Kalk had seen this play before. He'd interviewed with both the Cleveland Indians and St. Louis Cardinals in 2008, and been approached by a Chicago Cubs scout in early 2009. Kalk had ample experience in academia, but none in dealing with interest from professional baseball teams. It showed. "When I showed up to the Cleveland interview, I was wearing a full suit, tie, everything—it seemed like the safe thing to do. [Indians baseball operations director] Mike Chernoff shows up in a T-shirt and jeans. I was totally out of place." He was also charmingly naive about protecting his ideas, handing over seminal analyses to the Indians and Cubs. "Every little bit of information I had I gave to them, because *obviously* they were going to hire me."

He would try to be shrewder this time. After battling to get someone to cover his Wednesday class, he flew down to the Rays' spring training site in Port Charlotte and met with Click. After a few minutes, Kalk realized that the Rays had trained their eye on him for a while. A PITCHf/x expert could help them spot early signs of ineffectiveness, fatigue, or even possibly injury in a pitcher. Kalk next met with Andrew Friedman. Money was discussed. Would Kalk work for the Rays if they matched his professor's salary? He would. Five days later, on his birthday, Kalk got the official offer. He quickly accepted. Given how common Tommy John surgeries and rotator cuff tears remain in baseball, and how much money teams lavish on pitchers, Kalk's ability to break down the intricacies of a pitcher's delivery stood to save the Rays millions of dollars—maybe even tens of millions. All for the price of a Bluefield State professor.

Kalk didn't much care that his new bosses had just pulled off one of their most impressive feats of arbitrage. He'd landed his dream job in a major league front office. An unassuming guy from Sheboygan, Wisconsin, he wasn't one to gloat. But telling the baseball world he was on the inside would still be a lot of fun. The Rays were having none of it. Tell no one, they told the new guy. Send a cryptic good-bye to the blogosphere if you want. That's it. Not only was Kalk barred from revealing the identity of his new employer, but the Rays took the added step of leaving his name off their front-office directory. Tasked with the weighty responsibilities of improving the health and performance of the pitching staff and the pitch recognition skills of Rays hitters, Kalk was The Man Who Wasn't There.

"When they hired me, they wanted to portray a neutral image to other teams that they weren't studying this area hard or that area hard." He was learning just how zealous the Rays were about safeguarding their intellectual property, so much so that "they may have someone like me studying just fielding, and I wouldn't be aware of it."

That the Rays wanted Kalk's work—and even his identity—kept a secret was no surprise, given the background of Stuart Sternberg. The Rays' owner learned the importance of secrecy while working his way up to partner at specialist firm Spear, Leeds & Kellogg, then had those values reinforced while at Goldman Sachs. On Wall Street, Sternberg discovered, letting even the most innocuous details slip out risked compromising a company's competitive edge or scuttling a big deal. Let success speak for itself, and keep others guessing how you did it.

When Sternberg bought the team and put his friends Matt Silverman and Andrew Friedman in charge, the trio sought to carry on that tradition. Problem was, they quickly discovered, baseball is very different, in some ways at least, from Wall Street. The first obstacle to secrecy was the media. Investment banks similarly have to learn to keep the financial media at bay—but not for the better part of each day from February through October and through the off-season, the way baseball writers have to be handled. Baseball is also easier for outsiders to quantify: an astute baseball analyst can deduce if, say, a team is loading up on strong defensive players, then write an article or blog post describing the team's efforts to win that way. Not so for big banks, where a lack of transparency contributed to the collapse of the U.S. housing market and a nasty recession, with only a few voices in the wilderness spotting the signs of danger before it was too late.

The bigger roadblock to protecting intellectual capital in baseball comes from other teams. In dealing with other firms in his old job, Sternberg could feel secure in knowing that other parties had as much incentive to be discreet as he did. In baseball, he found, that wasn't the case. Government officials could run to the media after even the most preliminary of stadium discussions. In trade negotiations, other teams could leak information, whether to curry favor with go-to reporters, tilt a future deal in their favor, or just crow about an exciting potential deal.

Sternberg, Silverman, and Friedman set to work protecting their secrets. The first step was easy. Key personnel were told in no uncertain terms to keep their mouths shut. Once everyone else in the organization toed the line, the Wall Street trio devised their own media plan. They would be friendly and accommodating, but in a precise manner. No sharing of secret sauce on any key projects, whether on the baseball side or the business side. No on-the-record, impolitic words for anyone in the game. And certainly no sidling up to even the most venerable of reporters; no supposed inside information would be worth ruining their own deals. The approach was born primarily out of pragmatism. Rarely would details of a Rays trade be leaked before the deal actually went down, thus preventing last-minute bidding wars. But there was an additional incentive. The publication of *Moneyball* had triggered a wave of both reverence and disdain for Billy Beane: boardrooms and aspiring baseball execs lauded the A's GM, while Joe Morgan and his ilk ripped him for . . . something or other. The Rays honchos simply wanted to do their job in peace, while maintaining that coveted 2% edge.

"They're guarded with the proprietary way they do business," said *St. Petersburg Times* columnist Marc Topkin. "[Fellow *Times* columnist] John Romano tried to do an [investigative] piece. And I know, just anecdotally, how hard it was for him to get Andrew to the table. They literally had a lunch, and if you read that column, there's like two little tiny quotes in it."

Few resources prompt Rays management into secrecy more than the team's number crunchers. The advent of the *Moneyball* era accelerated a trend already under way in baseball: the seduction of overqualified young men into entry-level positions in front offices (they're almost never women). Most major league teams now employ at least some kind of full-time statistician as a counterweight to traditional scouting and player evaluation personnel. Many of those aspiring Billy Beanes, Theo Epsteins, and Andrew Friedmans carry impressive credentials: advanced degrees in mathematics or statistics, law degrees, or, in Kalk's case, a background in physics. They'd probably make a lot more money, advance further with their careers, effect more real-life change, or all of the above, elsewhere. But they chose baseball instead, many of them hoping to defy astronomical odds and claim one of the thirty MLB general manager positions on the planet. For all the sacrifices these gunners were willing to make, the Rays knew that such talent represents a huge bargain given the work they do. Moreover, Tampa Bay's brain trust knew that other teams with more resources could easily woo their star analysts away with a few more bucks or the promise of promotion. That's why they went to KGB-esque lengths to hide the identity and responsibilities of people like Josh Kalk.

The Rays were slightly less paranoid about James Click, though they still didn't shout his name from the rooftops. After graduating from Yale in 2000 with a degree in history, Click sought a career in a major league front office. His job search eventually took him to *Baseball Prospectus,* a place he felt could serve as a stepping-stone to the big leagues. There, Click absorbed the work of Keith Woolner, a skilled analyst noted for a number of key studies, including his ability to peg replacement-level talent in baseball; Clay Davenport, a meteorologist by day who'd developed new metrics for batting, defense, and other skills; Michael Wolverton, whose work with pitching gave baseball some of its first support- and luck-neutral stats that helped debunk the game's reliance on won-lost records; and Nate Silver, the inventor of the PECOTA projection system who went on to become a noted political writer and analyst. To keep pace with these and other leading lights at *BP,* Click knew he'd need to make significant contributions of his own to the world of sabermetrics.

One of his most notable efforts was park-adjusted defensive efficiency (PADE). Years earlier, Bill James had devised a simple but useful stat that tracked the frequency with which fielders caught balls hit into play that didn't go for home runs. Click realized that tracking down fly balls at Fenway Park was very different from patrolling the vast expanse of Coors Field's outfield, and that adjusting for those differences would help better evaluate fielders' ability.

In the book *Baseball Between the Numbers: Why Everything You Know About the Game Is Wrong* (a book I edited and co-authored), Click contributed several studies, asking offbeat questions such as "What if Pete Incaviglia had Rickey Henderson's legs?" It was a creative way to learn more about the value of base running and base stealing, subjects that many crusty old baseball men didn't fully understand properly and few analysts had studied with much depth. The chapter showed that even a base stealer as prolific as Henderson was scarcely more valuable on the base paths than a plodder like Incaviglia if he kept getting thrown out trying to steal or take an extra base. Dan Fox, another *Baseball Prospectus* author who went on to an MLB front-office job (with the Pirates), would later invent a stat called equivalent base-running runs, which quantifies exactly how many runs a player is adding or subtracting from a team's ledger based on his performance on the base paths.

The sabermetric community knew Click's work, and his name, very well. But many major league front offices did not. When Tampa Bay hired Click full-time in February 2006 (he'd consulted the year before), management tasked him with building a database that could track all major league and minor league players, blending scouting reports, statistical analyses, injury information, and multiple other components. If successful, the project could be used in any number of ways, whether to unearth hidden free-agent gems, make quick, but still informed decisions in the heat of trade talks, or help Joe Maddon and his coaching staff make informed on-field decisions based on tangible information rather than blind guesses. Working alongside Erik Neander, an intern who would later become the Rays' co-manager of baseball R&D, Click built a database that rivaled the Indians' oft-praised DiamondVision, as well as similar databases constructed by the Red Sox, Mariners, and other clubs.

"We want to take as many steps out of the decision-making chain as possible, minimize phone calls and mouse clicks," said Tony Blengino, special assistant to Mariners GM Jack Zduriencik. "When scouts are informed of stats, and vice versa, it makes the whole process go much more smoothly." Having a robust database, he said, "is huge." How huge? Blengino pegs the value of a robust, central database in the millions. But one MLB executive estimates the total cost of setting one up, between the human capital and technology, at just $500,000. Demand has grown so rapidly for all-in-one data depositories that financial giant Bloomberg entered the market with its own product in 2010, offering its Bloomberg Sports Pro tool to major league clubs that would prefer to buy rather than build. (Last note of this kind, promise: I write, edit, and consult for Bloomberg Sports.)

Click belongs to a cadre of Rays baseball personnel that's much smaller than the group that works for the Yankees or many other clubs. Depending on the time of year, Click can be found helping with draft preparation, Neander gathering information for a (rare) arbitration case, Kalk compiling pitching data for an upcoming series, baseball operations director Dan Feinstein researching minor league free agents, and Friedman negotiating a trade—with many of those roles liable to switch. It's a close-knit group that also often includes assistant director of minor league operations Chaim Bloom, another bright young mind and Yale graduate who cut his teeth at *Baseball Prospectus*. On any given night (except Friday), you might find Friedman, Feinstein, Bloom, Silverman, and Click holding spirited conversations at the Trop or over beers. The running joke is that peer pressure will eventually force Click to change his name to Clickstein.

What makes the combination work—aside from Manischewitz Night at local watering holes—is the buy-in throughout the organization. *Moneyball* chronicles how everyone from manager Art Howe to Feinstein, then the A's video coordinator, adopted the principles espoused by Billy Beane. With the Rays, Feinstein presides over a similar culture, only from a higher position (in essence, assistant GM). On any given night, especially late in a game, Joe Maddon will pull out his trusty three-ring binder. Inside, he can scan the usual scouting reports—as well as pitcher release point tips from Kalk, defensive tendencies from Click, and tidbits from Feinstein, the man who, A's assistant GM David Forst said, "has probably watched more video in the last fifteen years than anyone in baseball."

Like the rest of "the Mystery Men," Feinstein's contributions often go unnoticed by the masses. He excells in subtle areas such as arbitration. When the Rays defeated B. J. Upton in his 2010 arbitration case, that brought Tampa Bay's record to 4-0 in arb cases under the new regime. They have a rigid negotiation policy in place: as soon as both sides give their offers to the arbitrator, the Rays cut off communication on that case. Kendall Almerico, the agent for Rays catcher Dioner Navarro's 2009 case, said he's rarely heard of a team that refuses to talk once figures have been submitted. He's also rarely seen cases where a player and team go to arbitration over such a small gap. The Rays offered $2.1 million after Navarro's breakout 2008 season. Almerico countered with $2.5 million. Most teams would split the difference in a case like that; $200,000 is a rounding error for the Yankees or Red Sox. But the Rays work for every dollar. And they are supremely confident they will win.

Navarro was coming off a season in which he hit .295, threw out 36% of base-stealing attempts, and made the All-Star Game. By contrast, Royals catcher John Buck settled at $2.2 million the year before, despite owning a batting average 73 points lower. Through data compiled by Feinstein, Click, and others and an argument style that is both brutally effective and, as Almerico said, "handled with class," the Rays won their case anyway. Put an extra $200,000 in the bank.

For his part, Kalk's addition has enabled the front office's analytical power to better assist other parts of the team, namely the pitching coach and trainers. One month before the Rays snapped him up, Kalk published a *Hardball Times* article entitled "The Injury Zone." In it, he pushed Pitch f/x analysis to the next level, wielding it as a tool to try to predict a pitching injury several pitches before it happens. It wasn't hard for the Rays to see the implications of this study: by combining Pitch f/x input with an artificial neural network algorithm (a system that looks at everything from a lower arm slot to velocity changes and movement on a pitch), Kalk could spot early warning signs, call the Rays' decision-makers from anywhere, and warn of a potential injury risk for, say, David Price. Joe Maddon and Jim Hickey could then act on that information and save their star pitcher from harm, just in the nick of time. Conversely, Kalk's research could also reassure Maddon and Hickey if they wanted to push one of their young starters for an extra inning. Amid a growing trend of overcautiousness that has prompted the Yankees to institute the convoluted "Joba Rules" for right-hander Joba Chamberlain, and other teams to get less out of their young arms, early-career pitchers like Price, Matt Garza, Jeff Niemann, and Wade Davis can go deeper into games when the situation calls for it.

Other innovative on-field tactics have also gained traction, thanks to the influence of the Rays' Mystery Men. One of the most reliable ingredients in a typical lineup is a prevalence of opposite-handed hitters facing that day's pitcher—stack the order with lefties when a righty takes the hill, do the opposite when a lefty toes the rubber. It's such an ingrained, almost immutable baseball concept that *The Simpsons* once lampooned it. With the bases loaded in the bottom of the ninth, the Springfield Nuclear Plant team has lefty-swinging Darryl Strawberry due up to bat against a left-handed pitcher. Strawberry is the lone ringer left on a team full of regular Joes, one of the best baseball players on the planet dominating vastly inferior competition. Yet the manager, Mr. Burns, pulls Strawberry for a pinch hitter anyway, sending in the hapless (but right-handed!) Homer Simpson in his stead. When Strawberry protests—"But, Skip, I've hit nine home runs today!"—Burns pulls out the hammer: "It's called playing the percentages. It's what smart managers do to win ball games."

One of Neander's most visible contributions has aimed to turn that bit of orthodoxy on its head—and he's had Maddon's full cooperation. For the better part of two decades, Yankees right-hander Mike Mussina fared considerably better against left-handed hitters than he had versus righties. He showcased that ability again on April 7, 2008, yielding just one run on two hits against a Rays lineup that featured five lefty bats (including switch-hitters batting from the left side) in a 6–1 Yankees win. On May 14 of that year, Mussina whitewashed a Rays lineup that featured six lefties, giving up just a single run in six and a third innings en route to a 2–1 New York victory. On September 2, same story: lineup packed with lefties, six innings, two runs, eight strikeouts, Yankees win. Finally, in the Rays' fourth start of the season against Mussina, the Rays set Neander's plan into action. On September 13, the Rays stacked the lineup with six right-handed batters, including light-hitting catcher Michel Hernandez and seldom-used outfielder Justin Ruggiano; Rocco Baldelli, owner of an ugly on-base percentage below .300 against righties, batted *cleanup*. The Rays shelled Mussina, piling up eight hits and two walks and counting five runs in five innings, on their way to a 7–1 blowout win.

It was only one game, and the Rays knew not to put too much stock in small sample sizes—a terrible mistake in baseball, and in life. Still, they were intrigued. The next season, on the rare occasions when they would face a starting pitcher with large, backward splits, Tampa Bay started deploying same-handed lineups. But the Rays possessed tools that also went well beyond simple lefty-righty splits. Their data sets showed each batter's bat speed, swing plane, and the direction of all of his hits. Using that information, Neander could then dig deeper, looking for pitchers with particular pitch types and usage patterns who could be vulnerable to a lineup full of same-handed hitters. An obvious choice was Boston's Tim Wakefield, who had shown a career-long tendency to fare better against lefty hitters and had a go-to pitch, the knuckleball, that old-school and new-school baseball types alike claimed could be better hit by same-handed hitters. But the Rays weren't quite ready to take the theory beyond Mussina and an extreme knuckleball pitcher. At least not until they faced a heretofore anonymous young lefty named Dallas Braden.

On May 9, 2010, Braden, an A's soft-tosser who relied on command and a deceptive changeup, took the bump against the Rays. Less than a year earlier, White Sox veteran Mark Buehrle, another lefty who leaned heavily on his changeup, had thrown a perfect game against a Rays offense that ranked among the best in baseball. To the Rays' shock and chagrin, Braden matched Buehrle's feat, tossing just the 19th perfecto in major league history. If one time was a possible fluke, two times equaled a disturbing potential trend, and Neander wanted no part of it. A few weeks later, the Rays entered a stretch where they would face Shaun Marcum, a Blue Jays right-hander who threw his changeup more than almost any other starter in the game, twice in a span of seven days. The Rays loaded their lineup so heavily with righty batters that even the team's switch-hitters batted right-handed against Marcum, leaving just five lefty starters combined in those two Marcum starts. The Rays crushed Toronto each time, winning by a combined score of 17–4. Four days before the first of the two Marcum starts, the Rays faced White Sox lefty John Danks, another pitcher who relied on his changeup. Armed with every left-handed bat they could find on the active roster, the Rays battered Danks for eight runs and eight hits in four innings, cruising to an 8–5 win. The Rays blog DRaysBay called it "the Danks Theory," though given the idea's creator, it could have been dubbed "Neander's Notion."

The ideas generated by Click and Neander, combined with Maddon's open mind, have hatched other offbeat, in-game strategies. One such tactic is the Rays' approach to defensive shifts. Historically, teams shift their shortstop to the right side of second base against big, plodding, left-handed power hitters, leaving the third baseman to guard the entire left side of the infield. That tack goes back decades, at least as far as Ted Williams's heyday. It also misses the point. If "the Splendid Splinter" or David "Big Papi" Ortiz launches a ball into the upper deck in right field, only Superman would be able to track the ball down. But Maddon, Click, and company understand that the relevant stat in considering the utility of shifts is the frequency with which a batter hits ground balls to a certain side of the infield. The Rays thus have shifted frequently against a different Red Sox batter, J. D. Drew, a decent, left-handed power hitter who drives a high percentage of balls in the air to center and the opposite field—but hits an aberrantly high percentage of his grounders to the right side. Tampa Bay is credited with being the first team to regularly shift against Drew. The Rays have also been the first team to shift against Chase Utley, noted John Dewan, author of *The Fielding Bible* and an expert on defensive analysis. When the Rays repeatedly shifted against the Phillies' second baseman during the 2008 World Series, commentators wondered why they would do so against a relatively fast runner. What they should have noted was that Utley had hit 72% of his ground balls to the right side that year, making him a good candidate for a shift—even if he lagged slightly behind the extreme 80% hitters Dewan says make for ideal shifts.

The Rays' approach has taken the concept of defensive realignments well beyond the usual shift protocols. They once used four outfielders in a shift against Cleveland's Travis Hafner, a classic slow-footed, fly-ball-hitting bopper. They often shunt center fielder B. J. Upton way over to right-center against Derek Jeter, knowing that the Yankees' captain has built an entire Hall of Fame–caliber career around an inside-out swing that sends balls the other way. At the end of games, the Rays occasionally raise the ante. Instead of the usual outfield-in setup used by other teams, Maddon once brought Upton in to stand at second base and serve as a fifth infielder when any decently placed ground ball could have won the game. The Rays have answers ready if you try to shift against them too. Through the 2010 All-Star break, Carlos Peña, the most-shifted-against player on the team dating back several years, was

14-for-24 lifetime when laying down bunts—many of them shift-beaters.

Some concepts have taken time to refine before the Rays could make them work. For all the success enjoyed by the pennant-winning team of 2008, they weren't very good at base running. According to Baseball-Reference, the Rays took an extra base (for example, going from first to third on a single) 40% of the time, tied for eleventh in the majors. But they also made 68 outs on the base paths, the second-highest mark in baseball and a sign that they were being far too aggressive. Like Click's tale of Rickey Henderson versus Pete Incaviglia, the net result illustrated how harmful giving away outs can be: the Rays ranked just twenty-fifth in MLB in *Baseball Prospectus*'s catchall base-running stat, equivalent base-running runs. This was a puzzling outcome. The Rays employed several fast runners, including Carl Crawford, B. J. Upton, and Jason Bartlett. Click and others in the front office were acutely aware of the value of successful base running. And Maddon, Mike Scioscia's former bench coach with the Angels, had seen his former team complete one of the ten most successful seasons of team base running in documented history.

Addressing the club in spring training of 2009, Maddon told his players to remain aggressive in trying for that extra base, but also to be better aware of game situations. The players and coaches carried out that philosophy to some extent; no third-base coach in the game sent runners more frequently from third base on sacrifice flies than the Rays' Tom Foley. But overall, the Rays took the extra base just 38% of the time in 2009, a mark slightly lower than the team's '08 result and also below league average. The good news was that they also made 10 fewer outs on the bases, improving to league average in that category. Many of the Rays' best subtle advantages result from old-fashioned player development and instruction more than data crunching; their approach to base running fits that mold. In 2009, Maddon and the Rays' coaches implemented drills brought over from the Angels to help the team improve. The approach taken was both simple and unusual, said Morgan Ensberg, a former major league infielder who was in camp with the Rays that year.

"We had these drills on getting from first to third based on where the outfielders were," said Ensberg. "It wasn't as much about how you round[ed] the bag as much as where the ball was in the outfield and where the fielder was. They put three coaches out in center field and dropped balls in front of each of them, one runner at a time. If the coach got to the ball quickly, you shut it down. If he hadn't gotten to the ball, go to third. The emphasis and explanation were very clear and very good, and these were easy lessons to learn and use later. Most drills are stupid. It's so rare to have a good drill in professional sports, since people don't know how to teach the game. This was brilliant stuff. Just, 'We have speed? Let's go!' Even guys who don't—let's go!"

The full effect of the new base-running approach didn't kick in until 2010. According to Bill James's website, the Rays took 196 more bases than the average team, the best result by any club in the nine years the stat has been tracked.

Underpinning all the physical improvements the Rays made from the time Sternberg took over has been a new emphasis on the mental side of the game. The first season under the new guard ended with the Rays losing 101 games, their worst result in four years. Afterward, senior vice president of baseball operations and former Astros GM Gerry Hunsicker reached out to an old friend in Houston. Dr. John Eliot had worked as a performance psychologist with perennial baseball powerhouse Rice University, while also serving on the school's faculty. Would Eliot come work for the Rays and help the team improve its own mental approach, Hunsicker asked. Eliot jumped at the chance.

Major League Baseball requires all teams to have an Employee Assistance Program (EAP). That program gives each team access to a clinical psychologist, ready to treat anyone from players to the grounds crew. The MLB mandate was meant to deal primarily with, Eliot explained, "abnormalities." If a player has problems with depression, substance abuse, or spousal abuse, the EAP representative is there to help. The rep can also deal with specific kinds of on-field problems: if a pitcher comes down with Steve Blass Disease (can't find the plate, often throwing wildly to the backstop) or a catcher contracts Mackey Sasser Syndrome (can't throw the ball back to the pitcher), he can get immediate assistance.

The Rays' strategy—*again*—has been vastly different from the approach taken by most others. Maddon had worked with Ken Ravizza, an applied sport psychology professor at Cal State Fullerton, for several years. The focus of Ravizza's sessions with Maddon, and also with Matt Garza, was to get the most out of each man's abilities. For Maddon, that meant improving his ability to connect with players and set reachable goals for both himself and the team. Meanwhile, Garza was a supremely talented but highly emotional pitcher who would learn to rein in his frustrations through methods as simple as reading calming messages on the bill of his cap after a bad outcome. In both cases, it wasn't about treating abnormalities. Ravizza, like Eliot after him, worked to maximize his clients' potential by emphasizing focus, concentration, and visualization.

Eliot's focus was on getting the most out of the Rays' young talent. The Rays had invested tens of millions of dollars, thousands of man-hours, and many high draft picks to build a farm system they hoped would give them an edge over their rivals and enable them to catch up to much richer teams like the Yankees and Red Sox. But those prospects, Hunsicker, Maddon, farm director Mitch Lukevics, and others felt, would need the equivalent of finishing school to thrive in the big leagues. "Everybody talks about five-tool players," Eliot said. "The guys that are the best are six-tool players—guys with five tools, but also the mental game."

Eliot interacted with dozens of players at different levels. His favorite pupil, though, was Carlos Peña. A former top prospect, Peña had bounced around with several teams and was fighting for a job in spring training of 2007 when he met Eliot. "Doc, I want your help, teach me everything you know," he implored. For the first two weeks, Eliot and Peña would hang over the dugout railing, talking first about sports psychology, then about success in general and how to achieve it. Even with his uncertain status with the club, Peña made an impact on his teammates. Eliot saw what others saw—a relentlessly happy guy with an infectious smile—but also someone stressing over his future in the game. "I kept asking him, 'Why do you play?'" Eliot recalled. "It was to have fun. He needed to start playing the game like he was in Little League, to allow himself to love what he was doing. To stop being so stats-driven and mechanics-driven." Peña made the team that spring. Then he pummeled the rest of the league, bashing a career-high 46 homers. For the next three seasons, whenever the team would gather for a players-only meeting—to halt a losing streak or just make sure everyone was content and pulling their weight—it was Peña who would lead the way.

For the Rays, employing Eliot and other Mystery Men has been about getting a strong return on their investment. For a fraction of the cost of a major league minimum salary, the team can benefit from cutting-edge statistical analysis, a physicist's view of the game, or innovative psychological techniques. Richer rivals can build palatial stadiums, pay nine figures for Alex Rodriguez, or draw on the fandom of an entire region. Upgrading a terrible defense, addressing bad base running, providing counsel for talented, young players—all of these steps have been pointed toward a more modest, but equally important and beneficial goal: wiping out weaknesses.

"If you have a team that's at least average at everything," said the Mariners' Blengino, "you're going to be a pretty good club."

CHAPTER 11 DAVID VERSUS GOLIATHS

Everybody knows they're not going away.
—Theo Epstein

Matt Silverman sat on a stage with four of the brightest minds in sports management at the 2010 MIT-Sloan Sports Analytics Conference. The "Next-Generation Sports Management and Ownership" panel was just getting started, and a large crowd was eager to hear what the Rays' young team president and his dais mates would say. But Silverman kept shifting in his seat, looking uncomfortable. Suddenly, he stood up, grabbed a Red Sox jersey hanging right behind him, and set it on the ground.

"They're always looming," he quipped, bringing the house down.

Silverman had good reason to feel like the Red Sox and the Yankees were always looking over his shoulder. In 2008, the Red Sox played with a budget three times bigger than Tampa Bay's; the Yankees' payroll was nearly five times larger. The revenue streams in Boston and New York demolished anything the Rays could ever hope to achieve, even if Tampa Bay were to build five new stadiums and thousand-dollar bills rained daily from the Florida sky. The Rays don't hold any exclusive rights on brains either; the Red Sox and Yankees are stocked with savvy baseball people at all levels of their organizations.

"When Theo Epstein took over in Boston, he changed the industry," said Indians president and former GM Mark Shapiro. "Now we see the Red Sox and Yankees operating as if they're creative mid- to small-market teams, and it's widened the gap."

Pitted against two teams with realistic championship aspirations every year, the Rays, Blue Jays, and Orioles face a bigger challenge than any other clubs in major North American team sports. Sky Andrecheck, a writer for the sabermetric site Baseball Analysts as well as for SI.com, broke down all thirty teams based on a combination of factors, including market size and owners' willingness to spend. In his exercise, he had all thirty teams start from scratch with none of their current players on the roster, while also stripping out the quality of existing front offices and other related factors. With their massive resources and a Steinbrenner family that's readily opened its wallet for four decades, the start-from-scratch Yankees made the playoffs nearly six times out of ten in Andrecheck's simulation. The Rays, playing against the two behemoths in New York and Boston, with a much smaller home market than Toronto and weaker revenue streams and a thriftier owner than those found in Baltimore, were the least likely team to make the playoffs. According to Andrecheck's model, in any given year the theoretical Rays owned just a 7% chance of cracking the postseason.

The massive competitive advantages that the Yankees possess are exactly what makes it so tough for the Rays to compete and win. Running up a payroll that's multiple times bigger than Tampa Bay's is merely a symptom of the chasm between the Yankees and everyone else. *Forbes's* annual report "The Business of Baseball" looks at the franchise value, revenue, and operating income of every MLB team. Its 2010 report (encompassing the 2009 season) showed the Bombers pulling in $441 million in revenue; the Mets were number two at $268 million, and the Rays ranked twenty-sixth at $156 million. The Yankees also topped the list for franchise value at $1.6 *bil-*

lion; the Red Sox were second at $870 million, the Rays twenty-eighth at $316 million. Two teams, same division, one team banks nearly three times the revenue, with a business that's worth five times as much as the other.

Before anyone plays a single game, the Yankees already own a gigantic advantage over everyone else, playing in the biggest market, with the brightest brand name. With more than 19 million people living in the metro area, their customer base is much larger, making it easier to pack the stadium. Greater demand means higher ticket prices. The new Yankee Stadium, opened in 2009, heightened demand and prices even more. The Yanks banked $319 million in gate receipts alone in 2009, more than double the Rays' total revenue from all sources that year.

The Yankees' revenue stream would blow the Rays away even if Jeter, A-Rod, and company played their home games in a garbage dump on Staten Island—thanks to the Yankees Entertainment and Sports Network. For the first century or so of baseball history, teams collected almost all their revenue from ticket sales, concessions, and related items. Although the growth of baseball on the TBS and WGN superstations introduced new revenue streams, most teams remained stuck with limited moneymaking opportunities. The Yankees breezed through a string of cable deals, searching for the right regional sports network (RSN) opportunity. Three years after the Yankees and the NBA's New Jersey Nets formed a joint venture (brilliantly called YankeeNets), the two teams co-launched the YES Network in 2002. Three years later, YES became the most-watched RSN in the country. The hugely successful New England Sports Network (NESN) has similarly given a big boost to the Red Sox's top and bottom lines, as well as the total franchise value. No team nabbed higher local television ratings than the Red Sox in 2009.

Exactly how much the two teams reap from their RSNs every year is unclear. YES paid the Yankees an $84 million rights fee in 2009. The partnership yielded more than $100 million in dividend checks too. But the Yanks probably make a lot more than those reported numbers. They're not technically the owners of YES; the

Yankees' parent company, Yankee Global Enterprises, owns that stake. The Yankees wouldn't be the first sports franchise, or the last, to play a revenue shell game and dramatically underreport their take.

"RSNs are what gave rise to all the imbalance in the first place," said New York Mets GM Sandy Alderson. Before Billy Beane took the helm for the A's, Alderson ran that franchise on a tight budget, dreaming up innovative ways to keep pace with far richer opponents. In 1990, the A's owned the third-highest payroll in MLB, at a shade under $23 million, trailing the Red Sox and . . . the Kansas City Royals. "That was the inflection point, that's when the disparity among payrolls began to escalate." As the gap widened, some small-market clubs started deficit spending. For most of those teams, the strategy didn't work. "So they said, 'We're just not going to throw this money away anymore to stay with teams that have more revenue.'"

MLB took steps to curb the disparity between richer and poorer clubs. The league implemented more aggressive revenue-sharing, as well as a luxury tax, to try to prevent the Yankees—and to a lesser extent the Red Sox and their ilk—from steamrolling the competition. Rod Fort, professor of sport management at the University of Michigan, breaks down baseball's sharing efforts into three eras. Until 1995, all MLB did was share gate revenue, with 80% going to the home team, 20% to the visitor. From 1996 to 2001, baseball introduced pooled revenue-sharing, consisting of straight and fixed pools. As Shawn Hoffman, a *Baseball Prospectus* writer who became a Rays consultant, explained, straight pool funds are collected by taxing each team's net local revenue (total local revenue minus stadium expenses) at a rate of 31%. For the fixed pool, MLB takes a portion of its national revenue and distributes it unevenly among all thirty teams, with small-market teams getting more and large-market teams getting less. In 2002, the league added the competitive balance tax (luxury tax) and also wrapped in fresh revenue streams, including new media.

In 2009, the Yankees paid *out* well over $100 million in revenue-sharing; the Rays took *in* about $30 million. The thirty teams then split up a much larger pool of revenue stemming from national TV, MLB Advanced Media, and other sources, with a disproportionate amount going to smaller-revenue clubs. The Yankees have also paid the vast majority of luxury tax penalties, doling out just under $26 million in 2009 and $174 million of the tax's $190 million total from '03 to '09. By some estimates, the Rays received roughly $70 million to $80 million in 2009 without lifting a finger, while the Yankees shelled out well into nine figures.

Even these seemingly large redistributions of funds barely make a dent. The *Forbes* numbers that had the Yankees banking nearly three times as much revenue as the Rays in '09? Those figures already included revenue-sharing—and didn't account for, say, the possibility of a massive YES Network IPO. "There's no way revenue-sharing has improved balance—in the AL, the gap has only gotten bigger," said Fort. "We ask ourselves why. The answer is obvious: it wears pinstripes and stares us in the face every day. Yankees revenues just lap the field. Sharing isn't stopping that. The luxury tax may have just saved us from seeing how bad it could have gotten."

Another reason revenue-sharing isn't helping as much as it should, or could: poorer teams benefit less from revenue-sharing when they start winning more games. For a team like the Rays, this creates a tricky situation: win more games—as they have since 2008—and you get less money from the league. On the flip side, going from one of baseball's worst teams to one of its best should theoretically fuel a giant leap in revenue. But Tampa Bay's poorly located, aging stadium, combined with a litany of other factors, has prevented the Rays from realizing the kind of attendance gains they might have expected. After a huge jump in 2008, turnstile counts edged slightly higher in 2009, then fell slightly in 2010. Thus, the Rays will be severely challenged as they try to sustain their success. An overhaul in revenue-sharing that accounts for differences in market size but also incentivizes on-field success would be a welcome addition to baseball's next collective bargaining agreement.

That step aside, the best solution to the revenue disparity problem, said Fort and other experts, is to eat into advantages in market size. Add three more teams in and around New York—say, one in Brooklyn, one in New Jersey, and one in Connecticut—and you'd get closer to leveling the playing field. Add another team or two in New England and one in metro L.A. while you're at it. Practical solutions, in theory. In practice, the thirty teams maintain a delicate balance of competition among themselves and profit-seeking. If the commissioner took aggressive steps to knock down the competitive advantages of richer teams, he'd also nullify the entrepreneurial efforts those teams make to dramatically grow the value of their franchises. The whole thing would dissolve into a decade of lawyers billing enough hours to own a fleet of private jets.

Without such checks, though, the Yankees and Red Sox wield huge advantages over the Rays, Jays, and Orioles. The Rays would need to sell off nearly half their roster just to pay Alex Rodriguez's 2010 salary of $32 million—let alone the rest of his ten-year, $275 million deal. Stronger rosters in turn attract higher-caliber free-agent talent. When Marco Scutaro and Adrian Beltre hit the open market after the 2009 season, the A's offered three-year contracts to both. Scutaro and Beltre passed, signing less lucrative two- and one-year deals, respectively, with the Red Sox and giving themselves a better chance to compete for a World Series.

The Yanks and Sox have also figured out more subtle ways to exploit their big financial advantages. They can take sizable risks and easily write them off if they fail. The Yankees looked past Carl Pavano's history of injuries when they inked him to a four-year, $40 million contract after the 2004 season. Pavano made just 26 starts and won just 9 games during that span. New York made the playoffs in three of those four years anyway. In 2009, the Red Sox handed a combined $10.5 million to John Smoltz and Brad Penny, gambling on two pitchers with major age and injury concerns, respectively. Neither one panned out, Boston released both in August, and the Sox still sashayed into the postseason.

Even more nefarious has been the muscle both teams flex in the amateur draft. The draft was originally designed as a mechanism to save the owners money—with the side benefit of giving the worst teams first crack at the best high school and college players. But as the cost of signing top amateur talent has soared, many smaller-revenue teams have balked at paying big signing bonuses. The threat of reprimand from the Commissioner's Office has heightened weaker teams' reluctance to pay big bucks for the best of the bunch. The Yankees and Red Sox have taken full advantage, nabbing elite prospects twenty-five picks or more into the draft and paying them massively over recommended "slot value." Along the same lines, richer teams have also started going hard after top international prospects. The one area of the game that was supposed to be the great equalizer for the have-nots—drafting, signing, and developing your own talent to avoid paying megabucks in free agency—has become just another chance for the Yanks and Sox to push the little guys around.

"The draft and international market are no longer dispersing talent equally like they were intended to do," said A's assistant GM David Forst. "There are teams that budget two to three times as much as we do in the draft. How does that help, when they have the ability to spend so much more than we can?" There's more. MLB and the Elias Sports Bureau devised a rule that assigns values to various free-agents-to-be, such that teams that can't afford to retain their walk-year players can collect high draft picks as compensation. Unintended consequences abounded. Poorer teams have begun trading away players approaching free agency, usually to contenders. That shift allows rich teams like the Yankees and Red Sox to add even more premium young talent through the draft. They can then develop those players into potential stars or trade them for high-priced veterans. The strong get stronger, the weak get weaker. "All of this exponentially exacerbates the problem," Forst lamented.

The Yankees and Red Sox have ably achieved those two markers of baseball success, win now and win later. From the first post-strike season of 1995 through 2010, the Yankees made the playoffs fifteen times in sixteen tries, the Red Sox nine times. The two teams combined to win the World Series seven times in that stretch. That's despite playing in the same division, putting the onus on one of the two to win the AL wild-card spot every year. With a mountain of resources at their disposal and intelligent management at the helm, both teams can load up on veterans who can win in the short haul, then invest in the draft and international market to keep winning long-term. Can the Rays, Jays, and Orioles do the same?

"It's unlikely," said J. P. Ricciardi, the Jays' former GM. From 2006 to 2008, the Jays averaged more than 85 wins a season. Place them in the NL West in '08 or the NL Central in '06 with their win totals in those years and they win those divisions. And that's without accounting for the hellacious, AL East–heavy unbalanced schedules they played, which probably cost them a bunch of wins over that three-year stretch. "You can't just be good to make the playoffs, you have to be *great*. It doesn't mean Tampa can't get there or [the Blue Jays] can't get there. But even if you do, it's very unlikely that you will rattle off a few years in a row making the playoffs. The big monsters that sit in the division make that almost impossible."

In a span of two decades, Dave Dombrowski built the foundation of winning clubs in Montreal, Florida, and Detroit, including three World Series winners and a '94 Expos club that would've been a World Series favorite if not for that season's strike. The current Tigers GM has served as a head of player development and was also baseball's youngest GM when, at thirty-one, he took the Expos' reins in 1988. Few executives in any sport can claim Dombrowski's success in building winning teams from the ground up. "If you're Baltimore, Tampa Bay, or Toronto, you know that there's no sense in shortcutting what you're doing," he said. "If you're going to be good, you'd better build your foundation and take your time, because you're going to have to compete year in and year out. A lot of times what we all do is try to shortcut the process, speed it up, maybe continue building while trying to win. In that division, it's tough. I'm not sure you can do it."

Andy MacPhail led a similar homegrown effort as general manager of the Twins during their 1987 and 1991 championship seasons before moving on to the Cubs, and then later taking his current position as the Orioles' GM. Both his father, Lee MacPhail, and grandfather, Larry MacPhail, made the Baseball Hall of Fame for their contributions to the game. Like Dombrowski, MacPhail said shortcuts don't work and lucky breaks aren't enough. "You're not going to have a year [in the AL East] where you have 87, 88 wins and slide into the playoffs. You have to build it right—grow the arms, buy the rest. Free-agent pitching just does not want to come into this division unless they're getting paid full retail and then some, or going to Boston or New York."

With the odds constantly stacked against the Rays, the impact of every mistake is magnified. Cliff Floyd's departure after Tampa Bay's 2008 pennant run launched a search for a new DH. The Rays offered Bobby Abreu a two-year deal that topped any offer on the market, but Abreu opted to take a one-year, $5 million deal with the Angels instead. They looked into signing Adam Dunn, only to get outflanked by the Nationals, a far worse team and organization that made a two-year offer similar to the one the Rays floated. After weeks of research and negotiation, they finally settled on Pat Burrell, signing the longtime Phillies outfielder to a two-year, $16 million contract. The move was a disaster from the start. After averaging 31 homers and 103 walks a year in his previous four seasons, Burrell's power and on-base ability deserted him. He hit just 14 homers in his first season in Tampa Bay, playing in only 122 games, drawing just 57 walks, and hitting a miserable .221. No one was quite sure what the problem was. Nagging injuries, including persistent neck pain, took their toll. Critics wondered if Burrell was struggling against tougher AL East competition, feeling the effects of a tougher hitter's park, or even wilting as a designated hitter for the first time in his career. Whatever the cause, his struggles only worsened the next season. In 2010, Burrell posted a .202 average and .292 on-base percentage, and he hit only 2 homers in 24 games before the Rays kicked him to the curb. Adding insult to injury, Burrell became a key contributor for the playoff-bound Giants, who picked him up for next to nothing, then cruised to a World Series title.

That $16 million spent on a lineup cipher has had far-reaching effects. The Rays passed on high-priced talent at the 2010 trade deadline; they preannounced plans to slash payroll the following off-season; and flushing away that $16 million might even tighten future budgets enough to prevent them from signing a homegrown talent to a long-term deal or paying big bucks for draft talent. A cynic would note that the Rays had fewer picks to sign anyway: their two top choices in the 2009 draft, LeVon Washington and Kenny Diekroeger, both opted to play college ball rather than sign with the Rays. It will be years before we know how good Washington and Diekroeger will become, or whether they will have major league careers at all. The Rays received compensation picks for the 2010 draft that could work out just fine. But spending millions on hitters who don't produce and whiffing on the top of a draft are the kinds of moves that can scuttle a small-revenue team's efforts to close the gap on their powerful foes—if not now, then over the long haul.

"One bad contract can handicap you for years," said Forst, the A's assistant GM. He would know. Oakland signed rising star Eric Chavez to a six-year, $66 million deal in March 2004. Major shoulder injuries and surgery after surgery knocked Chavez out of the lineup for months at a time, sapping his hitting and throwing and leaving the A's with an albatross of a contract. Oakland offered Jason Giambi a six-year, $90 million pact after the 2001 season, following an MVP season and a second-place MVP finish. The Yankees outbid Oakland, locking up Giambi for seven years and $120 million. "We thought it would be a fair deal," Forst said. "But then, as we made the offer, we also thought, 'If we do this deal and it backfires, we could be screwed for the next six years.'" The Yankees watched Giambi deliver two miserable, injury-racked seasons out of the seven on his $120 million megadeal and saw Carl Pavano and Kevin Brown turn into pumpkins after getting big bucks, but never sweated much when these fat contracts blew up in their face.

Jed Hoyer has seen the Rays' monumental task from both sides, first as assistant GM of the well-heeled Red Sox, then as the head man in small-market San Diego. Ninety-five wins is almost a must to make the playoffs in the AL East, he said. That type of atmosphere forces the Rays—and the Jays and Orioles—to aim higher at everything they do: more aggressive spending on scouting, drafting, and development, more advanced analytical tools, more thoughtful management style both in the front office and on the field. Building slowly over a long period of time, as the Rays did with their LaMarera draft picks and a decade of losing, might be the only way to get it right. "Their patience was phenomenal," he said. "I don't think you could do a much better job building a small-market team. They never made moves just to fill holes. They looked at a team with the highest bullpen ERA and said, 'Why the hell am I going to fix it?' There's no point in plugging holes to win 70 or 75 games instead of 67."

No point in plugging holes—unless you work for an owner who won't tolerate losing. Or a fan base that won't. Or a demanding, always-in-your-face press corps that will roast you alive. "There are certain places where there's more latitude on the part of management to deal with the issue of competition," mused Alderson, the former A's general manager. "Places like Minnesota. Not that Minnesotans accept failure. But there's a long history of the Twins growing their own players, allowing them to leave, and at least staying competitive. So they have more latitude to get rid of, say, Johan Santana. Oakland, Tampa Bay, Florida—those types of places would be more forgiving. In other places—New York, Boston—it would be unthinkable. It would be unforgivable."

The quality of the top three AL East teams drives the emerging rivalry between the Rays and their richer competition in New York and Boston. But the haves-versus-have-nots nature of the teams can also cause friction. For the most part, Andrew Friedman and the Rays' front office do their jobs without worrying about macro issues like their limited resources, just as Brian Cashman and the Yankees and Theo Epstein and the Red Sox tend to their own daily operations. But it's easy to let your mind wander, to wish you had more money if you're the Rays, or wish you could deal with less scrutiny if you're the Yankees or Red Sox. Still, it's a healthy, respectful rivalry, said Hoyer and others, with each team motivated to match the high-level decision-making of the others.

The owners are a different story—especially where the Rays and Red Sox are concerned. John Henry and Stuart Sternberg both hail from Wall Street. But it's an awfully big street, one that includes wildly divergent investment strategies. Those different approaches to making money can make one man look upon the other's efforts with contempt.

Henry made his fortune selling commodities futures. As a young commodities broker and later the founder of investment management firm John W. Henry & Company, he learned the value of quick thinking, and also of agnostic thinking. In his world, the true value of a bushel of corn or a ton of soybeans doesn't matter. All that matters are the prevailing trends. Go long when market conditions dictate it. Go short when the market turns the other way. In Henry's world, the market is always right. Sternberg takes the long view. With Goldman Sachs and later in his own ventures, he went to great lengths to learn the intrinsic value of assets. When working on a merger, he would pore over both companies' operations, mining for synergies to exploit and redundancies to eradicate. When digging into a particular company, he'd consider every little edge in its supply chain, every rising star on its management team, every chink in rival companies' armor. He'd look for the ideal long-term investment, the value play that could produce big gains over a span of multiple years. In Sternberg's world, the market is often wrong, and it is his job to take advantage.

Those approaches are inherently at odds with each other. A successful commodities trader sees the big gains he's scored from his fast-acting strategy and wonders why someone would waste so much time doing painstaking research in the name of some nebulous, far-off goal. A successful long-term investor takes pride in the hard work he's put in to find the hidden gem. He sees much less skill, and no elegance, in a commodity trader's playbook.

Not everyone with those divergent backgrounds need become bitter combatants. But once both men joined the exclusive club of Major League Baseball owners, those feelings began to simmer. With the two teams playing in the same division, with vastly different revenue bases, the rivalry came to a slow boil. And when the Rays finally caught and passed the Red Sox in 2008, everything bubbled over.

The first signs of resentment cropped up in 2005, before Sternberg had even completed his buyout of Vince Naimoli and ascended to the role of managing partner. In the third round of that year's amateur draft, the Devil Rays drafted a high school pitcher named Bryan Morris. A big kid out of Tennessee, Morris had been regarded as a near-elite talent who would require more than third-round money to sign. At first, Tampa Bay was prepared to shell out to get their man. But with the Devil Rays' sale and ownership transfer pending, Sternberg changed his mind, opting not to go over slot for Morris in an effort to avoid upsetting anyone in the Commissioner's Office. Tampa Bay passed, Morris went back into the draft the next year, and the Dodgers scooped him up with their first-round pick. When Sternberg watched Henry and the Red Sox pay over slot for several players, both then and looking back at previous years, he felt duped. Why should the rich get richer, he fumed, when he's taking on one of the toughest rebuilding jobs in sports? When Tampa Bay picked right-hander Alex Cobb in the fourth round of the 2006 draft—from a Boston high school no less—Sternberg quickly authorized over-slot money to get him signed. The Commissioner's Office gave him a tongue-lashing, but Sternberg didn't care. He wasn't going to let niceties scuttle his goals again.

In 2006, the Rays believed that Boston was tampering with their free-agent-to-be, shortstop Julio Lugo. That August, Tampa Bay learned that the Sox wanted to trade for Baltimore catcher Javy

Lopez and that the asking price was young outfielder Adam Stern. The Rays claimed Stern on waivers, forcing Boston and Baltimore to work out the Lopez deal for a player to be named later—that player being Stern, thanks to the work-around engineered by the Red Sox and Orioles. Still, the message had been sent—don't screw with us, or we'll screw you right back. The Rays were far out of contention when they pulled that bit of gamesmanship, cementing the notion that they were just looking for payback against their rivals. The Red Sox weren't quite out of it when they made multiple waiver claims in 2010. Blocking the Rays from acquiring help was still a fun by-product.

Sternberg's disdain for Henry and the Red Sox soared in the 2006–2007 off-season. The Red Sox beat out multiple competitors that winter for the negotiating rights to Japanese star pitcher Daisuke Matsuzaka. The figures were mind-boggling: $51.1 million to the Seibu Lions just to grant Dice-K his freedom, plus a six-year, $52 million contract for him to play for the Sox. No way could the Rays afford to pay nine figures for any player, let alone one who'd never appeared in a major league game.

Meanwhile, no owner expressed more conflicting feelings about revenue disparity in baseball than Henry. While owner of the low-budget Florida Marlins, Henry stumped for more cash to flow his way so his small-revenue team could keep pace with the competition. After controlling the Marlins for three years, Henry won ownership of the Red Sox, landing in Boston after MLB engineered an elaborate plan that granted the Marlins to Montreal Expos owner Jeffrey Loria, made the Expos wards of the league until a lucrative franchise sale (to a Washington, D.C., group two years later), and awarded the Red Sox to Henry and his partners—despite other bidders offering more money. Once in control of one of baseball's glamour franchises, Henry suddenly developed mixed feelings about how to parcel out team revenue. A salary cap, he said, would be great for competitive balance in baseball, because hey, why should the Yankees get to spend so much more than everyone else? Henry's feelings on revenue-sharing were even more confusing.

"People seem to think I am opposed to revenue-sharing, but that has never been the case," he told NESN's Tom Caron in a 2009 interview, one of many public statements Henry made on the issue. "What I have said is there have to be limits when it comes to transferring assets, and there have to be incentives for all clubs to invest in their teams." Caron asked Henry about the Rays' 2008 run to the AL pennant, their win over the Red Sox, and whether it was good for baseball to have smaller-revenue teams rise up and knock off the big guys. Henry graciously praised the Rays' front office for their efforts: "Tampa Bay's turnaround was due to an excellent management team now running the club from top to bottom."

But after watching the Rays knock off a Red Sox team trying to defend its crown with a payroll three times smaller than Boston's, a tiny fraction of the total fan base, and a tinier fraction of the media exposure and history, guided by an owner who'd reaped the benefits of baseball's annual redistribution, with a chunk of that money coming right out of his own pockets, Henry couldn't resist a subtle, little dig. "It was also," he said, "a triumph of revenue-sharing."

For decades, the baseball world had watched the Yankees dominate the game. Other AL East teams had their time, wedging out periods where they triumphed over big, bad New York. Then, for the better part of fifteen years, the Red Sox became part of baseball royalty too. The two teams dominated the East, exchanging barbs, riling up fan bases, and bringing daily manna to columnists craving the latest controversies. All the while, Tampa Bay remained buried in the cellar.

Through meticulous planning, skillful player development, uncanny patience, and, yes, some high draft picks and shared revenue, the Rays threw off their last-place shackles and gunned down the two toughest behemoths of the sport. After years of irrelevance, they'd stirred up some good old-fashioned resentment from their once-bullying big brothers. New rivalries had begun, and the other guys wanted to beat their ass. On the field (if not off it), David had felled the Goliaths.

CHAPTER 12 THE PIT

*St. Pete is beautiful—a great little town with a
beautiful bay, beautiful beaches, and a beautiful
ballpark. Trouble is, the beautiful ballpark is
Al Lang Field.*
—JEFF MERRON, ESPN.com

If Warren Buffett targeted baseball teams instead of energy conglomerates, railroads, and soft-drink giants, he would have loved the Tampa Bay Devil Rays circa October 2005. For a skilled value investor, buying the team with the lowest franchise value and second-lowest revenues, in a sport where rapid growth was nearly assured, would have seemed a dream come true. Depressed assets were everywhere, including eight seasons of miserable baseball and a departing owner who had turned the community against him. But the biggest strike against the new owners was a stadium that was woefully outdated from the day they took over. It was obsolete the first time a home crowd craned their necks to watch a pitch and squinted their eyes to follow a pop-up's trajectory against the vast, white roof. Snatching up Tropicana Field wasn't buying low. It was free-falling into the Mariana Trench.

By the time Stuart Sternberg and Matt Silverman wrested control of the D-Rays from Vince Naimoli after the 2005 season, the giant white-domed monstrosity the team called home had become the most depressing pro sports venue in America. Paint was peeling off the walls. Bathrooms had fallen into disrepair. Concessions were a sorry lot, in-stadium attractions even sorrier. The lighting was dingy, the atmosphere funereal. But Sternberg and Silverman viewed the stadium the same way Andrew Friedman regarded a talented but flawed player. In the new regime's eyes, both offered potential.

"The stadium is not a hindrance to creating a successful business," Silverman said in a 2006 interview. "We're confident that once the marketplace latches on to our team and the players, Tropicana Field will be full of energy and excitement. It's a great place to watch a game. The empty seats are opportunities for us."

More than just a business opportunity, the D-Rays saw the Trop as a unique ballpark with unusual structural traits that could give the team a decisive on-field advantage.

"We already have great speed, and the turf creates an advantage there," Silverman gushed. "The white roof is something that our opponents may have trouble getting used to. When we get over 20,000 people here, it's extremely loud. We're urging people to come out and be the tenth man. The more people that come, the more that can have an impact on the outcome of the game."

Silverman had some cause for optimism. Attendance would surge 20% in 2006, the new group's first season. It would edge up 1% in 2007, then rocket 31% in 2008 as the Rays won the AL East. A better ball club (mostly) and better marketing would hike the number of butts in Tropicana Field seats from 1.1 million (14,000 a game) in the last year under Vince Naimoli to 1.8 million (more than 22,000 a game) the year the Rays won the pennant.

More fans, more *enthusiastic* fans, and the Trop's unique layout all fed into the Rays' growing home-field edge (predicted by Silverman). There was probably some luck involved too. But the numbers were dramatic. In 2008 and '09, the first two seasons in which the franchise had ever contended for anything but fourth place, the Rays went 109-53 at home and just 72-90 on the road.

After Tampa Bay swept the Red Sox in an August 2009 series, *Boston Globe* columnist Adam Kilgore made the feeling of opposing teams and fans clear. "Forgive the Red Sox if they were tempted to board their charter last night still wearing their uniforms, while the cowbells still rang in their ears and the fluorescent lights still stung their eyes. Forgive them if they ran from this place screaming. Forgive them for doing anything to leave behind Tropicana Field as fast as they could. . . . It is a baseball diamond trapped inside a demented theme park, where catwalks hang and cowbells clang. Playing here feels weird for invaders. It feels like home for the Rays."

It may have felt like home when times were good, but the stadium dubbed "the Pit" by Joe Maddon soon stopped looking like an opportunity and reverted to being a handicap. Attendance ticked up just 3% in 2009, a decent showing during tough economic times, but still a disappointment given the positive year-after effect that typically comes with winning a pennant. The economy and the fallback in the Rays' performance were also, of course, contributing factors to 2009's disappointing attendance. But the Rays failed to see a boost in 2010 too: the Rays ranked twenty-second in MLB in attendance, averaging just 23,000 fans a game. Despite winning their second AL East title in three years, the Rays' attendance finished slightly *lower* than in 2009.

Even the little quirks that drove opponents batty started backfiring. In an August 2010 series against the Minnesota Twins, the Rays averaged barely 18,000 fans for the first three games of the series. They drew 29,000 for game four, thanks to a special kids' camp promotion. But that game ended in absurdity when a ninth-inning Jason Kubel infield pop-up struck a catwalk high above the field, landed near the pitcher's mound, and cost the Rays the game.

"It's probably the perfect commercial advertisement for a reason to have a new ballpark," Maddon said afterward. "There's no better reason than that. I know it works both ways, but to lose a game in a pennant situation like that because of a roof truly indicates why there's a crying need for a new ballpark in this area, regardless of where they put it. It just needs to be a real baseball field where, if you lose the pennant by one game and look back at a game like that because the roof got in the way, we'd be very upset. So, again, there's no better reason than that."

In just four and a half years, the Trop went from an untapped commodity in ownership's eyes to the same old Pit, a stadium that couldn't draw fans even in a 96-win season, a building the manager would just as soon have burned to the ground. For a team that sees opportunity in everything, Tropicana Field is the one problem the Rays can't seem to fix.

The Howard Frankland Bridge, three miles long, is all that stands between Pinellas and Hillsborough counties and their anchor cities of St. Petersburg and Tampa. But for many residents on both sides of the bridge, that span might as well be 300 miles. St. Pete tends to get slighted when the two cities are compared. More provincial Tampanians gaze across the bay and see a town they imagine as overrun with retirees, and the area immediately around the Trop as a hive of crime and poverty. Both stereotypes are exaggerated: St. Petersburg's population base has grown progressively younger since a surge in retirees peaked in the 1970s, and urban revitalization has transformed the city center. But stereotypes die hard, especially when paired with other, larger inconveniences. The perceptions of residents outside St. Pete, combined with quirky geography and a woeful lack of infrastructure, turned Tropicana Field into an island within a peninsula that nobody wanted to drive to.

At the behest of St. Pete mayor Rick Baker, a group of local businessmen formed A Baseball Community Inc. (usually called the ABC Coalition) to study the viability of Tropicana Field as a major league ballpark. ABC found many of the usual deficits you'd expect in an aging sports facility, including a lack of state-of-the-art amenities, lucrative club lounges, and luxury suites. There were also many drawbacks specific to the Trop, including seats improperly oriented to the field, no natural light, poor sight lines from many seats, and those pesky catwalks that drive Joe Maddon nuts. But even if the Rays razed the Trop and built a palatial new home on the same site, they would still face the biggest problem of all—a terrible location.

Google Maps claims that it takes twenty minutes to drive the eighteen miles from Tampa's western edge to Tropicana Field, located in the southern portion of St. Pete. It just never works out that way. The Howard Frankland Bridge is the most-traveled route over the bay, and it's often packed. Congestion can slow the rest of the drive down I-275, the only major route from Tampa's main corridor to St. Pete, then choke the downtown exits leading to the stadium. Doubling Google's estimate is usually a good starting point.

And that's only for Tampanians who happen to live within spitting distance of the bridge. Fan out to population centers east of Tampa—Hillsborough County's fast-growing Brandon, for example—and you could be looking at two-plus hours, coming and going, to see a Rays game on a weeknight. Northern bedroom communities face similar hair-pulling commutes. Greater Orlando's 2 million–plus residents are theoretically within range, with a ninety-minute jaunt from its southwestern suburbs to the ballpark on paper—but that trip is an exercise in vehicular masochism for those who dare chance it during rush hour.

The greater Tampa Bay region is often regarded as a small market by MLB standards. But the population analytics website Demographics Now.com defines it as one of the fifteen largest in the country, with 3.25 million residents. Despite those healthy numbers, suburban sprawl and the Trop's unfortunate location paint a grim picture. Only 19% of Tampa Bay residents live within a thirty-minute drive of the Trop—by far the smallest percentage of any MLB market. Seattle, with roughly the same population base, counts two and a half times as many residents in a half-hour driving radius. Every market smaller than Tampa Bay counts at least half its residents within thirty minutes of the ballpark. The Denver area includes 800,000 fewer inhabitants than Tampa Bay, yet more than 1.9 million Denverites can make the thirty-minute-or-less drive to Coors Field versus just over 600,000 in Tampa–St. Pete–Clearwater.

"It all boils down to the worst-kept secret in Tampa Bay sports," wrote Noah Pransky, a reporter for Tampa's WTSP Radio who covers the Rays and other local sports franchises and their stadium issues in his blog, Shadow of the Stadium. "Tropicana Field was built on the wrong side of the bay."

If Sternberg could move to a new ballpark in Tampa tomorrow, the Rays would instantly become far more profitable, and have the cash flow they need to retain more top talent and expand the razor-thin margin of error for competing against the Yankees and Red Sox. But he can't, for many reasons. He can start by thanking Vince Naimoli. The Rays' former owner signed a thirty-year lease (technically a use agreement) before the team played its first game at the Trop in 1998. Forget skipping over to Tampa or another locale—the Rays are contractually obligated to stare at catwalks and a giant white roof in remote downtown St. Pete through the 2027 season.

Agreements can always be broken, so long as both parties consent. But reaching that point has been a long, excruciating process in other cities' stadium debates—especially for taxpayers.

Led by late owner Carl Pohlad, the Twins spent more than a decade haranguing the public into building them a new ballpark to replace the Metrodome, which was just thirteen years old when Pohlad started his campaign of pleas and threats. Local government stood strong at first, angering both Pohlad and Major League Baseball. What began as veiled whispers of dissatisfaction metastasized into threats of relocation, even contraction. Pohlad launched his career in the banking business by foreclosing on family farms during the Great Depression. After becoming one of the richest men in America, he ran the Twins on a shoestring budget, racking up revenue-sharing money despite a personal net worth that dwarfed those of all other MLB owners. When lobbying for a new stadium, he had no qualms about crying poor and shaking down local residents and politicians. Hand over $350 million in tax money to boost the owner's already fat profit margins, Pohlad's surrogates in Minnesota and on Park Avenue warned, or kiss your beloved Twins good-bye.

"Let's just concentrate on getting this done so we don't have to consider the alternative," Bud Selig said in an interview about the Twins' stadium impasse. He was speaking during Game 1 of the 2005 World Series, with not a Twin in sight.

In May 2006, the state legislature finally caved. Hennepin County would spend $390 million on the Twins' new ballpark, counting the cost overruns that inevitably occur during construction to give taxpayers one last kick in the nuts. The Twins kicked in $130 million—just one quarter of the total.

The Florida Marlins also needed more than a decade to strong-arm local politicians into building them a new stadium. At least they had a decent excuse. When Wayne Huizenga sold the Marlins to John Henry in 1998, Huizenga retained most of the revenue streams coming from the stadium. Thus, even if the Marlins had boosted their lousy attendance, the team wouldn't have derived much benefit. On the other hand, the lease was getting ready to expire, and the Marlins could have tried to renegotiate the lease. Instead, they tried to land that coveted public handout. After several attempts, though, Henry gave up his quest to get a new publicly financed ballpark. He transferred ownership to Jeffrey Loria in the shady MLB ménage à trois that gifted the Red Sox to Henry and the Marlins to Loria.

The methods Loria and his stepson David Samson employed in their own stadium gambit amounted to a giant con. They launched big publicity campaigns, calling out a number of potential sites for their new palace. They argued that a new stadium would bring enormous economic benefits to the area—a fact resoundingly debunked by many economists who note, among other things, that sports stadiums don't pump new money into the economy; they merely divert money from other points of sale. The Marlins' owners also got the poor-mouthing act down pat: *we're barely breaking even*, the deceitful duo pleaded to every public official within earshot.

This was, of course, a bald-faced lie. Despite playing in the seventh-largest metropolitan area in the country, the Marlins were blessed by MLB's deeply flawed revenue-sharing system with an orgy of cash. Deadspin and the Associated Press released leaked financial statements from the Marlins, Rays, and other teams in August 2010. The documents show the Marlins raking in more than $90 million in revenue-sharing for 2008 and 2009 combined. They perennially spend less on player salaries than nearly any other team in baseball. Even after accounting for all its other expenses and liabilities, the franchise makes big money—more than $29 million in net income in 2008 alone. And that's just the income we know about, let alone the annual appreciation in franchise value enjoyed by the Marlins, like most other teams.

The best way to build public support for a new stadium deal—other than threats—is simple (in theory, if not practice): win. That's just what the Marlins did when they knocked off the Yankees in the 2003 World Series. Soon after, the team, the city of Miami, and Miami-Dade County announced plans to fund a new ballpark. First, Miami proposed a baseball-only stadium for the Marlins at the site of the Orange Bowl. A few months later, Miami-Dade County commissioners agreed to contribute funding for the new stadium, which would cost roughly $435 million when combined with an adjacent parking complex. But in May 2005, the Florida legislature rejected a $60 million sales-tax rebate that would have helped pay for the stadium.

That setback, combined with the rising projected cost of stadium construction, prompted Loria and Samson to step up their shakedown. When their grandiose plans didn't inspire anyone who mattered, they brought out the big gun: extortion.

"There are no more deadlines," Samson warned. "No more fake deadlines. No more real deadlines. We need a place to play after 2010, and we don't have one. Baseball is no longer assured of staying in [south] Florida."

Loria and Samson made aggressive overtures toward San Antonio and other markets, vowing to move the Marlins if they didn't get what they wanted. The flirtation with San Antonio was at once amusing, maddening, and hollow: Loria had earlier (and ironically, as it turned out) played a role in MLB commandeering the one market capable of being more than a stalking horse for a struggling club like the Marlins—the Expos' eventual new home in Washington, D.C. But the region's feckless politicians, lousy poker players all, failed to read the Marlins' bluff. Apparently unaware of the many cases of MLB owners duping politicians into bankrolling new stadiums—and Loria's own past unscrupulous dealings in baseball—city and county leaders never demanded that the Marlins open their books. After years of browbeating, Loria and Samson finally convinced the city, county, and state to believe their lies, and the Marlins got their stadium approved.

"New stadiums are great for team owners so long as they're not the ones building them," said *Field of Schemes*' Neil deMause. "The whole model is to socialize the cost and privatize the profit."

The thing is, stadiums are not *net* revenue-positive. They're boondoggles that don't work. The reason teams make money off them is because cities pay most of the bill and teams collect most of the profits. St. Pete would be better off just writing Stu Sternberg a check for $100 million than building the Rays a new stadium: it's much cheaper that way.

The Marlins gained final approval for their stadium deal in December 2007, just a few weeks after the Rays made their own initial proposal. Sternberg sought to build Rays Ballpark on the site of Progress Energy Park (formerly Al Lang Field), a small spring training stadium sitting on a nine-acre downtown lot abutting the bay. If all had gone according to plan, the Rays would have played in the new park on opening day 2012. The design was ambitious and unprecedented. Resembling a huge sailboat, the stadium could be covered by retractable fabric, which a pulley system would be able to open or close in eight minutes. Sternberg pledged one third of the estimated $450 million construction cost. The Rays sought another $60 million from the same thirty-year state sales-tax rebate that benefited the Marlins. Most ambitiously, the plan called for Tropicana Field to be redeveloped into a major mixed-used complex that would include apartments, condos, offices, and hotel and retail space. The Rays claimed that the sale of the Trop's redevelopment rights, combined with new property taxes, could generate $800 million in new revenue for the city.

The plan failed for several reasons. Downtown residents spoke out against the idea of a huge, multi-year construction project in their backyard, not to mention 35,000 fans streaming into the park and back out onto the streets eighty-one times every year. Environmental factors also posed a challenge. The Rays originally envisioned filling in two and a half acres of Tampa Bay. They slashed that number twice—which still wasn't enough to satisfy critics. The Rays also misread the community's interest in paying for a new stadium. Having already watched the NFL's Tampa Bay Buccaneers saddle Hillsborough County with a hefty financial burden—and seeing the honeymoon period peter out for the Bucs and Raymond James Stadium—the Rays were unlikely to get the kind of sweetheart deal from the community that the Marlins had received. Indeed, a similar situation had unfolded in Seattle, where, after funding new buildings for the NFL's Seahawks and MLB's Mariners, the city was unwilling to bend over for the owners of the NBA's SuperSonics.

The biggest problem was the plan's timing. The Twins, Marlins, and other teams had shown that it often takes more than ten years merely to get a plan approved, sometimes fifteen or more to go from the germ of an idea to throwing out the first pitch. The Rays thought the Marlins had created a precedent for their own deal, but in reality there was no way that was going to happen. The Marlins' stadium was just one part of a gigantic, citywide endeavor that dwarfed even the Rays' ambitious proposal. It was an impossibly unlikely outcome at an impossible time, the kind of windfall that happens once in a lifetime. Florida's housing market was cratering, and Tampa–St. Pete would prove to be one of the regions hardest hit by the recession, with unemployment topping 13% in adjacent areas. To bypass the usual ten years of jousting would have been improbable. But introducing the idea as thousands of locals lost their jobs and their homes proved disastrous. The plan made it to a St. Petersburg city council vote, with the city agreeing to draw up language for an approval referendum in November 2008. But opposition had grown too intense, and the waterfront site had inherent, perhaps insoluble problems. Less than three weeks after clearing that first hurdle, the Rays suspended the waterfront plan indefinitely. The next spring, they abandoned it entirely.

"I wonder just the way the political climate is now, if there would still be opposition even if all the Rays asked for were road investments and infrastructure [as part of a stadium plan]," *St. Petersburg Times* columnist Marc Topkin said in a 2009 interview. "I really think there would be. They closed five elementary schools and two middle schools in Pinellas County this week. So, you can't come back the next day with a headline of 'Rays Want X Amount of Millions for Their New Stadium.' They're going to have to weather this out."

Not much has changed since. The Tampa Bay region continues to struggle with sky-high unemployment and sluggish growth even as GDP results have picked up nationwide. The economy has taken its toll on fans of other local teams too. The Buccaneers failed to sell out their first preseason game in 2010, marking the first time since the stadium opened fourteen years earlier that the NFL had to black out a game for that reason. Meanwhile, St. Pete's city council took what looked like a hard-line stand against the Rays' going anywhere. "We absolutely feel good about our position," said St. Petersburg mayor Bill Foster. "We all know that there are seventeen years remaining on their agreement to hold major league baseball games at [Tropicana Field]. I promise I will uphold my end of the deal. I expect them to do the same."

Foster had every right to draw a line in the sand. The stadium lease explicitly prohibits the Rays from even talking to cities outside St. Pete.

With the waterfront site dead, the Rays stayed quiet and let the ABC Coalition prepare its final report. The group's conclusions surprised nobody who'd been paying attention. Tropicana Field is a dump. The Rays need a new stadium with a retractable roof, better sight lines, and more of the modern "amenities" if they are going to generate the necessary revenues. Oh, and they need to get the hell out of St. Pete. In many ways, this was a curious set of conclusions. Leaked documents had shown that the Rays are generating a profit (albeit a small one) while also competing and winning in the toughest division in baseball.

The group also posited that the Rays could generate nearly $300 million in local economic impact for the region, not including intangible benefits such as raising Tampa Bay's national profile. Though such claims had been roundly debunked in other cities by virtually every independent study, the ABC's report still softened St. Pete government's stance considerably. St. Pete officials trusted ABC's findings above past studies by economists contradicting such claims, and they had no desire to see the team bolt. Foster eventually agreed to at least consider relocation . . . as long as the new site was in greater St. Petersburg and the city could annex that territory into its own purview if needed.

The mayor had good reason to change his tune. The alternative stadium sites that ABC suggested include several within the broader Carillon area, a big swath of land right near the bridge, though still on the St. Pete side of the bay. But the coalition's two other top choices are both outside St. Pete: the Westshore neighborhood, just over the bridge on the Tampa side, and downtown Tampa. For St. Pete, the thought of losing the Rays to Tampa represents not only a scary thought in terms of loss of revenue (if ABC's rosy estimates are to be believed) but a chance for Tampa to strike another major blow in a twin cities rivalry with a contentious history.

For a while, you could flip your radio dial to ESPN 1040 in Tampa during afternoon drive time and hear a sports talk show called *The Swarm*. Almost every day, host Marc Benarzyk would go on a rant about Joe Maddon. True to the show's name, the attacks came swarming in against the Rays' manager: too much lineup tinkering, too many bad bullpen choices, thinks he's smarter than the rest of us. B. J. Upton is a lazy pariah who should be shipped out of town.

Carlos Peña is a bum who can't hit. Typical sports talk fare. Get the haters on your side. Rile up your targets' defenders. Just make sure you're never, ever boring. But for Rays fans, the bashing in this case strikes a particularly sensitive nerve. The station took *The Swarm* off the air in the summer of 2010. But it still does not broadcast Rays games. ESPN 1040, headquartered in Tampa, Florida, broadcasts the New York Yankees.

The first sign you see crossing over the bridge to Tampa points drivers to George Steinbrenner Field, the spring training home of the Yankees. Much of the Yankees' brain trust, including the heart of its scouting and player development departments, works there. When the Bombers play at the Trop, crowds often swell to near sellout levels, with chants of "Let's go Yankees!" competing with the clanging of Rays fans' cowbells.

"There are Yankees fans everywhere," said Mark Newman, the team's head of baseball operations. "But here, they are more ensconced than you might find in other places because of what the Boss and his family have done for the community. I've been here more than twenty years. We were here long before the Rays."

While a fair number of Tampanians—transplanted New Yorkers or otherwise—side with the Yankees over the Rays, a far greater number see a rivalry between themselves and St. Petersburgers. It's a rivalry about as one-sided as Yankees–Red Sox pre-2004. Tampa and St. Pete fought for the regional airport. Tampa won. The Bucs' new stadium? Tampa won. The University of South Florida's main campus? Busch Gardens? The zoo? Tampa, Tampa, Tampa. The Tampa Bay Lightning's arena? Tampa won and inked a naming rights deal with the rival newspaper. That's right. To see an NHL game, you must drive to the St. Pete Times Forum—located in the heart of downtown Tampa. For St. Pete residents, driving over the bridge to Tampa, whether for work or to catch one of the city's many attractions, is routine. But unless they're headed to the beaches, most Tampanians rarely cross over the bay.

Most of the area's corporate headquarters are in Tampa; a lack of interest from the business community has tamped down season-ticket sales and left many premium seats at the Trop vacant. Tampa is far more centrally located than south St. Petersburg, relative to the region's major population centers. A proposed high-speed rail line from Orlando, originally routed all the way to St. Pete and the beaches, is (for now) slated to end in Tampa, with no possibility of crossing the bay until at least 2025. A new stadium in Tampa could pay far bigger dividends than one in St. Pete. But even if the Rays could Houdini themselves out of their lease, the political will and the capital simply don't exist to build a new ballpark in Tampa. Not with the county knee-deep in debt for the Bucs stadium and revenue shortfalls whacking the public and private sectors for as far into the future as anyone can see.

Meanwhile, St. Pete has its own problems. The same economic woes hurting Tampa have taken their toll across the bridge too. The BP oil spill in 2010 created another potential setback for the Rays' stadium chances. The Florida Gulf Coast was still sorting out the implications of the spill in October 2010, particularly with the area's annual hurricane season under way. Term-limited elected officials already have a bias against looking too far into the future. Looking five or ten years into the future to see how a half-billion-dollar stadium project might work is a much lower priority than, say, fixing the damage that a gigantic oil spill, or even the perceived threat of an oil spill, could inflict on St. Pete's beaches, tourism, fishing, and other industries. The spill may not be any more than a blip in the history of the Rays, but it is another setback they didn't want.

St. Pete and Pinellas County have taken tangible steps toward preparing for stadium discussions. A 1% hotel tax kicks $5 million a year in tourism funds toward paying off Tropicana Field's bonds. The 1% tax would have expired in September 2015, but the county agreed to extend the tax, creating a potential new funding source for any tourism uses it sees fit, including a new stadium. But that amount would be a drop in the bucket given the likely cost of a ballpark, sure to be considerably higher than the $450 million proposed for the St. Pete waterfront site by the time a future construction crew would break ground.

If St. Petersburg does eventually come to the bargaining table—as the city has said it will—the financial documents leaked by Deadspin and the AP create potential leverage . . . for both sides, depending on your point of view.

St. Pete might reasonably argue that the Rays made $15 million in net income between the 2007 and 2008 seasons. That's not counting the big boost that the 2008 World Series run provided for the Rays' franchise value, plus the enhanced visibility of the team's brand and the potential gains to be reaped as a result. Meanwhile, Sternberg and Silverman have focused on the negatives in the Rays' finances. At a January 2008 luncheon, Silverman told a group of local businesspeople, "We're cash-flow negative." The next month, Sternberg told Rays blog DRaysBay, "We've certainly run significant cash deficits the past two seasons." Those claims are contradicted by the leaked documents. Other accounting tricks could also obfuscate the Rays' finances, said deMause. If a group of investors borrows money to buy a team, it could then assign that debt to the team and count it as a drag on the team's books, even though it's really just part of the investment cost.

On the other hand, the Rays could point out that a $15 million net profit over two years—one of those a pennant-winning year!—is a lousy return compared with other, thriftier teams, not to mention other investment vehicles. They could note that even their World Series run in 2008 did little to help the bottom line. The Rays banked $161 million in revenue in 2008, up 20% from '07 levels. But expenses soared 31% year-over-year in 2008, to $146.7 million. By dramatically boosting player payroll and also hiking sales and marketing spending, the Rays were doing exactly what MLB would want a revenue-sharing recipient to do with its funds: investing in the team and trying to win a World Series. Yet net income actually dropped from 2007 levels, to $4 million from $11 million a year earlier. Even when the Rays climbed the mountaintop, knocked off the Yankees and Red Sox, and surged to the World Series, they barely broke even. That's a sign, they could argue, that new revenue streams—including a new stadium—are needed. Of course, the most likely way for those new revenues to outstrip the gigantic costs of building a new stadium and paying down its debt remains for taxpayers to pay for a huge chunk of the bill . . . which takes everyone back to square one.

Some of these shortfalls could resolve themselves organically. A better economy would certainly help. Time could also change the makeup of the Rays' fan base.

More endemic problems remain. As long as the Rays play at Tropicana Field, they'll be able to stretch their ticket prices only so far before running into resistance from already skeptical fans— whereas fans tend to be willing to pay higher prices at new ballparks. The 2009 team marketing report showed that the Yankees charge four times as much as the Rays for nonpremium tickets. For club seats and other premium tickets, the Yankees raked in more than eight times as much as Tampa Bay. Even if the Rays built a new, heavily subsidized stadium and charged much more for their tickets, their revenue streams would still be dwarfed by the Yankees'—especially considering the impact of the indomitable YES Network. The Rays could win five World Series in a row but still face a huge financial disadvantage against their rivals in New York and Boston.

If history is any judge, the Rays will eventually get that new ballpark somewhere in the Tampa Bay region. In the end, nearly every major league market has caved to such demands, doling out hundreds of millions of dollars for stadiums while trying to convince themselves that the investment will pay off. The exceptions are the Giants, who built AT&T Park mostly with private money; the A's, still trying to find a new home in the other Bay Area; a few cities where ballparks were renovated rather than knocked down in favor of a new stadium; and Montreal, which lost its team to a city that was willing to build a new park.

"Only one team has moved in forty years," said Rod Fort of the

University of Michigan. "The Rays' not getting something out of the [Tampa] bay area is not a zero-probability event. But I would suggest the odds are dramatically in their favor."

The big question is when, and will Sternberg be willing to wait that long? "I have been patient, if nothing else," Sternberg said in a June 2010 *Tampa Tribune* editorial meeting, one of the few times he's spoken at length about a new stadium. "I'm not banging on a table saying I need a new stadium tomorrow."

But?

"If I don't get the sense there's real cooperation, I'd sell the team."

Is Sternberg posturing for the kind of gift the Marlins got from taxpayers? Or would the huge baseball fan with a Wall Street competitive edge really take his ball and go home? This is the uncomfortable question Rays fans face.

For all the positive arbitrage pulled off in trades, all the forward-thinking scouting, drafting, and player development techniques, and all the innovative branding and marketing efforts, Tropicana Field remains *the* major obstacle standing between the Rays and an ascendance to the rarefied air the Yankees breathe—that of a potential dynasty. They still wouldn't be able to touch the Yankees' monstrous total revenue streams. But as long as Sternberg, Silverman, and Friedman remain at the helm, the Rays have a chance to compete with anyone, even more so if they can raise the funds to keep winning teams together—or at least replace missing pieces with new talent.

The question is: which road will the Rays' owner take? Sternberg could choose to slash expenses. Before the 2010 season even started, he vowed to drastically reduce payroll for 2011, whether the Rays won the World Series or finished last. Such thriftiness could all but guarantee healthy profits every year, the same way the Pittsburgh Pirates have funneled revenue-sharing funds into big profits. And like the Pirates, the Rays could lose big if the cuts are deep enough, despite the best efforts of front-office wizards.

The Rays' owner could also follow through on his promise and sell if he doesn't get the stadium deal he wants, and soon. If that happens, the wheels could fall off in a hurry.

Baseball will always have a place for bold, innovative thinkers like Stuart Sternberg, Matt Silverman, and Andrew Friedman. A game so wedded to tradition runs the risk of perilously falling behind the times if it's not infused with new ways of thinking. By mining for hidden sources of talent, Friedman and his compatriots put a better team on the field, and raised the quality of play for fans—the same way new ideas and new technologies keep the most successful companies ahead of the competition. But the free market allows the most talented minds in other industries to find the most attractive working environments, and Major League Baseball does the same. Silverman, Friedman, and the behind-the-scenes savants who helped build the Rays have succeeded despite astronomically long odds against them. At some point, though, the daily grind of trying to beat the Yankees and Red Sox with one hand tied behind their back might prove too much to bear.

The idea behind the extra 2%—finding ways to gain that little, but essential, edge on the competition—will always exist, in baseball as in business. It just won't always belong to the Tampa Bay Rays.

EPILOGUE

The New York Yankees had been embarrassed. For the first time in fourteen years, they had failed to make the playoffs. The last time that had happened, Mike Gallego was their shortstop. (Derek Jeter had never before failed to play in the postseason.) Even more mortifying, the Yankees hadn't just finished behind their well-heeled Boston rivals. When the curtain fell on the 2008 season, the Tampa Bay Rays—the American League's perennial doormats and a team with a payroll five times smaller than New York's—had won the American League East title, and the AL pennant.

This would not stand. The following off-season, the Yankees embarked on one of the biggest spending sprees in the history of sports. The three biggest signings, CC Sabathia, Mark Teixeira, and A. J. Burnett, inked contracts worth a combined $423 million— more than the GDP of four nations. The strategy—if leveraging the sport's most lucrative market and deepest pockets and outbidding everyone else could be called a strategy—worked. The Bombers won 103 games in 2009, reclaimed the AL East title they felt was rightfully theirs, and steamrolled the rest of baseball en route to their twenty-seventh World Series title. After laying waste the league, the Yankees then traded for Javier Vazquez, seeking to bolster their already strong rotation with one of the National League's best pitchers. The Red Sox, coming off a strong season and a wild-card berth, opened their own checkbook, signing John Lackey to a massive five-year deal that matched Burnett's. The Yankees' spending spree was especially conspicuous: the team would take a 2009 luxury tax hit of $25.7 million—or as the Yankees typically call a sum that size, a rounding error.

Baseball's intelligentsia was suitably impressed. Fox's Ken Rosenthal surveyed the already loaded New York and Boston rosters now buttressed with reinforcements, then looked back at the rest of the division, and gave his readers the bad news. His December 22, 2009, eulogy for the Jays, Orioles, and Rays was nearly as light on subtlety as the headline of said oeuvre: "Rest of AL East Should Just Give Up Now."

The Rays would do no such thing. They were going to challenge the Yankees and Red Sox using the most challenging of playbooks. Chuck LaMar claimed he couldn't follow ownership's directives and still stick to his multi-year plan; Dave Dombrowski said trying to win and build at the same time in the AL East was impossible. Yet that's exactly what the 2010 Rays set out to do.

The first casualty of the Rays' plan was public relations. Tampa Bay experienced success for the first time in franchise history in 2008. As the summer of 2009 wore on, the Rays found themselves looking up at the Red Sox as well as the reloaded Yankees. By August 29, the Rays sat four and a half games back of Boston in the wild-card chase. A tough mountain to climb? Sure. But the Rays' magical run in '08 had shown that anything was possible. With the stretch run upon them, the Rays gauged their situation, looked at their roster—and traded away the greatest pitcher in franchise history.

The locals howled. How could the Rays trade Scott Kazmir, the lefty with the electric fastball, the young ace with the balls to come out on the first day of 2008 spring training, after a decade of losing, and predict a Rays playoff run? How could Stuart Sternberg, that cheap New York carpetbagger, do this to us?

As with all of their decisions, Andrew Friedman and the Rays were simply playing the odds. With just thirty-four games left in their season, trailing a strong Red Sox squad, those odds were heavily against them—the website CoolStandings.com gave the Rays just a one-in-eight chance of making the playoffs. Kazmir had struggled with injuries and ineffectiveness earlier in the season, putting up an ERA over 5.00 with no bite on his pitches. He'd come back strong later in the year after working with pitching guru/*Moneyball* character Rick Peterson. The former A's pitching coach had helped Kazmir regain some of his lost fastball velocity and, more important for the lefty's success, rediscover his devastating slider. Friedman knew that Kazmir's recovery might not last long and that he might get only one more chance to sell high before Kazmir's injuries and poor performance returned. If they kept Kazmir, the Rays would be on the hook for nearly $24 million over the next two-plus seasons. If Kazmir's arm went south again, he'd become untradeable, saddling the low-budget Rays with a financial burden that could torpedo any efforts to get back to the promised land.

Ignoring would-be critics, Tampa Bay dealt Kazmir to the Angels. The lefty excelled down the stretch in Anaheim, only to collapse the next season, when his 5.94 ERA made him one of the worst starting pitchers in the majors. Derisively called a "money dump," the trade did indeed free up a huge chunk of cash, even more so by Rays' standards. But Friedman also reeled in some intriguing young talent, nabbing Sean Rodriguez, an up-and-coming infielder with power and speed; Alex Torres, a Venezuelan left-hander small in stature but big on results; and first-base prospect Matt Sweeney. Rodriguez would prove to be an important player for the 2010 Rays.

Meanwhile, J. P. Howell's shoulder injury and attrition elsewhere created multiple vacancies in a suddenly thin Tampa Bay bullpen. But the Rays tended to build their bullpens on the cheap, and they seemed unlikely to break the bank. Ahead of the 2009 winter meetings, the Rays had made only minor moves—but with extra points for creativity. Second baseman Akinori Iwamura, the man who had stepped on second base to send the Rays to the World

Series the year before, played just sixty-nine games in 2009 owing to injury. The thrifty Rays seemed unlikely to pick up Iwamura's $4.25 million club option. Under baseball's arcane rules, ranging from draft pick compensation to contract-tender deadlines, the Rays were probably doomed to let Iwamura go for nothing; unlike in the NBA, sign-and-trade deals never happen in baseball. Of course, Friedman never says never. Hurting for a second baseman, the Pirates expressed interest in Iwamura, and a deal was soon consummated. In return, the Rays got Jesse Chavez, a right-handed reliever with a 94-mile-per-hour fastball but largely unimpressive numbers. He was a body to add to the mix, nothing more. Or so it seemed.

A month after that unusual but seemingly innocuous deal, Tampa Bay media began grilling Stuart Sternberg about the team's Swiss cheese bullpen. Would he open his wallet and throw serious bucks at a relief pitcher? How about a closer? Sternberg was quick to snuff out that idea.

"There's no $7 million closer showing up," he told inquiring media.

Or so he said. In fact, the Rays were about to hatch one of their most nefarious schemes. The same free-agent compensation rules that make sign-and-trade deals nearly nonexistent also bind teams' hands when it comes to signing free-agent relief pitchers. You can justify sacrificing a first-round draft pick if it means wooing Albert Pujols to your team. But GMs' increased awareness of the value of picks made it rarer to see a relief pitcher with that Type A designation signed away from another club. Still, the Braves figured someone would sign their likely-to-depart closer Rafael Soriano. Braves management saw little risk in offering Soriano arbitration, figuring someone would grab the fireballer with 27 saves, 102 strikeouts, and a 2.97 ERA. If that happened, Atlanta would gain a valuable comp pick. Instead, Soriano shocked the team by accepting arbitration. Suddenly the Braves had a budget crisis on their hands. They became desperate to find a taker for Soriano.

No one picks up the scent of desperation faster than Andrew Friedman. In short order, the Rays yanked Soriano away from the

Braves. In return, they sent back that unassuming, innocuous afterthought, Jesse Chavez.

The Rays gave up virtually nothing in player value to land their closer. And by trading for Soriano after he accepted arbitration rather than signing him as a free agent, they had avoided sacrificing the kind of high draft pick that had become the lifeblood of the organization.

There was one final twist to Friedman's master stroke. Soon after Soriano's acquisition, the Rays agreed to a one-year deal with their new stopper. The cost? A tick over $7 million. Don't ever play poker with Stuart Sternberg is what we're saying.

The Soriano heist triggered a sequence of events that saw the Rays do almost no wrong through the rest of that off-season and into 2010. Three months after nabbing their closer, the Rays tossed a minor league deal to Joaquin Benoit, a thirty-something relief pitcher coming off major arm surgery. The Rays saw Benoit's track record of high strikeout rates and solid command and figured he'd be worth a flyer. For the tiny cost of $750,000, they got one of the best setup men on the planet, a lights-out eighth-inning man who teamed with Soriano to form one of the most devastating late-inning duos in baseball.

The plan to build and win at the same time also depended heavily on the contributions of rookies and other young players. Every one of them seemed to click. Matt Joyce earned a June promotion, won a platoon role in right field, and became a late-inning terror, winning several games in the late innings, including a couple with monumental home runs. Rodriguez, part of the booty in the Kazmir trade, flashed an excellent glove, deft base running, and periodic power in becoming the team's new Ben Zobrist, a dangerous super-duper utilityman. Once relegated to afterthought status in the Rays' farm system, John Jaso finally got a chance to play and promptly snatched the Rays' starting catcher job, becoming an on-base machine who gave opposing pitchers fits. Wade Davis, the starting rotation's heir apparent after Kazmir left, enjoyed a big second half for a rookie fifth starter in a pennant race.

EPILOGUE

The Rays' usual arsenal of scrap-heap finds did their thing too. On August 28, 2010, a year less a day after the Kazmir deal waved the Rays' white flag, Dan Johnson smoked a tenth-inning, walk-off home run to beat the Red Sox and push the Rays closer to another playoff berth. This was the same Dan Johnson who had hit perhaps the biggest homer in team history, a game-tying shot against Jonathan Papelbon and these same Red Sox two years earlier, propelling the Rays to their first division title. Unable to find any takers in the big leagues, he had left for Japan in 2009, only to end up back in Triple A Durham in 2010 and eventually back on the Rays' major league roster. So acute was Johnson's ability to rise up out of nowhere, smite the Red Sox, then return to obscurity that he earned a new nickname. The ginger-locked slugger became "the Great Pumpkin."

Everything else fell into place. The Rays' core players excelled, with Evan Longoria and Carl Crawford putting up near-MVP-level performances and David Price emerging as one of the top five starters in the American League. Joe Maddon, aided by the reams of data fed to him by Rays number crunchers, brought out his usual tricks. Three straight times in a late July series against Detroit, Maddon faced the prospect of pitching to beastly Tigers slugger Miguel Cabrera while nursing a one-run lead. Each time, he gave Cabrera a free pass, loading the bases and setting up potential disaster for the Rays. All three times, the plan worked.

"All I could think of was that sign [in the clubhouse] that says FORTUNE FAVORS THE BOLD," Carlos Peña said afterwards. "So I was like, 'Hey, Joe, let's go with it. That's living the sign.'"

Peña himself embodied the other ingredient in the Rays' success: luck. Even the boldest, most astute, best prepared teams need some 50-50 odds to roll their way if they are to achieve success. Plop the league's two scariest teams into your division, have them continue to run much bigger payrolls—the Rays would spend more than $70 million in salaries in 2010, less than half what the Red Sox would shell out and about one-third the size of the Yankees' payroll—and you'll need good fortune on your side. Peña might have never played a game in a Rays uniform if not for random chance. In spring training 2007, the Rays released Peña, opting to go with journeyman Greg Norton at first base instead. Mere hours after making that decision, Norton came up lame. Frantic, the Rays buzzed Peña and asked him back. Installed as the team's first baseman that year, Peña smoked a franchise-best 46 home runs and established himself as the team's vocal leader. Though Peña would suffer a down year in 2010, you couldn't help but look at the Rays—the reclamation project setup man, the litany of kids playing beyond their years, the Charlie Brown creature come to life—and wonder if destiny was simply on their side.

On the very last day of the season, the Yankees lost, giving the Rays their second AL East title in three years. To a generation of fans who remembered the Vince Naimoli years, one crown seemed wildly improbable. Winning two was downright impossible.

But there was one bad decision that lingered, festered, and may have cost the Rays their chance at breaking through and winning their first World Series. Pat Burrell had been a disaster in his first season with the Rays, not only failing to hit at anywhere near the perennial 30-homer pace he had shown in Philadelphia but also saddling Tampa Bay with a financial burden that made other moves incredibly tough. The Rays could have accepted that Burrell wasn't going to work out and gone after a new DH. Instead, they passed on several far more attractive options, including Jim Thome—who swatted 25 homers in just 276 at-bats with the Twins and emerged as the team's most dangerous hitter, helping them back into the playoffs—for the princely sum of $1.5 million. After a few more weeks of failure in Tampa Bay, Burrell got kicked to the curb. He promptly signed with the Giants, instantly resurrected his career against inferior competition, and blasted 18 bombs in 96 games to push San Francisco to an unlikely NL West title. Meanwhile, the Rays pondered several big-ticket moves at the trade deadline, figuring an all-in season might warrant a major deal and bigger spending. But hampered in part by the remnants of Burrell's ugly two-year, $16 million contract, which the team still had to honor, the Rays passed on several would-be upgrades, including coveted left-hander Cliff Lee.

Thrust into the postseason with the best record in the AL and the league's number-one playoff seed, the Rays ran into an upstart Rangers club. Texas used killer left-handed pitching to tie Tampa Bay's lineup in knots for the first two games of the series. With a huge hole where Burrell's right-handed bat would have been, the Rays resorted to Rocco Baldelli in one of those games, leaning on a player whose fortunes had fallen so far that he'd semi-retired, become an instructor in the Rays' system, then returned for just 24 big league at-bats and somehow earned a spot on the postseason roster. The pitcher who finally did them in was the best left-hander in all of baseball that year, the very same Cliff Lee. Lee's Rangers would make it to the World Series, where they would fall to the National League's Cinderella story . . . Pat Burrell's Giants.

The vagaries of small playoff samples, bats slumping at the wrong time, and the greatness of Cliff Lee all played a big role in the Rays' falling short in their quest. But the Burrell debacle's far-reaching effects also showed that a single mistake could set a team up for failure—and much more so when that team lacked the resources to wipe away mistakes the way the penthouse-dwelling Yankees and Red Sox could. Disappointing attendance, a lack of corporate support, and a regionwide backlash against spending for everything from a new ballpark to public transit for St. Pete—these setbacks overshadowed another fairy-tale Rays season, at least in some people's eyes.

But the biggest hand-wringing was happening in New England, not in Florida. The Red Sox, they wailed in Boston and Providence and Manchester and Augusta, were now an old, boring team, unable to beat the hated Yankees or even the poorhouse-dwelling Rays. Those cries would die down quickly. When the Red Sox traded for elite slugger Adrian Gonzalez, Boston fans rekindled some optimism, while Rays fans worried that Tampa Bay might struggle to stay in the wild-card race. When the Sox then snatched Carl Crawford out of Tampa Bay's hands, paying an amazing $142 million to do it, the doubters came out in full force. When word hit just before press time that the Rays were about to lose another major piece by trading Matt Garza to the Cubs as part of a prospect-laden, eight-player deal, many fans just lost it. Forget making the playoffs, they howled. How much longer would the Rays go without contemplating a move out of town?

"AL East Back to Normal," blared the *Boston Herald*'s headline. "Welcome to 2010 and the ramping up of the Red Sox–Yankees rivalry," crowed the *Boston Globe*'s Dan Shaughnessy. The implication was obvious: those pesky little Rays had their fun. It was time for the big boys to take over again.

On the surface, Andrew Friedman appeared to adopt the same defeatist attitude. Revenue problems persisted. The Rays had bagged the fifth-best local TV ratings of any MLB team, an encouraging development that might have helped the team overcome its lousy attendance and weak corporate support. But having recently reupped their television deal, the Rays wouldn't be able to capitalize on that surge in interest for several more years. Even if their finances improved dramatically, the Rays could never remotely approach the resources available to the perpetually flush Yankees and Red Sox. Still, the Rays had won the AL East twice in three years, pulling off one of the greatest feats in recent sports history given the bottomless list of factors working against them.

Asked about trying to compete in the AL East, Friedman lamented, "It was always nearly impossible, and it's probably getting closer to impossible."

Then he paused.

"But it's doable."

ACKNOWLEDGMENTS

There are so many people who played a role in making this book happen, either directly or indirectly. I'm going to do my very best to acknowledge each and every one of you. If I miss anyone, please know that it was not intentional and that I will make up for it by springing for a tasty beverage of your choice.

Rob Neyer is the nicest guy in this business. He's kind and encouraging to young writers and quick to credit anyone who does good work, regardless of their pedigree. Rob did first reads for the book, scrutinizing every word before chapters even made it to the publisher. He didn't merely find a few typos. He helped me organize my thoughts and develop new ideas that never would have made it onto these pages if not for his help. I am a better writer now than I was when I started this project, and Rob's the reason why.

This book's editor, Paul Taunton, has the patience of a saint and the wisdom of years of successful projects behind him. He was understanding when deadlines had to be stretched, and he knew exactly which story lines to play up and which ones to toss. Steve Wulf of ESPN Books drew from a lifetime of writing and editing experience, helping me shape many of the seminal concepts that inform this book. Mark Tavani of Ballantine was another trusted and respected guide.

My literary agent Sydelle Kramer had been pushing me to write my first solo book for years before *The Extra 2%* came along. She's full of great ideas, has a keen sense of the publishing industry, and works hard to find the best projects for her clients. I'm lucky to have her on my side.

Twenty years ago, a writer starting a book about a team he had barely covered would've had a steep learning curve. Today sharp bloggers cover every major league team . . . and few teams boast a better collection than the Tampa Bay Rays. Tommy Rancel and Erik Hahmann met me on my first trip to St. Pete. Since then, we've had thousands of conversations about the Rays, their methods, and their history. As I write this, I'm already looking forward to seeing my next Rays game with them. Add up all the instant-messenger conversations I had with R. J. Anderson about the Rays—Joe Maddon's managerial tactics, Andrew Friedman's trades, and, of course, B. J. Upton—and you could fill five books. R. J. has become a respected colleague and a friend. Jason Collette and Steve Slowinski chimed in with valuable thoughts on the Rays and with support during the whole endeavor. Visit DRaysBay.com, TheProcessReport.com, and DockoftheRays.com if you're a Rays fan, or just a fan of intelligent baseball commentary.

As I mentioned in the notes section, I conducted about 175 interviews for this book. Fortunately, I found a crew of diligent folks willing and able to help transcribe many of those interviews. Warren Margolies, Fred Katz, Andy Hutchins, Minda Haas, Sagiv Edelman, Kyle Dickinson, Cedric de Jager, Adam Gotts, Jamie Vann Struth, Forrest Carpenter, Alex Walsh, Peter Garavuso, Cal Lee, Jason Sykes, and Matt Swain formed an all-star team of transcribers. If you ever get a chance to hire any of my new e-migos, do it. They get my strongest recommendation.

When I first talked to Stuart Sternberg about this book, he was enthused. Sorry, did I say enthused? I meant not happy at all. The title of this book comes from a Sternberg quote: the Rays must do everything 2% better than the competition if they're to succeed against long odds, and they do everything they can to protect that competitive edge. Throwing back the curtain and letting a writer learn all their trade secrets would've run counter to that philosophy, and I fully understand and respect his point of view. The Rays could have easily shut me out entirely during my nearly two years of reporting, but they did no such thing. I spent several days with the team in spring training 2009 and acquired a wealth of material. Andrew Friedman and Matt Silverman sat down for a lengthy interview, then graciously answered follow-up queries. They were as cooperative as two people who needed to not be *too* cooperative could possibly be. Same goes for James Click and Chaim Bloom, two former *Baseball Prospectus* colleagues who have become key cogs in the Rays' operation, even if few people outside the team's offices know of their valuable contributions. I'm grateful to Josh Kalk, Shawn Hoffman, and Phil Wallace for sharing their thoughts, on the record and off. Another former (Devil) Ray, Chuck LaMar, discussed not only his success but also his failures during those tumultuous first eight years of team history. He did so with candor and grace.

Thanks to every player who took a few minutes to answer questions. Five players went well above and beyond the usual quick chat: Gabe Kapler, Fernando Perez, Joe Nelson, Dioner Navarro, and Ben Zobrist. Much of the material from my conversations with these five players, and many other key figures, never made it into the book. I'll publish these and other Q&As at this book's companion site, TheExtra2Percent.com.

I spent a delightful spring day in his hometown of Hazleton, Pennsylvania, learning all about Joe Maddon. The people I met couldn't have been nicer or more accommodating. Thanks to the many members of the extended Maddon clan, with whom I had great chats at Third Base Luncheonette (try the hoagies, they're amazing) and in their homes. Special thanks to Beanie Maddon, Joe's sister Carmine, and the other two members of the Three Amigos, Jeff Jones and Willie Forte, for sharing many amazing stories.

Marc Topkin and Marc Lancaster helped frame much of the historical content about the Rays and their history in St. Pete. Rick Dodge and Rick Mussett played crucial roles in bringing Major League Baseball to Tampa Bay and bringing me up to speed on how it all happened. The expertise of Neil deMause, Maury Brown, Noah Pransky, Bob Andelman, Vince Gennaro, and Rod Fort informed many of the business concepts discussed in this book, especially regarding stadium financing and the business of baseball.

My former *Baseball Prospectus* colleagues provided an incredible education in how to think and write about baseball. Thanks Nate Silver, Steven Goldman, Dave Pease, Gary Huckabay, Michael Wolverton, Keith Woolner, Christina Kahrl, Will Carroll, Dayn Perry, Clay Davenport, Jeff Bower, Ryan Wilkins, Mark McClusky, and John Erhardt. Rany Jazayerli and Joe Sheehan are the reasons I got into *BP* in the first place. Rany took pity on a downtrodden Expos fan, while Joe took a chance on an eager Canadian raised on Bill James books. Other colleagues past and present to acknowledge: Chris Gessel, Juan Arancibia, and David Chung at IBD; Bill Squadron, Bo Moon, and Jay B. Lee at Bloomberg Sports; Sam Walker, Geoff Foster, and Adam Thompson at *The Wall Street Journal*; and David Schoenfield at ESPN.com. I've already worked with my friend Greg Foster of IMAX on one project and hope to do so on another, very soon.

I've been fortunate to meet and befriend some of the brightest names in the industry. Dave Dameshek, John Manuel, Jeff Passan, Jorge Arangure, Bomani Jones, Amy Nelson, Kevin Kaduk, Dave Cameron, David Appelman, Derek Zumsteg, Keith Law, Craig Calcaterra, Bill Simmons, Kevin Goldstein, Bernie Miklasz, Tommy Bennett, Ben Kabak, Joe Pawlikowski, Derrick Goold, Bob Elliott, King Kaufman, Will Leitch, Henry Abbott, Tommy Craggs, Matt Meyers, and Mark Simon, thanks for your continued support. Thanks also to the people who aid and abet my blabbing on radio and other forums, including: Elliott Price, Shaun Starr, Denis Casavant, J. P. Peterson, Toby David, Shaun King, Justin Lewis, Dave Ortiz, Brian Drake, Bobby Curran, Alan Miya, Gene Winters, Bruce Drennan, Nate Ravitz, Jeff Erickson, Matthew Berry, Jay Soderberg, and my Vegas partner in crime, Chris Liss.

Two more luminaries played big roles in making this book better. I called Michael Lewis to ask him for advice, figuring he might have a minute to sum up his experiences working on *Moneyball*. He gave a lot more than that, helping me lay the groundwork for the reporting in this book. Mark Cuban contributed a thoughtful and thought-provoking foreword. Cuban runs the Dallas Mavericks in much the same way Sternberg, Silverman, and Friedman run the Rays, making him a perfect fit to offer (more than) a few words.

While writing this book, I became the father of twins(!). I had to lean heavily on friends and family members to help care for the kids and generally keep me sane. Those friends are too numerous to mention, so I'll extend a blanket thank-you to all of them and hope for plenty of road trips, pickup hoops, and good times to come. As for family, Dad, Roz, Mom, Drew, Dan, Stephanie, Katie, Theo, Quinn, Samantha, Lauren, Nicole, Bubby Gertie, Chaim, Bess, and everyone else, thanks for all you've done, and all you do. Also, a nod to Andrea Buccini, Catherine Phillips, et al. for enabling me to work many sixteen-hour days.

Finally, Angèle, Ellis, and Thalia, thanks for filling all my days with joy. You sacrificed a lot for me to write this book, and for that I'll always be grateful. So excited to spend long hours in the park, or just lounging around the house, looking at your smiling faces. I will always love you.

NOTES

The foundation of this book was laid in the approximately 175 interviews I conducted with various players, front-office executives, politicians, fans, media members, and other key parties.

In a few cases, I also drew from prior interviews from other publications, both print and online. Those publications included the *St. Petersburg Times*, the *Tampa Tribune*, *The New York Times*, DRaysBay, and ESPN.com.

Other valuable sources included The Process Report, Dock of the Rays, Rays Index, *Baseball America*, *Baseball Prospectus*, Baseball-Reference, FanGraphs, SI.com, Bill James Online, Baseball Think Factory, Baseball Musings, *The Hardball Times*, The Book Blog, Shadow of the Stadium, MLB.com, Bloomberg Sports, *Stadium for Rent* by Bob Andelman, *Moneyball* by Michael Lewis, and *The Numbers Game* by Alan Schwarz.

ABOUT THE AUTHOR

JONAH KERI is the co-author/editor of *Baseball Between the Numbers: Why Everything You Know About the Game Is Wrong* and has written for ESPN.com, SI.com, *Baseball Prospectus, The New York Times, The Wall Street Journal,* and other publications. He has covered the stock market for *Investor's Business Daily* for more than a decade and is the lead baseball analyst for Bloomberg Sports. Follow him at JonahKeri.com and on Twitter @jonahkeri. Also, check out The Jonah Keri Podcast, at JonahKeri.com and on iTunes.

ABOUT THE TYPE

This book was set in Fairfield, the first typeface from the hand of the distinguished American artist and engraver Rudolph Ruzicka (1883–1978). Ruzicka was born in Bohemia and came to America in 1894. He set up his own shop, devoted to wood engraving and printing, in New York in 1913 after a varied career working as a wood engraver, in photoengraving and banknote printing plants, and as an art director and freelance artist. He designed and illustrated many books, and was the creator of a considerable list of individual prints—wood engravings, line engravings on copper, and aquatints.